··

PRIVATE RENTING IN TRANSITION

Peter A Kemp

··

Chartered Institute of Housing
Policy and Practice Series
in collaboration with the
Housing Studies Association

The Chartered Institute of Housing

The Chartered Institute of Housing is the professional organisation for people who work in housing. Its purpose is to maximise the contribution housing professionals make to the well-being of communities. The Institute has 18,000 members across the UK and the Asian Pacific working in a range of organisations, including housing associations, local authorities, the private sector and educational institutions.

Chartered Institute of Housing
Octavia House, Westwood Way
Coventry CV4 8JP
Telephone: 024 7685 1700
Fax: 024 7669 5110

The Housing Studies Association

The Housing Studies Association promotes the study of housing by bringing together housing researchers with others interested in housing research in the housing policy and practitioner communities. It acts as a voice for housing research by organising conferences and seminars, lobbying government and other agencies and providing services to members.

The CIH Housing Policy and Practice Series is published in collaboration with the Housing Studies Association and aims to provide important and valuable material and insights for housing managers, staff, students, trainers and policy makers. Books in the series are designed to promote debate, but the contents do not necessarily reflect the views of the CIH or the HSA. The Editorial Team for the series is currently: General Editors: Dr. Peter Williams, John Perry and Peter Malpass, and Production Editor: Alan Dearling.

ISBN: 1 903208 36 X

Published by the Chartered Institute of Housing
Cover photographs by Jon Walter
Printed by Latimer Trend and Co. Ltd., Plymouth

Contents

Acknowledgments

This book examines the development of the privately rented housing market over the past century and the nature and characteristics of the sector today. It draws on government statistics and the publications of numerous other authors, but also on the research projects that I have conducted on the privately rented sector over the past two decades. I would like to thank my co-workers on those studies. Special thanks are due to Professor Tony Crook, with whom I have undertaken a succession of highly enjoyable research projects on private landlords over much of that period. I am grateful to a number of organisations for funding my research on the privately rented sector, including the Department of the Environment, the Economic and Social Research Council, the Joseph Rowntree Foundation, the Lewis Cohen Trust, the Scottish Executive, and Scottish Homes. I am especially grateful to the Joseph Rowntree Foundation and particularly its Director, Lord Best, not only for financial support, but also for giving me the opportunity to participate in numerous 'Chatham House rules' discussions and seminars on private renting. Betty Johnstone, Tilly Wright, Julie Morgan, Margaret Johnson, Joanne Gatenby, and Laura Clark provided invaluable assistance at various stages. I have benefited greatly from the assistance of Lisa Goode in preparing the final manuscript. I would also like to thank Alan Dearling, John Perry and Peter Williams for their comments on the first draft of the book and for their patience in waiting for its arrival. My family has given me considerable encouragement along the way. Needless to say, responsibility for the contents is mine alone.

The book is dedicated to my mother and to my late father.

P. A. Kemp
York, May 2004

Peter A Kemp is a Professor of Social Policy and the Director of the Social Policy Research Unit at the University of York.

Foreword

At the beginning of the last century the private rented sector was by far the dominant form of tenure in the UK but by the late 1980s just seven per cent of households rented privately. Over the last 15 years or so we have seen a modest but significant revival which started with the introduction of the concept of the assured shorthold tenancy in the Housing Act of 1988 and which has been boosted by the arrival of buy to let. Tenant demand for privately rented housing is expanding at present because of affordability constraints and confidence issues in the owner occupied sector and because of contracting supply in the social rented sector. Some housing analysts predict that it will need to expand by as much as 40 per cent over the next ten years in order to satisfy growing demand.

Buy to let was first launched in 1996. It is a concept that has developed such that it now represents funding to private landlords across the whole sector from more than 50 lenders. Lending on private rented housing just ten years ago was seen as simply another form of commercial mortgage finance for a specialist group of property investors. They were offered no special products or terms and rates and fees were prohibitively expensive. Today buy to let represents close on seven per cent of gross mortgage lending in the UK and property investors are offered attractive products with criteria tailored to meet the requirements of a landlord looking to expand their portfolio to meet demand.

With the regeneration of the sector, easier availability of competitive finance and the decline of equity based investments, we have seen the emergence of a new cadre of property investors. These are individuals who are investing for the long-term and who understand that tenant demand is the key driver to the success of their business. They are therefore careful about the selection of property, they refurbish to a high standard and are concerned about taking care of the tenants' interests. As a result we have seen the quality of the stock improve and choice expand which in turn has helped create a much more positive image for renting.

The private rented sector is no longer a back-water in UK housing populated by ruthless landlords and exploited tenants. It has a crucial role to play in filling the growing gap between social renting and owner occupation. It is critical that legislators, regulators, lenders, landlords and the population as a whole understand more about the history and the prospects of this market. This book will provide the involved and interested observer with the context and knowledge that is vital to assist in planning for the future at whatever level they intersect with private renting.

John Heron
Managing Director
Paragon Mortgages Ltd

CHAPTER 1:
Introduction

Private renting is a housing tenure in transition. For most of the twentieth century, the number and proportion of households renting from private landlords was in decline. The statistics of this decline are well known. Private renting accounted for around nine out of ten dwellings in Britain prior to the First World War, but for only about one in ten by the end of the twentieth century. Owner occupation and, to a lesser extent, social rented housing, have overtaken private renting as the dominant forms of housing tenure in Britain.

Yet, despite or perhaps because of this long-term social change, by the 1970s perceptions of the sector had become somewhat ossified. The image of the private landlord, though it had never been glorious, had become firmly associated with the image of 'Rachmanism' or at best the rather seedy resident landlord Rigsby of the TV sitcom *Rising Damp* (Kemp, 1987b; Kemp and Rhodes, 1997). 'Private renting' conjured up images of damp and squalid, furnished and often multi-occupied property, let at high rents on insecure terms to vulnerable tenants by greedy or even unscrupulous landlords. To be a private tenant beyond a certain age was somehow to have failed or at least something to be explained, rather than a 'normal' state of affairs. Instead, it was considered normal to be an owner occupier or, failing that, a council tenant. At best, private renting was a temporary state of affairs through which households passed on their way to something much better. It was scarcely thought of as a tenure of choice, but rather more as something to be endured, preferably for as little time as possible.

These pervasive images of private renting were largely based on caricatures, which scarcely reflected the variety of circumstances that existed within the sector. Even to the extent that this social construction was firmly grounded in material circumstances, it was an ahistorical and ethnocentric image of the private rental housing market. It was ahistorical because, all too often, discourse about the tenure took it for granted that private renting was always like that; that private renting was, by definition, inevitably an inferior tenure, that rents were always high, that conditions were invariably poor, that most landlords were grasping, and that the landlord-tenant relationship was by definition an exploitative one. It was an ethnocentric social construction because the implicit assumption was that was how it must be in other countries too.

During the 1990s, however, both the image and, to some extent, the reality of private renting began to change. After decades of more or less continual decline, the sector ceased shrinking in size and in fact underwent a modest expansion. Public perceptions of the privately rented sector also began to alter. The image of private landlords and of what it meant to be a private tenant, were to some extent rehabilitated. Private renting was seen much more as a life style choice, at least for middle-class households, a change reflected in the sitcom *This Life*, about a group of young urban professionals sharing a house. The newspaper property pages included regular features about the merits of renting compared with buying one's home and whether rental property was an investment worth exploring. Mortgage lenders began to advertise loans aimed at landlords. Political debates about the sector also shifted in tone and in emphasis. There were signs that a political consensus had developed about the need for a healthy privately rented sector (Best *et al.*, 1992). The Labour Party, hitherto antagonistic or at best indifferent to the sector, began to see private renting and private landlords in a more positive light. The New Labour government, which came to power in 1997, made it clear that private renting was central to its housing policy (Armstrong, 1997).

Hence both in a long-run sense and in recent years, private renting is a housing tenure in transition. Indeed, private renting may well be at a crossroads; it may be moving away from one trajectory, associated with long-run decline, onto a new path of development; away from being a 'stagnant backwater of the market economy' towards a more healthy and acceptable, if still small-scale, part of the housing market. The old regulated sub-sector is being replaced by deregulated tenancies. The 'buy to let' market may be bringing a new breed of landlords into rental housing. While the legacy of the past decline still hangs heavy over the sector, the prospects for private renting are now better than at any time since the Second World War.

The purpose of the book is to examine this transition in the privately rented housing sector in Britain. It explores the long-term decline of private renting that took place during most of the twentieth century, as well as the more recent, modest revival. It examines key aspects of the private renting today, but locates them within the context of the development of the sector over the past century. An understanding of the historical development of the tenure is crucial in order to fully appreciate the nature of the privately rented sector today. This is not only because many of the current features and problems of the sector are in important respects a product of, or at least affected by, that history; but also because it reveals that perceptions of private renting have changed over time. Housing tenures are to some extent historically specific and not immutable over time and space (Kemp, 1987a).

In the present context, the 'privately rented sector' refers to accommodation, other than that owned or managed by social housing landlords, let to occupiers who are not the owners of the property. Private landlords are the owners and private tenants – who in some cases are in fact only licensees – are the occupiers of such accommodation. Private landlords could be defined more elegantly as people or organisations that let residential property in exchange for the payment of rent (Kemp, 1980; Allen and McDowell, 1989). But the problem with that definition is that it excludes property that is let rent-free, including much tied accommodation and some property let to friends or relatives of the owner. However, in the majority of cases, landlords let the right to occupy the accommodation for a period of time to the tenant in return for the payment of rent, more often than not in order to make a profit out of the transaction. Over time, the state has become involved in regulating the terms of this transaction, for example, in defining how much rent may be charged or the circumstances in which the landlord may regain possession. The changing nature of this intervention over time is explored in this book.

Chapter 2 outlines some of the most important features of the privately rented housing market before the First World War. It concludes with a discussion of the Edwardian housing slump and considers whether this was a largely cyclical recession or the collapse of the structure of housing provision associated with private landlordism.

Chapter 3 examines the impact of the First World War on the fortunes of private renting and the subsequent development of the sector between the wars. This was a critical period in its history, for rent controls were introduced for the first time in 1915 and remained largely in place for much of the 1920s and 1930s. The construction of new privately rented houses failed to recover in the 1920s; and although a revival did take place in the 1930s, the Second World War brought it to a halt. Meanwhile, owner occupation and local authority housing had become powerful competitors to the private landlord.

Chapter 4 looks at the development of the privately rented sector from the Second World War until the late 1970s. These were years of decline and decay as the sector shrank in size and failed to compete with the rising standards and greater security offered by owner occupation and council housing. These were also years in which the composition of the sector changed fundamentally, as it slowly ceased to provide 'family housing' and increasingly catered for niche groups in the market including those who could not afford to buy or did not have enough 'points' to be allocated a council house.

Chapter 5 examines the development of the sector and of policy towards it under the Conservative governments from 1979 to 1997 and the subsequent New Labour governments. During this period, the sector witnessed a modest but significant revival in its fortunes.

Chapter 6 focuses on the stock of privately rented dwellings. It looks at recent trends in the supply of privately rented homes and the characteristics of the stock today. It also examines the condition of the stock and the reasons why a substantial minority of it is below standard. Houses in multiple occupation are also considered, not only in terms of their prevalence and condition, but also who lives in them.

Chapter 7 looks at private landlords. It examines who they are, why they invest in housing to let, how they acquired their properties and how they view them. It examines the evidence on landlords' rates of return and compares these to the returns on alternative investments. The chapter also develops a typology of private landlords.

Chapter 8 considers the people who rent their homes from private landlords. It looks at the characteristics of the tenants and the roles that the private rental sector plays in the modern housing market and how these have changed in recent years.

Chapter 9 examines access to the sector including the difficulties that some people face in finding a home within it. It looks at accommodation search, as well as the payment of rent in advance and deposits. It also explores landlords' letting strategies as these can affect who gains access and who does not.

Chapter 10 looks at rents and the affordability of privately rented accommodation. It also examines the role and problems of housing benefit for private tenants.

Chapter 11 looks at the management of privately rented housing including landlord-tenant relations. It explores the role of managing agents, landlords' management policies and practices, harassment and illegal eviction.

Finally, Chapter 12 reviews the development of private renting over the past century, summarises some of the most important recent developments, and looks at the future prospects for the sector.

Part I
History

CHAPTER 2:
Private renting before
the First World War

Introduction

Chapter 1 emphasised the importance of understanding the privately rented housing market in historical perspective. The aim of this chapter is to begin to provide such an historical perspective by sketching out the nature of private renting in the late nineteenth and early twentieth centuries. The subsequent two chapters then track the development of the sector from the inter-war years to the late 1970s. Chapter 5 charts developments since 1979 to the present.

In devoting only four chapters to the evolution of the sector since the late nineteenth century, it is necessary to gloss over many details and stick to certain key features and the most important milestones. Nevertheless, in order to understand the private rental sector today it is essential to be aware of how it has developed over the past century as this has affected the nature, role and condition of the tenure and accounts for much of the legacy of decline and decay which remain.

The late Victorian housing market

In contrast to today, the dominant housing tenure in the nineteenth and early twentieth centuries was private renting, not owner occupation. Before the First World War, the housing market in Britain was based upon the renting of accommodation from private landlords. Nationally, something like nine out of ten dwellings were rented privately, most of the remainder being owner occupied. Local authorities accounted for only about 20,000 dwellings (Merrett, 1979). The proportion of the stock that was rented from private landlords varied from one town to the next but was dominant almost everywhere. Rates of private renting have historically tended to be higher in towns and cities than in the countryside. If the evidence from other countries is anything to go by (Harloe, 1985) the proportion of the housing stock that was rented privately rather than owner occupied probably increased as urbanisation progressed in the course of the nineteenth century.

In the nineteenth century, renting accommodation from private landlords was seen as the normal means of obtaining somewhere to live (Kemp, 1982a). This was as true of the wealthy as it was of the poor. For the mass of the working population prior to 1914, home-ownership was not financially feasible. In the first place, house prices were, as now, too high in relation to wage levels so that very few households could afford to buy a house outright. The average price of a new dwelling (including land) in 1907, for example, was around £300. This compared with average weekly earnings of men in full-time manual work, in various trades, of from £1.35p to £1.70p (27 to 34 shillings) a week (Cairncross, 1953). In order to become an owner occupier, it was therefore necessary to take out a mortgage.

However, although building societies were not unimportant prior to the First World War, they did not operate on a scale sufficient to fund home-ownership on a mass basis. In 1907, for example, they accounted for only 8.5 per cent of all mortgages advanced in the UK, and much of their lending was to private landlords and not just to home owners. Moreover, as well as being low, earnings were prone to fluctuation and employment in many trades was precarious. Hence, most working people at this time did not have an income level that was sufficiently assured for them to take out a mortgage loan.

The late nineteenth century British economy was subject to seasonal and cyclical fluctuations that resulted in a lack of security of employment and income level for many working-class households. The Royal Commission on the Housing of the Working Classes reported in 1885 that:

> *In considering the rate of wages, whether high or low, ...sight must never be lost of the precarious condition of the earnings of many of the working classes. Evidence has been given to show how uncertain is the employment of the majority, how a period of comparative prosperity may be followed by a period of enforced idleness, and how consequently their existence and subsistence can only be described as from hand to mouth. But even if employment was regular, the wages are so low that existence must be a struggle at the best of times.*

In these circumstances, therefore, buying a house on a mortgage was simply out of the question for most people. Instead, they had to rent their accommodation from a private landlord who invested in housing for the financial returns it offered.

Yet renting accommodation was not simply the result of necessity, for many people who could have afforded to buy their house chose not to do so. Instead they preferred to rent their accommodation. In fact, many private landlords were themselves tenants of other landlords. Before the First World War owner occupation was not considered to be important by many well-off people and was seen as just another investment (Daunton, 1977). For the well-off, home-ownership was not regarded as socially necessary. It is also significant that many of the financial attractions of home-ownership that were so important in the 1970s and 1980s – such as the effect of high rates of inflation on mortgage repayments, real house price appreciation, and the provision of mortgage interest tax relief – were of much less relevance before 1914. Inflation was not a problem, house prices went down as well as up, and most people did not pay income tax and therefore did not benefit from tax relief on interest payments. Social conceptions of home-ownership and of private renting were thus very different from what they are today (Kemp, 1987a). This important point is often forgotten or not realised in debates about the growth of home-ownership and the decline of private renting.

Where owner occupation did exist, it was mainly concentrated in the more expensive parts of the housing market. Nonetheless, there is evidence of working-class home-ownership, though even here it was confined to the better off workers in the more secure occupations. Working-class home-ownership seems to have been most frequent in small towns that were dominated by a single firm or industry or where there was a large amount of company housing (Rose, 1981; Kemp, 1982b). However, some of these working-class owner occupiers were also landlords. And despite these pockets of owner occupation, renting was by far the dominant housing tenure before the First World War.

The rental market

While renting was the norm, the privately rented housing market was very different before the First World War from what it is today. One illustration of this point concerns the length of tenancies before the First World War. In urban England and Wales, most working-class people held weekly tenancies, though monthly and even quarterly tenancies were not uncommon among the better paid and more regularly employed workers. Middle-class households usually took out yearly leases, while better off households took out leases for a term of years, such as 7, 14 or even 21 years (Kemp, 1987a).

In a relatively inflation free housing market, the security of tenure provided by leases for a term of years effectively made owner occupation unnecessary for the well-to-do. Moreover, unlike owner occupation, renting accommodation did not involve tying-up capital that could be invested more profitably elsewhere (Lloyd, 1978). When moving home, the renter did not face costs as high as those faced by owner occupiers. While tenants did not benefit from any rises in house prices, neither did they suffer from any falls that might also occur. Finally, tenants renting for a term of years were relatively free of interference from the landlord (Kemp, 1987a).

Yearly leases in England and Wales specified a quarter or even half a year as the period of notice to quit by either the landlord or the tenant. This had to expire at the same time as the lease was taken out. Failure to meet this requirement meant that, unless both landlord and tenant agreed otherwise, the lease ran for a further year (Cox, 1853). Weekly tenants had virtually no security in law and could be evicted at one week's notice. The Small Tenements Recovery Act, 1838, had made it much easier than previously was the case to evict tenants who were unwilling to leave. Under this Act, landlords of dwellings with an annual rental of up to £20 had only to apply to the nearest JP to secure a warrant for possession after 21 days (Nevitt, 1970; Englander, 1983).

Weekly lets only became widespread with the development of industrial capitalism and the rapid urban growth that accompanied it (Nevitt, 1970). In pre-industrial England and Wales rented dwellings appear to have been much more commonly rented by working people on yearly leases (Englander, 1983). In feudal times, many householders enjoyed tenure rights that covered the span of their lives, while widows and children had rights to succession. However, these social relations of occupation changed with the industrial revolution and the rapid urban growth of the late eighteenth and early nineteenth centuries. With the shift of the population from the countryside to the rapidly growing towns and cities and the emergence of a much more mobile labour force, the new urban workers found themselves renting on weekly tenancies and, in effect, occupied their accommodation at the will of the landlord (Nevitt, 1970).

While weekly tenancies were very insecure in law, landlords had an interest in keeping their good tenants. In the nineteenth century, rental income on tenanted property was widely regarded as an attractive investment (see below). Unlike today, the market value of tenanted dwellings was no less than that of vacant ones. Indeed, if anything, selling a tenanted property was easier because it was the rental income that most house buyers were after: a house with a tenant indicated that such an income would be forthcoming. Hence, provided they paid the rent and did not knock the place about, tenants were unlikely to receive an eviction notice (Kemp, 1987a).

Landlords and letting agents in England and Wales were generally in favour of weekly tenancies on working-class property. In the first place, collecting the rent weekly, as opposed to monthly or quarterly, increased the likelihood of the rent being paid, since it fitted in with the payment of working-class wages and household budgeting (Daunton, 1983). Second, weekly lets meant that persistent non-payers of rent, and tenants who were otherwise deemed to be 'unsuitable', could be evicted at very short notice. Hence landlords could rid themselves of the tenant before arrears got out of hand, thereby minimising the loss of rental income.

The growth of weekly tenancies was still occurring in the early years of the twentieth century and was even beginning to penetrate into the lower middle-class reaches of the housing market. But while the owners and managers of working-class property were broadly content with weekly tenancies, they were less than happy about their spread into middle-class housing (Daunton, 1983). Since rent payments were rather more certain from middle-class tenants, the main advantage to landlords of weekly tenancies did not apply in this part of the housing market. The growth of weekly lets among middle income tenants reflected the desires of tenants, not of landlords, for the latter wished to resist this development (Kemp, 1984).

At the same time, weekly tenancies had a number of disadvantages for landlords. They incurred greater rent collection costs than on property let on longer tenancies. Moreover, weekly tenancies tended to incur a higher level of tenant turnover than property let at longer intervals. This increased wear and tear on the property. It also meant that vacancies had to be advertised – and if an agent was used for this purpose, it involved paying a commission – prospective tenants had to be interviewed and references possibly followed up. Furthermore, in order to attract good tenants it was often necessary to redecorate the dwelling every time it became vacant, which again increased landlords' costs (Kemp, 1984). Hence management and maintenance costs were particularly high on weekly let property.

Weekly tenancies were a reflection of the relative insecurity of employment and of the income level of many working-class households (Kemp, 1982a). The main advantage to tenants of renting their accommodation on weekly tenancies was that it allowed them to be mobile. The freedom to move should their circumstances or preferences change was very important for many working people because of the nature of the economy at that time. In contrast to the comparatively stable feudal economy, where crises were more often the result of natural disasters or war, cyclical crises were an endemic feature of the nineteenth century capitalist economy in Britain (Aldcroft and Richardson, 1969). In combination with seasonal fluctuations in certain trades, these cyclical oscillations resulted in a lack of security and income level for many working people (Money, 1912).

The pre-1914 economy was also characterised by much casual employment. It has been estimated, for example, that casual workers and their families accounted for as much as 10 per cent of the population of London in the 1880s (Stedman Jones, 1971). Casual workers by definition had no security of employment and could be employed on a day-to-day, or even an hour-to-hour, basis. This resulted in an irregular flow of earnings and low wages (Anderson, 1982). In these circumstances, renting their accommodation by the week or month made economic sense, for it enabled working-class tenants to '…get rid of their house as soon as it becomes an encumbrance to them,' as a witness to an official enquiry put it in 1886 (quoted in Kemp, 1987a, p8). In this way, households could adjust at short notice their level of expenditure on housing or their residential location in response to changes in their employment, income or other circumstances (Kemp, 1982a).

Before the First World War the urban working-class moved frequently and often over very short distances. For example, one letting agent with a portfolio of 771 dwellings at rents up to £26 a year in Merseyside in 1906 had 263 changes of tenancy during the year (Kemp, 1987a). In Liverpool one-third of intra-urban house moves in the late nineteenth century were of less than a quarter of a mile (Pooley, 1979). In contrast to the working-class, middle-class households moved infrequently, but when they did it tended to be over longer distances (Dennis, 1984).

Not all moves were prompted by a change of circumstances, whether financial or otherwise. Among better off working-class households, the reason for moving was sometimes to obtain a new or a recently decorated house and leave one that had become shabby. Indeed, landlords would sometimes redecorate a house or make some other improvement in order to keep a good tenant. At the other extreme, some house moves were the result of a need to avoid the rent collector (Englander, 1983); in many cases this was itself due to these tenants' precarious position in the labour market and was just another aspect of their every day struggle to survive (Kemp, 1987a).

Another way in which tenants could economise on rent was to let out part of their home to lodgers. The practice of taking in lodgers was widespread among working-class tenants in the nineteenth century (Sokoll, 1997). Very often lodgers were provided with meals as well as accommodation. Letting part of the home to lodgers supplemented the tenant's income and may have been especially useful to those not in regular or any paid employment (see Rowntree, 1901). The net result was that significant numbers of low-income tenants were informal resident landlords, even if they did not see themselves as such.

Households with the least secure employment and income level were also those who were obliged to live in the worst conditions and take on the most insecure tenancies. For example, the casual workers of Covent Garden lived in abject poverty outside of the short-lived fruit season and resided in common lodging houses – in effect, commercial hostels – the tenancy of which was only nightly. Similarly, in Liverpool the casual dock workers were heavily concentrated in the common lodging houses and run-down streets of houses adjacent to the waterfront (Treble, 1979).

In Scotland, unlike England and Wales, yearly leases appear to have been more common among working-class households, except for the very poorest tenants (Englander, 1983). However, working-class tenants envied English tenants their freedom to move and would have preferred to rent their accommodation on similarly short tenancies. For the predominance of yearly leases north of the border was the result of the preferences of landlords and their managing agents (or house 'factors' as they were known) rather than of tenants. While many Scottish tenants wished to rent their accommodation on short tenancies, landlords refused to let on any other terms than yearly on property with a rental value above £5 a year. They also commonly insisted that tenants sign their lease four months in advance of the date of entry or renewal (which was normally fixed at 28 May), thus binding them to a house for up to 16 months (Damer, 1980; Englander, 1983).

The system of yearly lets north of the border caused considerable hardship to many working-class tenants and was one of the reasons for their growing antipathy towards private landlords in Scotland. After prolonged agitation by tenants for short lets, the government set up a committee of enquiry to investigate the matter, which reported in 1907. The main grievance voiced by tenants was that, while they were paid weekly or fortnightly and could be dismissed at a week's notice or even on the spot, they were tied to their houses for up to 16 months; this also prevented them from taking up better employment opportunities if it involved moving house. In 1911 the government gave way and passed legislation which replaced the system of yearly leases with monthly tenancies on dwellings of up to £26 rental a year in Scotland. But this concession came at a high price: the same legislation gave Scottish landlords powers for the summary eviction of non-paying tenants after 48 hours' notice (Englander, 1983).

Investment in rental housing

The dominance of privately rented housing in the nineteenth century required not only people who wished or had no alternative but to rent their homes, but also investors willing to let accommodation to them. House-builders tended to sell their dwellings to investors rather than retain them for letting themselves. Building for sale to landlords meant that builders could get their money back quickly, pay off their debts – to the developers from whom they acquired the land, those who had lent them the capital, and the builders' merchants who had supplied them with materials on credit – and construct more dwellings (Ball, 1981, 1983; Kemp, 1980, 1982a). Provided there was no over-supply in the local housing market, builders had little trouble in finding a market for their products.

Private rental housing was a popular investment prior to the First World War. The phrase 'as safe as houses' originally referred to housing to let as an investment. At the turn of the century, one-sixth of all personal wealth was held in the form of dwelling houses and it was the second major form (after stocks and shares) in which wealth was held (Kemp, 1982a). Rental housing provided returns that were competitive with alternative investments (Damer, 1976; Kemp, 1982b). Moreover, 'bricks and mortar' was a tangible asset over which the owner had control and one not subject to the decisions of a remote board of directors (Spensley, 1918). It was an investment that struck a chord with Victorian ideals: it was 'real' property and had 'emotional overtones' (Gauldie, 1974). Like much Victorian sentiment, it had roots in economic reality:

> *Before the establishment of limited companies the small capitalist was restricted (in practice if not in opportunity) to a very few investments and, of those, house property and mortgages on house property were the most popular; house property was expected to improve in value, it was tangible, it satisfied a sense of proprietorship and it was one of the very few forms of security available to trustees* (Spensley, 1918, pp196-7).

The ownership of rented houses was spread across all levels of wealth ownership, but was particularly important for those owning relatively small amounts of capital (Kemp, 1982a). It was one of the few investments available to people whose savings or inheritance were not substantial. While management problems could be a hassle, they could always be off-loaded onto a 'house agent', as they were known at the time in England and Wales or 'factor' as they were referred to in Scotland.

The few studies that have been carried out into the ownership of rented housing indicate that private landlordism was a mainly small-scale business, as it still is today. For example, Daunton (1977) found that between 70 and 90 per cent of the landlords in the various suburbs of Cardiff in 1884 owned less than six houses to let and the average holding per landlord was only 4.2 dwellings. Only half a dozen landlords in the entire city owned more than fifty houses. In Liverpool, the average holding in 1849 varied from 3.0 to 9.6 dwelling houses across the 16 wards in the city (Treble, 1971). In some localities, however, large landlords could play a major role. In the Newcastle-upon-Tyne suburb of Benwell in 1880, for example, landlords with more than fifty dwellings accounted for only three per cent of owners but 27 per cent of dwellings (Benwell CDP, 1978). The average portfolio size was larger in Glasgow than in these English cities. In 1900, the average holding was 3.6 tenement properties, which represented about 22 flats (Morgan and Daunton, 1983).

Once the houses were let, the income from rental housing was steady and dependable, if not spectacular (Damer, 1976). According to one contemporary expert, the going rate of profit on weekly let property in the provinces before the First World War was five per cent, but in London this was not considered sufficiently remunerative – perhaps because of the greater investment opportunities that existed in the capital. In London, the average return was said to have been from six to seven per cent on freeholds and eight per cent on leaseholds (Kemp, 1982b). Private rental housing was not, however, a uniform investment. Contemporary comment suggests that there was a broad trade-off between the rate of return on the one hand and the quality of the accommodation and the level of management costs on the other (Urlin, 1902).

At one extreme, property let on leases for a term of years involved little by way of management and maintenance outgoings and the tenant was usually responsible for repairs and general maintenance (Ernest, 1905). However, while less remunerative than other types of letting, such property was '…generally considered to be as safe as Consols, and [hence was much in demand from] trustees of charities and others with whom security is the first consideration' (Urlin, 1902, p15). (Consols are UK government undated securities.)

At the other extreme, property let weekly entailed very high management and maintenance costs, more defaulting on rent, and greater tenant turnover than property let at longer intervals, but higher returns. One Victorian commentator complained that owning weekly-let property was often 'almost a business rather than an investment' and that, given the management difficulties it involved, the going rate of six or seven per cent was not a sufficient inducement to invest in it. Indeed, some investors held weekly property in contempt, though it was not necessarily slum property (Griffin, 1893-94). The eminent economist Edwin Cannan (1914, p556) claimed that working-class dwellings were regarded as undesirable by the '…well-to-do, respectable investor' and that the ownership of it was generally left to people with small amounts of capital, though the returns were on average 'somewhat above that obtainable on other home investments.' A contemporary expert agreed with Cannan that working-class dwellings could give a higher return than other types of property and were '...remunerative to local men who can sharply look after it' (Urlin, 1902, pp32-33).

Between these two extremes of property let on long leases, which incurred few management costs but a low return, and property let weekly, which involved very high management outgoings but a fairly high rate of profit, was property let to the lower middle-class, often on quarterly or yearly leases. On this type of property, management costs were lower than on weekly lettings and the tenant was responsible for the less substantial repairs. One contemporary expert noted that:

> *The return will be less from a better class of house property, such as premises... let to small traders, clerks, and annuitants – people who on the whole pay with regularity and take much better care of their holdings; but these houses are more likely to be unlet for a quarter or even half a year or more, now and then...* (Urlin, 1902, pp32-33).

Hence property let to the lower middle-class represented a safe middle ground for investors. It involved fewer management problems than weekly let property and returned a higher rate of profit than property let on long-term leases to middle and upper-class tenants. On property let on leases of a year or more, the tenant was responsible (in England and Wales) for the less substantial repairs, but with weekly property the landlord was responsible for all repairs and general upkeep, including decorations such as wallpapering and internal painting (Griffin, 1893/94; Ernest, 1905).

Although the private landlord has been referred to in the singular, it was not uncommon for there to be a number of 'interests' involved in even one house. Indeed, on leasehold property, between ground landlord and tenant there often stretched a whole series of intermediaries held in their contracted order by a series of subleases which divided responsibility for the maintenance and upkeep of the property (Dyos and Reeder, 1973) and which determined who appropriated what proportion of the rental income. In fact, it was not unknown for working-class tenants themselves to sublet part of the dwelling in which they were living, a strategy that was commonly used when times became difficult.

Many witnesses before the Royal Commission on the Housing of the Working Classes (1884-85) complained about the activities of 'house farmers' who purchased the leases of vacant houses that had originally been let to middle-class tenants, which they then let by the floor or the room to working tenants. Today, this type of property would be described as 'houses in multiple occupation' (see Chapter 6). The problem of house farming was said to be particularly common in central London. The dwellings were usually let just as they were bought, unaltered and unadapted, the tenants sharing the fixtures and facilities previously used by only one household. In this way, the lessee house farmer could obtain the maximum rent with the minimum outlay. The result was overcrowding, insanitary conditions, property deterioration and, according to contemporary observers, a greatly enhanced total rental income. The Royal Commission was told that leases on subdivided property of this kind were much sought after and 'recommended by some as the safest 8 per cent investment that exists at present' (quoted in Kemp, 1982b, p20).

Landlord finance

It was usual for private landlords to borrow money when investing in housing to let. Witnesses before the Departmental Committee on the Increases in the Rental of Small Dwellings (1915) variously claimed that between two-thirds and ninety per cent of dwellings in Glasgow were mortgaged. South of the border, a one-time president of the Property Owners' Protection Association estimated that 80 per cent of housing to let was subject to a mortgage (Cairncross, 1953; Kemp, 1982b; Offer, 1981). This is a higher proportion than is the case today, which is nearer to 50 per cent among the stock of lettings (Crook and Kemp, 1996b). The modern development of buy to let lending (see Chapter 5) is in some respects a return to Victorian practice, albeit involving institutional rather than privately organised finance. Borrowing enabled landlords to gear up their investment and obtain a higher return on the equity they had invested than would otherwise have been possible (Kemp, 1982b).

The main sources of mortgages in the housing market prior to 1914 were not building societies or banks, but private individuals and trust funds such as marriage settlements and bequests (Offer, 1981; Treen, 1982). Private mortgages offered the lender a regular flow of income without any of the management problems associated with property ownership. If such lenders were disinclined to speculate directly in house purchase themselves, then a 'mortgage on the speculation of others appeared to provide absolute security for their investment and a guaranteed return' (Lloyd, 1977, p132). Estate Duty statistics show that private mortgages on house property and business premises accounted for 6.8 per cent of all personal wealth held in the UK (Kemp, 1982a; Daunton, 1983).

Insurance companies were an important if diminishing source of mortgages during the late nineteenth century, though a minority of such loans were secured against house property. For the insurance companies, mortgages were seen as securities that did not fluctuate much in value but which offered a relatively high rate of return at a time when the stock market was relatively under-developed. However, as the range and security of alternative investments widened during the late nineteenth century, the insurance companies began to diversify their portfolios and mortgages gradually became a less important outlet for their funds (Gunn, 1902).

The building societies were also important providers of mortgages. Throughout the nineteenth century, as permanent societies gradually superseded terminating ones, the building societies made gradual, if at times faltering, progress as financial institutions (see Cleary, 1965). By 1890 there were 2,422 registered building societies, with a total mortgage book of £48 million; by 1913 the number of societies had fallen by a third, to 1,611, while their combined mortgage assets had increased by more than a quarter, to £62 million (Kemp, 1984). However, many building societies were apparently poorly managed (Urlin, 1902), they were sometimes accused of misleading their borrowers about the rate of interest they charged on loans (RCHWC, 1884-85), and fraud by officials was not unknown (Cleary, 1965; Worthington, 1893).

Building societies were an important source of mortgages for owner occupiers and, indeed, such lending was the main reason why they had been set up. Nevertheless, they also loaned substantial sums to private landlords and, to a lesser extent, to builders. To judge from the pages of the *Building Societies Gazette*, the societies had trouble finding sufficient outlets for their funds during the 1870s and 1880s and perhaps much of their business was of necessity with private landlords (Kemp, 1984). Thus, although the Leeds Permanent Society preferred to lend to working-class people, it nonetheless loaned considerable sums to 'the wealthier classes' who wished to invest in private rental housing (Select Committee on Town Holdings, 1888).

Building society and private mortgages were invariably made on a fixed rate basis. Nevitt (1966) pointed out that private mortgages had several important advantages over building society loans for private landlords. Whereas with building society mortgages, the annual payments involved both principal and interest, private mortgages involved interest-only payments, the principal being repaid either at the end of the term or if the loan was recalled. The effect of this difference was that landlords could obtain a higher rate of return by borrowing money privately than by getting a loan from a building society, a fact of which the societies were acutely aware.

Building society mortgages were usually taken out for a defined term, often ten years or more, during which the loan could not be recalled. By contrast, private mortgages, which were generally for terms of less than ten years, could be recalled at any time, but subject to six months' notice. However, because of the ready availability of private individuals and trust funds willing to lend money during the nineteenth century, the fact that loans could be recalled at short notice did not generally present landlords with much of a problem (Kemp, 1984).

The Edwardian property slump

In the half century up to 1914, investment in new housing went in long waves of around 25 years, with a boom in house building being followed by a slump. Hence, late nineteenth century housing markets were subject to cyclical fluctuations, with periodic gluts and shortages (Saul, 1962). These cyclical fluctuations affected the amount of rent that could be charged by the owners of houses to let, particularly on new dwellings (Weber, 1960). Indeed, it appears that larger speculative builders took into account in their profit calculations the likely effect that their addition to the supply of dwellings in a particular locality would have on the level of rents that could be charged and hence on the amount that landlords would be prepared to pay for the dwellings (Sargant, 1886). Dyos and Reeder (1973) pointed out that the most obvious consequence of over-supply in the Victorian suburbs was the occasional row of new, untenanted and perhaps unsold houses; a temporary fall in house prices and in rents; and an increase in bankruptcies amongst builders and landlords.

The last house-building boom in the nineteenth century peaked in the late 1890s and early 1900s. Like its predecessors, it was then followed by a slump, but this time on an unprecedented scale. Between 1903 and 1914 house-building fell by as much as 70 per cent. By the outbreak of the First World War, the output of new houses had fallen to a level that had not been seen for sixty years. From 1914 until the end of the twentieth century, house building for the private rental sector – apart from a short-lived resurgence in the 1930s – was negligible.

The origins of this decline of investment in private renting housing have been much debated. Some authors have argued that the decline began with the introduction of rent control in 1915 (see Chapter 3). For example, Damer (1980) argued that the 1915 Rent Act cut off the flow of capital into rental housing and was the *sine qua non* for the introduction of Exchequer subsidies for council housing in 1919. The continuation of rent controls after the war, it is claimed, prevented the private rental sector from reviving and signalled its demise (Byrne and Damer, 1980).

Others have argued that the decline began with the Edwardian housing slump, that is, before the First World War and, therefore, *before* rent controls were introduced. For example, Ball (1983) argued that the structure of housing provision associated with private landlordism collapsed before the war, thereby creating the need for new structures of housing provision. On this view, rent controls should be seen merely as another nail in the landlord's coffin. Proponents of the rent control school, however, would claim that the Edwardian housing crisis, far from being terminal for the landlord, was instead simply a cyclical crisis, the recovery from which was prevented by the introduction of rent controls. Others have additionally blamed the increasing burden of local rates, which reduced landlords' profits. On this view, the private landlord was sacrificed for political reasons (Daunton, 1983, 1984).

The resolution of this debate is of considerable significance to our understanding of the origins of the decline of the private rental sector in Britain. An examination of the contemporary evidence shows that both arguments have some truth in them but that both are somewhat over-stated (Kemp, 1984). Some of the causes of the crisis – such as the rise in both interest rates and building costs – were cyclical in that costs did eventually fall, although not for some considerable time. The boom in overseas investment, which drew off capital (and effective demand for house-room) from the house-building sector, was also cyclical in nature. But other elements of the crisis were more long-term and therefore unlikely to be reversed. Most obvious of these secular forces was the emergence of an increasing range of investment outlets, consequent upon the growth of joint stock companies and the developing banking system. It was inevitable that, with an increasing number of outlets being open to small investors in particular, rented housing as an investment would lose some of its attractions (Kemp, 1980).

At the same time, there had been a long-term trend before the First World War towards a withdrawal of house-building from the bottom end of the market. As many contemporary observers pointed out at the time, private enterprise was failing to provide new dwellings for the lowest income groups. The main problem was that of low wages. With an economy that, prior to 1914, was based more upon exports than the market for domestic consumption, low wages were related to Britain's commercial success. For as Dyos and Reeder (1973) have pointed out, 'the slums were part of this argument for the economy of low wages, and one of their practical functions was therefore to underpin Victorian prosperity.'

Thus, if there had not been a world war in 1914-18, some restructuring of the housing market would almost certainly have taken place. This was because of the increasing failure of private enterprise to provide for the very poorest households. At the same time, it seems evident that house-building would have revived, even if only in respect of middle-class dwellings and the better off working-class. Contemporaries viewed the Edwardian slump as a crisis of *house-building* but not of the whole structure of housing provision associated with private landlords. It is probably the case, however, that, had there been no war, Exchequer subsidies would have been introduced. Certainly, Wilding (1972) has found evidence that this was being seriously contemplated in government before the war. But even so, the precise *form* that such subsidies would have taken is an open question. In other countries, for example, while state subsidies were introduced at this time, they did not necessarily go to municipal authorities, but often to private landlords and sometimes to housing associations (Harloe, 1995). Moreover, the *scale* of any subsidies that would have been introduced is also an open question, but if anything would probably have been relatively modest (Kemp, 1984). However, in the event, the First World War did take place, and it had a most fundamental effect upon the subsequent development of housing policy and housing tenure in Britain. This is examined in the next chapter.

Conclusions

This chapter has shown that the privately rented sector in late Victorian and Edwardian Britain was very different from what it is today. It was the dominant form of housing provision for all households, not just for the poor, the young and the mobile, but also for families and the wealthy. Private renting encompassed, not just the slum housing occupied by the very poorest households, but also well-constructed middle-class dwellings, mansion flats and large houses occupied by the well off. It was part of a whole 'structure of housing provision' (Ball, 1981), involving not just tenants and landlords, but also house agents, mortgage lenders and house-builders whose day to day livelihoods were based around housing to let.

CHAPTER 3:
Private renting
from 1914 to 1939

Introduction

This chapter sketches out the development of private renting from 1914 to 1939. It proved to be a critical period in the history of the tenure. If the First World War did not mark the beginning of the decline of private renting in Britain, it certainly signalled (to paraphrase Churchill) the end of the beginning of that decline. Rent controls were introduced in 1915 and remained largely in place for the rest of the period. The construction of new dwellings for private rental failed to recover after the war and remained negligible until the early 1930s. Meanwhile, subsidised council housing and private building for owner occupation became the main tenures for new building. In the 1930s, private house building soared and, while there was a return of building for private rental, it proved in retrospect to be an Indian summer rather than an enduring revival.

The introduction of rent control

The private rental sector ceased to be an unregulated market in December 1915. At that date, rent control was introduced and, although the actual extent of control within the sector has fluctuated over time and is now quite limited, it has remained in place ever since. The control of house rents was introduced when rent strikes and tenant agitation in Glasgow and other centres of munitions production had threatened to undermine the war effort. The tenant unrest was a response to rent increases imposed by landlords taking advantage of the acute shortage of accommodation caused by the war, especially in centres of munitions production (Byrne and Damer, 1980; Dickens, 1978; Melling, 1980). Britain was not alone in introducing tenant protection at this time, for every other country involved in the war also did so (Kemp, 1984; Harloe, 1985). As a study of post-war housing problems in Europe by the International Labour Office observed in 1924:

> If the housing market [in the belligerent countries] had been left free, tenants would have suffered from an intolerable rise in rents and inopportune notices to quit. Against these two dangers threatening the economic and social stability of the civilian population a barrier had to be erected – tenant protection.

The 1915 Act in Britain restricted the rents on working-class dwellings *and* landlords' mortgage interest rates to their August 1914 level. The full title of the legislation was the Rent and Mortgage Interest (War Restrictions) Act 1915. However, it was private lenders rather than building societies that were affected by the restriction on mortgage interest rates. After lobbying by the Building Societies Association, loans that were repaid by instalments over a term of more than ten years from the creation of the mortgage were excluded from the scope of the Act. This concession effectively meant that building society loans were not subject to mortgage interest restrictions (Kemp, 1984). But although building society mortgages were more or less exempt from interest rate restrictions, the introduction of rent control made private landlords a riskier customer for the societies compared with owner occupiers.

The 1915 Rent Act was due to expire six months after the cessation of the war. The control of house rents was thus originally conceived as a temporary measure made necessary by the war. In the event, rent control was extended in duration and widened in scope in both 1919 and 1920. For by the end of the war, the housing shortage was far worse than it had been when controls were introduced in 1915 (Bowley, 1945).

A committee of inquiry was set up in April 1918 under Lord Hunter to examine the Rent Act 1915 in relation to the housing of the working-classes after the war. In evidence to the Hunter Committee, the majority of the representatives of both tenants *and* landlords argued in favour of an extension of the Rent Act after the war. That the property owners' associations should argue in favour of keeping rent controls in place (albeit temporarily) after the war might at first sight seem surprising. But as we have seen, the 1915 Act controlled not only rents but also landlords' mortgage interest rates. Since mortgage rates on their controlled dwellings were thereby held well below the market rate, then as the manager of one large company put it to the committee, '…if the Act were removed altogether the mortgages would be called in wholesale and this would result in forced sales and disaster to owners' (quoted in Kemp, 1984).

Thus, the 1915 Act provided protection both to tenants and to landlords. The real losers were the mortgagees who provided landlords with loans, for their interest rates were controlled. In addition, mortgagees found that the real value of their loans had been significantly eroded by wartime inflation. Conversely, inflation eroded the real value of landlords' outstanding mortgage debts.

The Hunter Committee recommended: (i) that the restrictions should remain in force until three years after the war; (ii) that landlords and mortgagees should be allowed certain increases in rents and interest rates (see Table 3.1); and (iii) that the restrictions should not apply to new dwellings. These recommendations were substantially accepted by the government and were incorporated in the 1919 Rent Act. The main difference was that, in the face of growing pressure and concern about profiteering by landlords, the government doubled the rateable value limits to which controls applied so as to include most middle-class dwellings (Kemp, 1984).

Table 3.1: The Rent and Mortgage Interest Restriction Acts 1915-20

Year	Scope: houses with rateable value not exceeding:			Maximum permitted increase	
	London	Scotland	Elsewhere	Rent	Mortgage interest
1915	£35	£30	£26	-	-
1919	£70	£60	£52	10%	0.5%[1]
1920	£105	£90	£78	40%	1.0%[2]

Source: Kemp (1984), p198.
Notes: 1. maximum interest rate: 5%
        2. maximum interest rate: 6.5 %

As well as extending rent controls after the war, the government also introduced Exchequer subsidies for local authority housing in 1919. The need to introduce subsidies had been increasingly recognised during the war (Merrett, 1979; Swenarton, 1981). It was realised that, not only would there be very considerable excess demand for accommodation at the end of the war, but building costs would also be abnormally high, yet could be expected to fall after a few years. This seemed to imply that, irrespective of the long-term prospects for a return of investment into rented housing, in the short-term investors would hold off from purchasing new house property until after building costs and house prices had fallen, for otherwise they would have suffered a capital loss. Hence, in turn, builders would be very unlikely to construct houses, since their traditional customer, the private landlord, would probably not buy them (Kemp, 1984). In these circumstances and in view of the likely social unrest that the housing shortage would generate, the government accepted the need to provide some kind of subsidy to house building until 'normality' had returned (Merrett, 1979; Swenarton, 1981).

It is worth reflecting upon why the Exchequer subsidies were provided to local authorities rather than, as happened in other countries such as the Netherlands and West Germany, to private landlords or to non-profit housing associations (Harloe, 1995). First of all it is clear that many working people and their representatives were demanding state housing (Merrett, 1979). Secondly, it would have been politically impossible to subsidise private landlords. Their public image had deteriorated considerably during and immediately after the war as a result of the shortage of accommodation and what was perceived to be profiteering by them (Kemp, 1984). Finally, although the 'public utility societies' (an early form of non-profit housing association) did receive some subsidy, they were not considered sufficiently able to cope with the likely scale of the problem after the war (Kemp, 1984; Malpass, 2000). For their part, local authorities not only had local knowledge, they also had some relevant expertise. Moreover, a few local authorities at the forefront of 'municipal socialism' had provided a limited amount of housing to rent, estimated to total about 20,000 dwellings nationally in 1914 (Merrett, 1979).

The shortage of housing at the end of the First World War was considerable. Leaving aside the pre-war shortage, the government calculated that at least 500,000 dwellings were needed just to make good the shortage created by the war. But because the building industry was extremely slow to revive, the shortage got even worse in the immediate post-war years. By January 1920, for example, the government estimated that the shortage had increased to 800,000 (Bowley, 1945).

As we have seen, in order to mitigate the effects of a marked excess demand for housing, rent control had been introduced in 1915 and extended in 1919. However, while rents were restricted, house prices were not. As a result, the selling price of houses increased dramatically – but only if the house was vacant or if vacant possession could be obtained. A gap therefore opened up for the first time between vacant possession and sitting tenant prices in the housing market. Consequently, many landlords were no longer prepared to re-let vacant property but instead preferred to sell to whoever would buy. By selling to owner occupiers, landlords could take advantage of the short-term increase in house prices and thus make a capital gain before prices fell to a more 'normal' level once the building industry had recovered from its slump and the shortage had abated (Kemp, 1984).

For their part, households in need of accommodation were prepared to buy, even at greatly inflated prices, simply in order to secure a roof over their heads. Owner occupation was in this way a personal solution to a general housing shortage. One tactic to which some people were prepared to resort was to buy a tenanted property from a landlord and then evict the tenant in order to use it for their own occupation (Kemp, 1984).

At the same time, many middle-class tenants whose dwellings were above the rateable value limits for rent control were being told to 'purchase or quit' as their leases came to an end, a problem that was particularly acute around London, while others were forced to pay greatly increased rentals. In these ways, middle-class tenants were beginning to experience some of the unfamiliar insecurities characteristic of working-class life. Consequently, pressure built up for a further extension of the scope of the Rent Acts to include even more expensive houses. Profiteering in housing was at this time a prominent issue both in the press and in parliament. One MP, for example, asked whether the Minister of Health was '…aware of flats in London where the rents had been increased from £150 to £350 a year?' but the Minister admitted to being '…aware of even worse cases…but, under the law as it stands at present, we have no power to deal with them' (quoted in Kemp, 1984, p190).

A further committee of inquiry, under Lord Salisbury, was therefore set up '…to consider the operation of the Rent Restriction Acts, and to advise what steps should be taken to extend, continue, or amend these Acts.' After examining the evidence, the committee concluded that rent control should not be allowed to expire but should be renewed for a further period. It also recommended, however, that the ceilings on rent levels and mortgage interest rates allowed under the Rent Act should be raised. The Rent and Mortgage Interest (Restrictions) Act, 1920, which followed not only extended the duration of rent control, but also raised the rateable value limits such that nearly all dwellings were included with the scope of the restrictions. The rent allowable under the Act was raised to a maximum of 40 per cent above the August 1914 level, while mortgage interest rates under the Act were also raised (see Table 3.1).

Another committee of inquiry into the operation of the Rent Acts was set up in 1922 under Lord Onslow. It argued that rent controls should be phased out in three stages by 1925 and that decontrol should occur wherever there was a change of tenancy ('creeping decontrol'). However, while the newly elected Conservative government was keen to put these proposals into effect, the general public was less happy. The Onslow Report, published in February 1923, was met by '...a great outcry from those who are likely to be affected' – the tenants (quoted in Kemp, 1984). So unpopular were these proposals for rent decontrol that the government lost three by-elections in safe Tory seats. All three by-elections and in particular the one at Mitcham, where the Minister for Health, A.G. Boscowan, was standing, were fought in a blaze of publicity. They were contested on two main issues: rent decontrol and the lack of houses. In the face of this 'revolt of the middle-classes', the government backed down (Kemp, 1984).

The 1923 Rent Act postponed decontrol by class of house until 1925 when the position was to be reassessed in the light of house-building progress (itself to be aided by government subsidies). But decontrol on vacant possession was included in the Act, thereby transferring the basis of rent control from the building to the tenant.

House-building between the wars

During the 1920s, the building industry recovered from the slump into which it had entered during the late 1900s, a recession much exacerbated by the war. A prime cause of the initial slump was the downturn in the attractiveness of house letting as an investment. The recovery of house-building during the 1920s, however, was based not on private rental but on owner occupation and local authority housing; two tenures that had been of considerably less importance before 1914. This recovery was greatly stimulated by the provision of Exchequer subsidies to new local authority housing and to private builders, as provided by the Housing Acts of 1923 and 1924 (Bowley, 1945; Merrett, 1979, 1982).

It is important to examine here why the construction of new private rental dwellings did not revive in the 1920s when it had previously been so dominant. The Onslow Committee had suggested that the Rent Acts had adversely affected the provision of new houses. However, although the Rent Acts probably had some impact, it is important not to exaggerate this effect during the 1920s. For the evidence suggests that, even if there had been no controls on rents, new private rental provision at this time would have been limited.

In the first place, during the inter-war years, rent controls did not apply to new dwellings, only those built before April 1919 (Kemp, 1984). The owners of new dwellings could therefore charge a market rent. Of course, it could be argued that rent controls could have affected the supply of new dwellings at this time, either by acting to dampen the rents that could be obtained on new accommodation (because the level of controlled rents fixed the amount that tenants would pay for a house of a given type in a given locality) or by creating a fear that controls might be extended to new dwellings at some later date.

The possibility of rent controls being extended to new dwellings during the 1920s and 1930s was in fact fairly remote (Holmans, 1987; Kemp, 1984). It was not proposed by any of the committees enquiring into the operation of the Rent Acts between the wars and nor was it a prominent demand of the tenants' organisations. Moreover, the whole thrust of the debate on rent control in the 1920s centred around the timing of *decontrol*; there was no question of control being extended to new private housing. The Conservative government's 1923 Rent Act implemented a programme of gradual or 'creeping' decontrol; while the Labour Party's policy at this time was for a '…distant but fixed date of decontrol' (quoted in Kemp, 1984). Finally, the Rent Acts were all meant to last only a few years; the continuing shortage of accommodation forced governments to either extend the duration of the Acts when they expired or introduce a new Act.

The argument that the controlled rents of previous rental housing dampened the rents obtainable from new private housing in the 1920s is more plausible. In the post-war years, the large gap between new economic rents and controlled pre-war rents would no doubt have inhibited many of those living in controlled dwellings from moving into a new one, assuming that they could afford to pay an economic rent. But those who could afford economic rents, and who were also without somewhere to live, would not have been so inhibited. As we have seen, many households in this situation had to pay quite substantial rental premiums or house purchase prices in order to obtain accommodation. Moreover, households were willing to buy newly built homes, despite the likelihood of a capital loss in due course, in order to secure a roof over their heads. This implies that, because of the severe post-war housing shortage, it was unlikely that the existence of controlled rents would have acted to depress the rents that landlords would have been able to charge on new properties.

However, even if there had been no rent control on pre-1919 dwellings, the economic environment of the 1920s was such that the production of new private rental dwellings would probably have been quite limited in any case. This was particularly evident during the immediate post-war years of 1919-22, when building costs and interest rates were very high. But even after the return to some kind of 'normality' in 1923, when the immediate effects of the post-war boom and slump had been felt and building costs had stopped falling from their 1920 peak, the prospects for investment in new private rental housing were poor. Interest rates and building costs were still at higher levels than they had been before the war. Building costs, for example, were 88 per cent higher in 1924 than they were in 1914. While the cost of living index was up by 81 per cent over the same period, wage rates had increased by only 69 per cent. Moreover, the index of wages applied only to those workers in full-time employment; but during the depressed 1920s, short time working was common and unemployment at a very high level. In 1924, for example, unemployment was 10.2 per cent, while the average for 1921-29 was 11.8 per cent (Bowley, 1947).

Thus, wages had not sufficiently kept pace with the increase in building costs since before the war, and the average working-class tenant may not have been able to afford the economic rent of a new dwelling. As Table 3.2 shows, very little private working-class housing was produced in the 1920s. The building industry was forced to move upmarket in order to sell its products. Those who could afford the cost of new private housing tended to become owner occupiers rather than remain in the rented sector. In addition, the builders' traditional market – the private investor – was no longer prepared to buy new rental housing. 'The investor has been almost extinguished', remarked one prominent estate agent. Nobody, claimed the National Federation of Property Owners and Ratepayers (NFPOR), now wanted to invest in new working-class housing:

> *In the first place, they cannot produce them to let at a rental which is within the pocket of a working class man in these days of unemployment and uncertainty. In the next place, they cannot be sure of getting a mortgage on that class of property. There is no one now inclined to take it* (quoted in Kemp, 1984, p217).

Not only was it no longer profitable to buy new working-class housing to let, it was also becoming socially undesirable. The respectable housing investor wanted out. The property owner, claimed the NFPOR's President, '...has been held up as such a blood-sucker, such a profiteer and such a despot, that no respectable decent man likes being put in that position if he can possibly avoid it, and he gets out' (quoted in Kemp, 1984, p217). In addition to the value gap between the price of tenanted and vacant property – which *was* a product of rent control – this disapprobation of landlordism was another reason for disinvestments from the housing market by private landlords.

Table 3.2: The stock and flow of private dwellings in England and Wales, 1919-39

Rateable value	1919 stock of dwellings %	Dwellings completed January 1919 to March 1939 %
Up to £13	67.6	1.3
£14 to £26	20.9	65.8
£27 to £78	11.5	32.9
Total	100.0	100.0

Source: Bowley (1945, pp272-273).

The private landlord also faced competition from the new, subsidised local authority rental sector. Of the 599,000 new 'working-class' dwellings (i.e. those with a rateable value of £13 or less) produced in England and Wales between 1919 and 1931, 98 per cent were built for local authorities and only 2 per cent for private owners. Moreover, the new local authority housing – built to higher standards and let at subsidised rents – did not house the poorer tenants, those most in need. On the contrary, they were let to '…the better off families, the small clerks, the artisans, the better off semi-skilled workers with small families and fairly safe jobs' (Bowley, 1945, p129). The rents of the new council houses, even with the subsidy, were simply too high for the poorer paid or unemployed households.

For the investor, alternatives to rental housing became more attractive or readily available after the First World War. Interest rates were much higher in the 1920s than they had been prior to the war. This not only meant higher rents and house prices, but also high returns from money lending investments such as government stock and building society share and deposit accounts. At this time there was also a marked change in the structure of the firm, the typical Victorian family concern increasingly giving way to the joint-stock company. This was in turn accompanied by an important development in the capital market, which became more geared towards the financing of home industry. As a consequence of these changes, the smaller-scale investor was able to invest money into a wider range of securities than before the war. Moreover, they were investments that, compared with housing to let and private mortgages thereon, were more liquid, less 'lumpy', involved far fewer management problems and promised fairly high rates of return. The growing habit of investing in shares on the stock market was stimulated by government propaganda during the war and the trend was further reinforced by the domestic new issue boom of 1919-20 (Thomas, 1978).

After the First World War a combination of rent controls, the investment environment and the tarnished image of investment in housing to let, had helped ensure that a revival of new building for private rental did not occur in the 1920s. But people had to be housed. New methods had to be developed for providing new housing. When the building industry did eventually get back on its feet, from 1923 onwards, the recovery was not based on private renting, but on local authority housing and owner occupation. This recovery of house building was greatly stimulated by the reintroduction of Exchequer subsidies for local authority and private housing in the Housing Acts of 1923 and 1924 (the subsidies introduced in 1919 had been axed in 1921). Whereas the 1923 Act passed by Chamberlain favoured the private sector, the 1924 Act passed by Wheatley favoured local authority house building (Holmans, 1987; Merrett, 1979).

The 1924 Act is particularly important because it helped establish council housing as part of the more permanent machinery for the provision of working-class houses (Bowley, 1945). Unlike the subsidies introduced in 1919, it had little to do with slogans about 'homes for heroes'. Nor was the 1924 Act seen as a solution to the temporary, 'after the war' problem by Labour's Minister of Health, John Wheatley. Instead it was recognition of the collapse of private investment in working-class housing to let. Accused of interfering with private investment in housing, Wheatley pointed out that '...there is no investment in working-class homes... Are we to remain without houses merely because people who have money to invest refuse to invest that money directly in working-class houses?' (quoted in Kemp, 1984, pp246-247). In fact, Wheatley's 1924 Act did provide subsidies for private rental construction. But the investment environment for such housing was so unfavourable at this time that in the first five years after the Act only 4,202 units were built with the aid of these subsidies (Kemp, 1984).

The recovery of the private housing sector in the 1920s was based on owner occupation (Ball, 1983; Merrett, 1982). Much of the growth of owner occupation in the new housing market was the result of necessity. The lack of investment in new private rental housing meant that anyone who wanted one of the new, modern 'labour-saving' houses that builders were beginning to put up had to buy one or go without. However, home-ownership had certain attractions in the 1920s. Whilst private renting was a reasonably attractive proposition for middle-class households prior to 1914, the uncertainties and shortages of the war and early post-war years quickly highlighted its disadvantages. Buying one's home was thus a means of ensuring stability and security (Kemp, 1984).

Moreover, the building societies were awash with money after the First World War (Cleary, 1965). Indeed, many of the people who before the war would have invested in private mortgages or in house letting, after the war put their money into building society share and deposit accounts. As one of their representatives later pointed out, the societies '...sought to create a desire for home-ownership by publicising its benefits and virtues. If many bought from sheer necessity, many others purchased from choice' (Ashworth, 1957, p22). Of course, this increase in owner occupation would not have been possible had not there been an important increase in people's ability to buy (Ball, 1983; Cleary, 1965; Merrett, 1982). This was a product of increasing job security, the growth of 'white collar' employment and rising real incomes for those in work between the wars (Pollard, 1969).

Thus in the inter-war years there was a major shift in social attitudes towards owner occupation (Cleary, 1965; Jackson, 1973). This shift was reinforced during the 1930s when there was a massive private house building boom, based largely on owner occupation. This building boom was a unique development, stimulated by a set of circumstances that was peculiarly favourable to house building (see Richardson and Aldcroft, 1968). The slump in Britain and in the world economy brought with it rising real wages for those in work, agricultural depression and hence low land costs, very low interest rates (2 per cent from 1932 to 1939), low building costs, low returns from alternative investments generally, and almost a glut of mortgage funds. Low house prices and generous lending terms meant that an increasing number of households could, for the first time, afford to buy rather than rent their own home (Ball, 1987). And the fact that the vast majority of those purchasing in the 1930s were first-time buyers meant that they did not have to sell their existing home in order to buy a new one (Merrett, 1982).

Building for private rental: an Indian summer, 1933-39

The conditions which made it possible for so many people to become owner occupiers also helped make investment in private rental housing more attractive. As well as low interest rates and building costs, the Ministry of Health's index of working-class rents increased during the 1930s, making rental yields relatively attractive. As a result there was a notable revival of new private rental house building in the 1930s (see Table 3.3). Between 1934 and 1939, an average of 66,000 private rental dwellings with rateable values of up to £26 were built each year. In total, over 350,000 new dwellings were built for private letting in the five and a half years from September 1933 and March 1939, together with a substantial but unknown number of more expensive ones.

Table 3.3: Private dwellings built for letting in England and Wales 1933-39

Year to 31 March	Dwellings built up to £26 rental value[1]	
	Number	% of all new private dwellings
1934[2]	22,730	21.4
1935	55,710	22.1
1936	60,475	25.3
1937	71,148	29.8
1938	74,396	33.1
1939	68,189	34.6

Source: Ministry of Health statistics cited in Kemp (1984, p298).
Notes: 1. In Greater London, rental values up to £35.
2. 30 September 1933 to 31 March 1934 only.

The demand for new housing to rent privately seems to have come from opposite ends of the market. At the lower end of the housing market, there was a demand from those unable or unwilling to become owner occupiers. At the upper end of the market, there was a considerable demand for self-contained, 'labour-saving' flats, particularly in and around London and along the south coast in retirement and holiday towns like Brighton and Hove. As was the usual practice prior to the late 1950s, the vast majority of these flats were let on leases of up to 21 years, and only in a very few cases were they actually bought by their occupiers (Kemp, 1984).

Many of the investors in this new rental housing were private individuals. However, an important and to some extent novel feature of this return of investment in private rental housing was that much of it was by newly formed property companies. Property company formation seems to have taken off in 1932 after the shift to a policy of low interest rates. Property companies began to emerge towards the end of the nineteenth century, but only seem to have gained real significance in the 1920s (Benwall CDP, 1978). A *Property Companies Year Book* even appeared in 1928, which noted that '...the past few years has witnessed the multiplication of property investment companies.' Its directory listed a total of 478 companies (Kemp, 1984).

These new property companies were different from the typical Victorian private landlords, who tended to be individuals. And this new form of landlord tended to involve a larger scale of operations, had access to a different form of capital financing, and could be expected to be more economically rational in outlook. Data on new property company formation show the extent to which there was a surge of investment after the conversion to cheap money (i.e. low interest rates) in mid-1932. New capital issues by property companies virtually doubled between 1931 and 1932, three-quarters of the increase taking place after the shift to cheap money in mid-year (Nevin, 1955). By the following year, new capital issues more than doubled again. However, not all of these capital issues were devoted to residential property; shops and offices were also important.

The big insurance companies and financial houses were also keen investors in these blocks of flats, but were not interested in small dwelling houses. At the annual meeting of the Prudential insurance company, for example, Sir Edgar Horne reported that, 'The low yield on suitable Stock Exchange securities has led us to invest a somewhat larger proportion of our new funds in the property market, where the return obtainable is, on the average, somewhat higher.' Investment by insurance companies in land and house property increased from £59.2 million in 1929 to £83.4 million in 1935 (Kemp, 1984, p299).

Conclusions

At the end of the 1930s, the private rental sector appeared to have experienced a modest recovery, at least when compared with the previous decade. At that stage it was still by far the largest housing tenure, accounting for nearly three out of every five dwellings. It is true that the sector had declined in relative importance between the wars, as owner occupation and council housing developed as important housing tenures. But even in the 1930s, when owner occupation underwent a massive house-building boom, over 66,000 units a year were produced for private renting. To put that figure in perspective, it is a bigger total than was then, and is currently, being constructed for social housing.

Moreover, rent control had been gradually relaxed during the 1920s and 1930s in Britain, as in other European countries where it had been introduced during the First World War (Harloe, 1985). While it was much less often the tenure of choice for better off households, private renting seemed to have a reduced but nonetheless reasonably secure future. In 1939, few people would have predicted the pace and extent to which the privately rented sector subsequently declined in Britain.

CHAPTER 4:
Decline and decay: 1939 to 1979

Introduction

This chapter outlines the development of private renting in Britain from the Second World War until the election of the Conservative government of Mrs Thatcher in 1979. This was a period of almost continuous decline and decay for this ravaged and highly controlled sector of the housing market. It was also an era in which political debate about the tenure became highly polarised. Meanwhile, public perceptions of landlords and of privately rented accommodation became increasingly unattractive and also suffused with stereotypical images. Before examining the development of private renting during this period, the chapter sketches out the broad dimensions of the decline in the size of the sector and the main reasons for it.

Private renting in decline

The Second World War marked an important turning point for the privately rented sector in Britain. From 1945 the sector declined rapidly, both in relative and in absolute size; and to a greater extent than in most other advanced industrial nations. Whereas in 1938 the privately rented sector accounted for 6.6 million dwellings or 58 per cent of the housing stock in England and Wales, by 1975 it contained only 2.9 million dwellings and represented only 16 per cent of the stock (Table 4.1). Though separate figures are not available for Scotland, a similar decline occurred north of the border. During this period, therefore, private renting in Britain was transformed from being the most common tenure to being a relatively small and residual part of the housing market.

While the relative importance of the various factors behind the decline of private renting is still a matter of debate, the way in which the decline has occurred is clearer. As Table 4.1 shows, the pre-war, *existing stock* of privately rented sector dwellings was denuded in three main ways in the period up to the mid-1970s.

First, the major source of loss from the privately rented sector was sales of dwellings to the owner occupied housing market. Between 1938 and 1975, 2.6 million dwellings were sold into the owner occupied sector. This process accounted for a substantial share of the growth in owner occupation over this period (DoE, 1977). If private landlords had not been so keen to disinvest, the growth of owner occupation would have been much slower and would have relied relatively more upon new construction.

Table 4.1: Housing tenure in England and Wales in 1938 and 1975

Tenure	1938		1975	
	millions	% of total stock	millions	% of total stock
Privately rented	6.6	58	2.9	16
Owner occupied	3.7	32	9.9	55
Local authority	1.1	10	5.2	29
Total	11.4	100	18.0	100

Sources:DoE, *Housing Policy Review, Technical Volume I*, HMSO, London, 1977, p39; Inquiry into British Housing, *Supplement*, NFHA, London, 1985, pxii.

While many of these transfers into owner occupation involved vacant properties, substantial numbers were sales to sitting tenants. For example, surveys carried out following the 1957 Rent Act (see below) found that, of the houses then being sold by private landlords, half were bought by sitting tenants and half were bought with vacant possession (Donnison *et al.*, 1961). It has been estimated that, over the period 1914 to 1975, about one in four transfers of privately rented dwellings to owner occupation involved purchases by sitting tenants (House of Commons Environment Committee, 1982).

Table 4.2: Components of change of the PRS in England and Wales 1938-75 (millions)

1938 stock	6.6
Dwellings sold into owner occupation	- 2.6
Dwellings sold to local authorities	- 0.3
Demolitions and changes of use	- 1.2
New building and conversions	+ 0.4
Net change	- 3.7
1975 stock	2.9

Source: DoE, *Housing Policy Review, Technical Volume I*, HMSO, London, 1977, p39.

Second, 1.2 million dwellings were demolished in slum clearance schemes or – to a much lesser extent – were switched from residential into commercial uses such as offices. Slum clearance by local authorities began to occur nationwide on a significant scale in the 1930s, during which period more than 270,000 dwellings were either demolished or closed under slum clearance schemes in England and Wales (Bowley, 1945). In the decade after the Second World War, clearance was given a low priority in the face of the housing shortage, but from 1955 it expanded considerably. In the decade from 1955 to 1964, an average of 58,000 houses were demolished each year, while in the decade from 1965 to 1974 it averaged 78,000 (calculated from Merrett, 1979). It has been estimated that eight out of ten dwellings demolished in slum clearance schemes were privately rented (House of Commons Environment Committee, 1982).

Holmans (1987) points out that nearly 30 per cent of the stock of dwellings rented from private landlords in 1939 had been demolished or destroyed by 1981. Most of these dwellings had been built in the nineteenth century or even earlier. Many had been constructed before the introduction of building bye-laws in the late nineteenth century, lacked some or all of the standard amenities, and were now considered unfit for human habitation. Years of inflexible forms of rent control had made it uneconomic for landlords to keep their properties in a good state of repair. Meanwhile, the excess demand for rented accommodation meant they had little need to do so in order to find tenants for them (DoE, 1977).

Third, a further 0.3 million dwellings were acquired by local authorities. In many cases, this acquisition of privately rented dwellings by local councils involved compulsory purchases necessary to effect developments such as road traffic improvements. But in some cases it was part of an explicit 'municipalisation' strategy (see below), particularly in Labour-led inner city local authorities such as Islington in London. Following the 1974 Housing Act, an unknown quantity of privately rented dwellings were acquired by housing associations undertaking inner city rehabilitation schemes, particularly in Housing Action Areas (see Kemp, 1981, for a local case study).

In addition to the decline of the existing stock, there was very little *new construction* for private renting following the Second World War (see Table 4.2). This lack of new construction in the post-war period is a key feature of the decline of private renting in Britain. It is also something that marks it out from most other advanced industrial nations, where new building for private rental was not uncommon. One important reason for this difference was that, unlike Britain, some other countries in Europe were willing to provide property subsidies and tax incentives to private landlords to construct new housing to let (Harloe, 1985).

Reasons for decline

The decline of private renting has been the outcome of a complex set of factors (see Hamnett and Randolph, 1988; Holmans, 1987; Kemp, 1993), the relative importance of which has varied over time. These factors operated on both the demand and supply sides; and they reflected elements of choice and constraint for both landlords and tenants. One crucial nexus of factors in this decline has been the housing finance system – that is, the ways in which housing has been taxed, subsidised and priced – and, therefore, the way in which the state has intervened in housing provision. Thus, the state has been deeply implicated in the decline of private renting (Kemp, 1997).

One of the more salient features of the housing finance system that has affected decline is rent control. These have existed in one form or another since 1915 and affected more or less of the sector. Rent control helped to reduce the rate of return from private letting. It gave landlords an incentive to sell their property on vacant possession to the owner occupied sector and place the proceeds in more remunerative investments (see Maclennan, 1982; Robinson, 1979). Although some critics of rent control have over-emphasised its importance to the decline of private renting, it has nonetheless been a crucial factor. It is not just the fact that rents were controlled that was important; it was also the highly inflexible way in which (prior to 1965) they were controlled that accounts for the very sharp decline in Britain compared with many other countries.

The growth of demand for owner occupation has also helped account for the decline of private renting. Quite apart from any inherent advantages which ownership may have over renting (see Whitehead, 1979), it had two important financial attractions for much of the post-war period. First, high rates of inflation meant that mortgage repayments on loans taken out in previous years fell quite quickly in real terms. Second, on average house prices increased broadly in line with average earnings and faster than the rate of inflation for most of the post-war period. Consequently, owner occupiers were able to make significant capital gains, a possibility not open to those who remained as tenants (Saunders, 1990). The result was that most people who could afford to buy their own home did so rather than rent it privately. Many of the people who remained as private tenants could not afford to pay a rent that would have given landlords an economic rate of return (House of Commons Environment Committee, 1982).

The provision of tax relief to the owner occupied sector up to the late 1990s also helped to shift demand away from private renting and to home-ownership. Further, to the extent that tax relief was capitalised into house prices, it increased the rent that a landlord required in order to continue letting the accommodation rather than selling it to the owner occupied sector.

In combination, rent control, the tax incentives to home-ownership and the low-incomes of many private tenants, helped to create a value gap between vacant possession and sitting tenant prices (Doling and Davies, 1984; Hamnett and Randolph, 1988). This gave landlords an incentive to sell when they got vacant possession. It also meant that landlords seeking to disinvest made less money by selling with a sitting tenant than they could with vacant possession. Landlords' inability to regain possession at the time of their choosing – a result of the security of tenure provisions of the Rent Acts – was therefore a disincentive to investment in rental property.

Further, the value gap also gave an incentive to speculators to buy tenanted property and then sell to owner occupiers – sometimes after renovation works had been carried out, often with the aid of an improvement grant (Crook and Martin, 1988) – as soon as the tenant could be persuaded to leave. The value gap therefore helped to generate problems of harassment and insecurity of tenure for tenants, which in turn made renting from a private landlord less attractive (Kemp, 1988).

Rent controls, the low-incomes of many private tenants and, according to Nevitt (1966), the lack of depreciation tax allowances, made it difficult for landlords to adequately maintain or improve their properties. Although improvement grants were available in one form or another from 1949, the extra rent that landlords were able to charge after improvement tended to be insufficient to cover their share of the cost of improvement works. Moreover, improvement policy was essentially remedial in nature, that is, concerned with remedying defects rather than preventing them from arising in the first place (SHAC 1981; Thomas, 1986).

Since 1919, governments have provided subsidies to social housing landlords, which have enabled them to provide housing at a lower rent (for comparable accommodation) than private landlords have been able to do (Milner Holland Committee, 1965). In Britain, governments (even Conservative ones) have generally been reluctant to provide subsidies to private landlords. Leaving aside improvement grants, prior to 1979, the only subsidies provided to private landlords were Exchequer grants payable on new housing built for letting under Labour's Housing Act 1924 (Kemp, 1984).

One reason for the reluctance to provide such subsidies was the negative image of private landlords in Britain. This image was encapsulated in the phrase 'Rachmanism', defined in the *Concise Oxford Dictionary* as the 'exploitation and intimidation of slum tenants by unscrupulous landlords.' In this imagery, poor or unwilling tenants were perceived to be renting substandard property from inefficient or even disreputable landlords. In turn, this poor image reduced both the demand for private renting from those able to afford owner occupation or gain access to social rented housing and the willingness of 'lily-white' organisations such as pension funds to invest in new supply within the sector.

The private rented sector was also the subject of what was at times intense and emotionally charged political debates about its future and appropriate policy responses to its decline (Duclaud-Williams, 1978; Cullingworth, 1979). While housing to let is essentially a long-term investment, governments and their policies come and go. The political uncertainty surrounding the future of private renting added an element of political risk to investment in the sector. This almost certainly increased the rate of return (and hence the rent) that landlords required in order to invest in private housing to let (Whitehead and Kleinman, 1986, 1989).

Control and disinvestment, 1939-53

The post-war housing shortage and the election of a Labour government in 1945 were important reasons for the lack of new construction for private renting. One consequence of the post-war housing scarcity was that blanket rent controls were continued after the hostilities had ended. The 1939 Rent and Mortgage Interest Restrictions Act had extended rent control to virtually all rented housing and froze rents at their September 1939 level. The second Ridley Committee, which reported in 1945, recommended that, in view of the post-war housing shortage, rent control should be continued for a considerable period. The committee also proposed, however, that rent tribunals should be established to determine 'fair rents' on properties in the unfurnished privately rented sector. Another significant proposal was that new construction should be exempt from rent controls, as it had been between 1919 and 1939 (Ridley Committee, 1945).

While the post-war Labour government accepted the recommendation that rent control should be continued, it did not exempt new construction from rent controls and nor did it take up the Ridley Committee's proposal on rent tribunals for unfurnished housing. The failure to exempt new construction from rent controls made it almost inevitable that little *new construction* for private rental would be undertaken in the post-war years. And the failure to address the anomalies produced by previous, relatively inflexible forms of rent control or to introduce a more flexible system such as rent tribunals, made it highly likely that the *existing stock* would decline in size as rents fell in real terms.

While the existence of rent controls on new construction was obviously a major deterrent to building for private rental, it was not the only factor. As Minister of Health, Bevan persuaded the Labour government (against considerable opposition in cabinet) to focus the post-war building programme very largely on council housing. Whereas the Conservatives had promised to provide subsidies for both private and local authority house-building (Kemp, 1991), Labour reserved them exclusively for local authorities. Under the system of building licences, local authorities were expected to provide 80 per cent of new construction. Given the existence of rent controls, the lack of subsidies and the limited permission to build (Merrett, 1979), it was hardly surprising that the private sector focused its output on the market for owner occupation rather than housing to let.

The Housing Act 1949 introduced improvement grants for privately owned dwellings, including those owned by private landlords. Improvement grants had been introduced for rural dwellings in 1926, and the 1949 Act extended them to urban properties. There was at this time considerable discussion about the morality of giving grants to private landlords. Bevan made it clear that these grants were *not* intended to '...permit landlords to make good the arrears of repairs that they should themselves have carried out long ago' (quoted in Cullingworth, 1979, p75). Instead, they were for *improvements* such as the installation of baths or inside WCs.

When the Conservatives returned to office in 1951, the housing shortage was still very great and hence so was the political imperative both to maintain rent controls on the existing stock of privately rented dwellings and to increase the output of new houses. As a 'plannable instrument' it was hardly surprising that local authorities continued to dominate the construction of new houses. The Conservatives at this time were more concerned with reaching the target of 300,000 new homes per annum that they had promised in the 1951 election campaign than by whom the houses were built (Holmans, 1987). With private housing construction gradually recovering as building controls were removed, it was difficult to argue a case for the extension of subsidies to the private landlord.

Meanwhile, private sector rents were frozen at their September 1939 level, which in many cases was the August 1914 level plus 40 per cent. The result was that private rents fell in real terms as house prices, earnings and retail prices all increased following the war. The consumer price index increased by 105 per cent between 1939 and 1951 and the price of building maintenance trebled (Holmans, 1987). Frozen rents and rising property values meant that rental yields fell substantially. With a significant gap opening up between tenanted and vacant possession house prices, many landlords took whatever opportunities arose to sell up and invest elsewhere. The continuing housing shortage, combined with an increasing appetite for owner occupation and growing numbers of households able to afford to buy, meant that landlords had a ready market for their properties (Hamnett and Randolph, 1988). Between 1939 and 1953, an estimated half a million dwellings were sold by private landlords to owner occupiers in England and Wales. A further 1.2 million were sold in the period from 1953 to 1961 (Holmans, 1987).

Decontrol and disinvestment, 1954-63

While the new Conservative government sought and succeeded in raising housing output to 300,000 a year by 1953, it also began to focus attention on the condition of the existing stock of (mostly privately rented) houses, much of which was seriously sub-standard. As Merrett (1982) has pointed out, the Conservatives' white paper *Housing – the Next Steps* (MHLG, 1953) saw the problem of sub-standard housing as one of the privately rented sector. Apart from the age of the stock – 30 per cent of which was a 100 years or more old – the white paper identified two causes of '...the neglect which privately-owned houses have suffered in recent years' (MHLG, 1953, p6). These were (i) controls on building works and materials such as timber and steel, and (ii) 'the more serious cause', rent control.

The structure of rents in the privately rented sector was described in the white paper as 'hopelessly illogical', with, for example, different rents being charged for identical houses in the same street. In addition, many rents were insufficient to enable landlords to maintain their houses in adequate repair. Since the housing shortage was still sufficiently severe as to prevent rents from being completely decontrolled, 'The main question resolves itself, therefore, into the most equitable way of allowing such increases in the rents of privately-owned houses as will enable the landlord to keep the house in good repair' (MHLG, 1953, p7).

The subsequent House Repairs and Rents Act 1954 permitted limited increases in the rents of dwellings which had been let before September 1939 and which had been maintained or put into a good state of repair (Doling and Davies, 1984). The size of the permitted increase varied according to the extent to which the landlord was responsible for repairs and decoration. The aim was to give landlords an incentive to increase their expenditure on repair and maintenance. In addition, rent control was lifted from newly constructed and converted dwellings.

The 1954 Act also eased the rather restrictive conditions on discretionary improvement grants administered by local authorities. The take-up of grants under the 1949 Act had been quite low: between 1949 and 1953 only 7,000 grants were awarded in the whole of Britain (Cullingworth, 1979). With the help of a publicity campaign, the take-up of improvement grants increased following the 1954 Act, such that, in the five years up to 1959, a total of 154,000 were awarded. However, only one in ten went to private landlords. Most were for the installation of baths and hot water (Thomas, 1986).

Some dwellings were beyond repair. From the mid-1950s the Conservative government began a new drive towards the replacement of the slums (Merrett, 1979). This new approach involved the large-scale clearance of mainly privately rented terraced housing, much of it built to low standards in the nineteenth century and suffering from inadequate maintenance expenditure because of the low rents produced by decades of crude rent controls. The cleared stock was replaced by new council housing, built to modern standards and with the help of substantial subsidies from the Exchequer, which made it much more attractive for tenant households than privately rented accommodation. This process further hastened the decline in the privately rented sector.

Although rents on new construction had been decontrolled, there is little evidence that this led to a resurgence of building for private rental. The demand for new private housing was focused on the owner occupied market. Decades of rent control in the private rented sector and large subsidies for council housing had created a low rent environment that was not easily shed. Rent-to-income ratios in the 1950s were relatively low. The provision of subsidies to the privately rented landlord seems to have been politically out of the question, even for Conservative governments.

The unwillingness of the Conservatives to provide subsidies to private landlords in the way that other west European countries had done reflected the political controversy that surrounded the privately rented sector from the mid-1950s onwards. This period witnessed a growing polarisation in political debates on the privately rented sector. These debates were often marked by the use of stereotypical images of both landlords and tenants.

The Labour Party became actively opposed to the privately rented sector. Its 1956 conference resolved, for example, that '…private landlordism had failed' (quoted in Wicks, 1973). It had evidently failed because slum housing was owned and let by private landlords. Hence the problem of the slums was seen as being due, not so much to the facts that the dwellings were old, had been built before the introduction of building standards, and had been constructed without state subsidies for tenants who could not afford to pay for anything other than poor quality housing. Nor was the failure due to decades of inflexible rent controls, which made it uneconomic to maintain such housing in an adequate state of repair. Instead, it was largely seen as being a function of *ownership*, of the fact that it belonged to private landlords.

The answer to this perceived failure of private landlordism was seen to be 'municipalisation' (as it was called) of the existing stock of privately rented housing. Local authority ownership was seen as the solution to the problem of private landlord ownership. That municipalisation should be seen as the best way to deal with the problems of the privately rented sector was a reflection, not only Labour's distrust of the private landlord, but also the statist welfare regime which marked Britain out from many other west European countries (see Dunleavy, 1989). In housing policy, this statist approach during the 1955 to 1975 period was reflected in the heavy reliance on local authorities – rather than voluntary organisations or the private sector – to provide new, subsidised rented housing (Harloe, 1995). At the same time, it reflected the tendency in housing policy in Britain towards uniform solutions being applied to what were often diverse housing problems. This was a period when the public tended to respect and trust public officials and when local authorities were seen as being at the cutting edge of housing management (Kemp and Williams, 1991).

From 1953 official Labour Party policy on privately rented housing involved 'comprehensive municipalisation' of the sector. Under this policy, it was envisaged that local authorities would be given powers to compulsorily purchase rented housing from private landlords. This remained the official line until 1961 when it was replaced with 'selective municipalisation' on default where there was persistent neglect by the landlord (Wicks, 1973). Although there was little prospect, on cost grounds alone, of a policy of large-scale municipalisation being put into practice, it can only have added to the political risk surrounding investment in the privately rented sector. It also reflected a view that the decline and indeed the death of the private landlord was a desirable, if not an inevitable, outcome and that nothing should be done to encourage this unwanted species. In the meantime, rent control was necessary to prevent unscrupulous landlords from exploiting their tenants by charging 'exorbitant' rents for slum housing.

For the Conservatives, the privately rented sector had not failed but, if problems existed, it was *because* of rent controls. By keeping rents at below the market level, rent control made disinvestment from the sector inevitable. Rent control also meant that private landlords could not afford to undertake the necessary repairs that they would otherwise have done. It was imperative, therefore, that such controls should be lifted as soon as the housing shortage had sufficiently abated to make that politically feasible. Once controls were lifted, it was argued, rents would rise, the sector would be profitable once again and investment would return. It followed from this argument that, since the problem was rent control, decontrol would be sufficient to revive the fortunes of the privately rented sector; subsidies were neither necessary nor desirable.

This polarisation of views was exhibited most clearly in the debates surrounding the passage of the 1957 Rent Act. One of the most controversial measures to be passed in the 1950s, the parliamentary debates on the Rent Bill, as Cullingworth (1979, p117) has pointed out, had '...a curious air of unreality about them.' Similarly, Barnett (1969) has noted that these debates were heavy in '...political symbolism in which myths about landlords and tenants defied rational discussion' (quoted in Stafford and Doling, 1981).

The impact of the 1957 Rent Act was much less dramatic than many of its supporters hoped or its opponents feared (Cullingworth, 1979). A study funded by the Joseph Rowntree Memorial Trust found that many landlords increased their rents (some by a considerable amount), but others did not, even though they were allowed to do so under the legislation (Donnison et al., 1961). Decontrol did not bring a halt to disinvestment by landlords. Rather, landlords continued to get out of the sector by selling to owner occupiers, including their own sitting tenants. Indeed, it seems that the rate of disinvestment by landlords actually increased rather than decreased after 1957. In the 62 months between April 1951 and June 1956, the privately rented sector in Britain shrank from 6.2 to 5.4 million dwellings, a decline of 154,000 per annum. Yet, in the 66 months from June 1956 to December 1961, the sector shrank to 4.1 million dwellings, a rate of decline of 236,000 per annum (see Table 4.3). In only six and a half years (June 1965 to December 1961) the privately rented sector had fallen from over a third to a quarter of all dwellings in Britain – an unprecedented rate of decline.

Table 4.3: Estimated number of privately rented dwellings in Great Britain, 1951-61

Date	No. of dwellings	% of housing stock
April 1951	6.2m	45
June 1956	5.4m	36
December 1961	4.1m	25

Source: Francis Committee (1971) *Report of the Committee on the Rent Acts*, HMSO: London, p80.

Disinvestment from the privately rented sector by sales to owner occupation was facilitated and accelerated by the Housing and House Purchase Act 1959 (Merrett, 1982). This Act made loans from the Exchequer available to building societies for lending to buyers of pre-1919 – and hence mainly privately rented – houses. As Holmans (1987, p155) points out, 'It was part of a policy to promote improvement of older houses, but by making them more readily saleable it could only accelerate the transfer of houses out of private renting into owner occupation.'

The 1959 Act also introduced mandatory improvement grants for the installation of five basic amenities: fixed bath or shower, wash hand basin, WC, ventilated food store, and hot and cold water supply. Although take-up increased still further, once again the great majority of these new grants were awarded to owner occupiers rather than landlords. One important obstacle for landlords was that they were not allowed to recoup their share of the cost of the work by raising the rent of the improved dwelling. The 1961 Housing Act permitted landlords to raise rents by 12.5 per cent of their contribution to the cost of improvement. While this might seem a relatively large increase, if (as was often the case) the initial rent was very low because of rent control, the post-improvement rent was still relatively low. Moreover, because landlords were not allowed to offset the improvement expenditure against their tax liability, the net return was much lower, especially on properties that had a relatively short life (Cullingworth, 1979; Nevitt, 1966). At any rate, in the five years to 1964 private landlords received only one in five grants awarded (Thomas, 1986) despite accounting for the great majority of eligible properties.

Partly in response to the failure of the 1957 Rent Act to halt the decline of the privately rented sector, the Conservatives introduced an initiative in the 1961 Housing Act to encourage 'new style' housing associations. This involved £25 million of Exchequer loans to approved housing associations that were to operate on a cost-rent basis and, so the government hoped, would '…serve to show the way to the investment of private capital once again in building houses to let' (quoted in Cullingworth, 1979, p118). However, a number of reports commissioned by the government at about the same time demonstrated that it was not possible to provide new houses built to modern standards without subsidies and still obtain a competitive return (Holmans, 1987). The 1964 Housing Act increased to £100 million the amount of Exchequer loan available for housing associations. However, the emphasis was shifted from stimulating a revival of investment in private letting, to '…the development of a housing society movement which will build and manage houses for people at large who are able to meet the cost' (quoted in Cullingworth, 1979, p118).

Thus, from the early 1960s the Conservatives began to encourage the development of the housing association sector, in the first instance as a stimulant to the return of investment in new privately rented housing, and then when that failed, as a cost-rent alternative to the privately rented sector. The development of this 'third arm' of housing provision (that is, in addition to owner occupation and council housing) was seen by the Conservatives as being especially important to counter the growing monopoly of council housing as the privately rented sector shrank and municipal housing increased through new building (Cullingworth, 1979; Malpass, 2000). The option of providing subsidies to enable the private sector to build new housing to let seems not to have been given serious consideration. This was perhaps hardly surprising given the political controversy surrounding the 1957 Rent Act and the subsequent Rachman scandal in the early 1960s.

It was not until the early 1960s that many of the darker consequences of rent decontrol became apparent, partly because some of the 1957 Act's provisions were postponed until 1961 (Kemp, 1987b). By then, the housing shortage in pressure areas such as inner London was acute, especially at the bottom end of the market. With controlled rents well below market levels, creeping decontrol (that is, decontrol on vacant possession) gave landlords an incentive to remove their sitting tenants by whatever means they could, in order to charge a higher rent. Because of the gap between sitting tenant and vacant possession house values – though this was not due to the 1957 Act – they also had an incentive to get rid of their tenants and sell their properties in the owner occupied housing market, a process that (as noted above) was facilitated by government measures which made it more feasible to obtain mortgages on pre-1919 dwellings (see Hamnett and Randolph, 1988).

In the late 1950s and early 1960s, stories began to appear in the local papers in London about intimidation of tenants, evictions and homelessness. The issue became highly politicised as a result of the publicity – which emerged in the wake of the Profumo scandal in 1963 – surrounding the activities of the West London landlord Peter Rachman. It turned out that one of the call girls involved in the Profumo 'sex and security' scandal had earlier been Rachman's mistress. The addition of slum landlordism to the already potent media cocktail of sex and national security allowed the press to inject new life into the controversy. The fact that Rachman was dead by this stage conveniently removed fears of libel writs being issued that might otherwise have restrained the media. For a couple of weeks, the public was fed a daily dose of stories about the violence and intimidation that Rachman was said to have used against his tenants (Banting, 1979). This publicity confirmed and strengthened the negative image with which private landlordism had come to be associated in Britain (Kemp, 1987b).

The Labour party made considerable political capital out of the episode, which it linked to the Conservatives' 1957 Rent Act and its approach to housing policy (Banting, 1979). Labour generalised the problems that the Rachman scandal had highlighted to the privately rented sector as a whole. It was yet more proof that private landlordism had failed (Kemp, 1987b). Indeed, the new Labour leader, Harold Wilson, appeared to sum up the view of many people on the left of the party when he argued that '...rented housing is not a proper field for private profit' (quoted in Cullingworth, 1979, p61).

In the wake of the Rachman scandal, the ailing Macmillan government was forced to set up the Milner-Holland Committee to investigate the problems of housing in London (Banting, 1979). The committee's report, which was published in 1965, concluded that there was an acute shortage of rented housing in London. The surveys commissioned by the committee found that, although most tenants were satisfied with the way their landlords treated them, landlord abuse was too common to be treated as an isolated problem. The committee also demonstrated that, because of the tax and housing subsidy arrangements then in place, an identical house would cost a household less to buy with a mortgage or to rent it from a local authority than it would to rent it from a private landlord (Milner-Holland, 1965).

Crossman's legacy

The Labour Party, which came to power in 1964, pledged to reintroduce security of tenure for private tenants. Later the same year it passed a temporary measure, the Prevention of Eviction Act, in order to fulfil that promise (Banting, 1979). The Rent Act 1965 incorporated the security of tenure provisions of the 1964 Act and introduced 'regulated tenancies' and 'fair rents' assessed by independent rent officers. Although much criticised, the system of regulated tenancies and fair rents remained intact for nearly a quarter of a century until it was abolished for new lettings by the Housing Act 1988.

Labour's new system of rent regulation was an attempt to provide a fair balance between the interests of landlords and tenants. It aimed to restore tenants' security of tenure while providing landlords with regular rent increases (Donnison, 1967). The expectation was that rents would largely be set by the market, but that where landlord and tenant disagreed, either or both could refer the rent to the new rent officer service. Rent regulation was seen as a significant departure from the previous, rather crude system of rent control that had prevailed in Britain up until 1965. David Donnison – an advisor to the Minister for Housing, Richard Crossman, and one of the backroom architects of the new system of rent regulation – argued that:

> *Unlike rent* control, *which was designed to freeze a market, thus eventually depriving its prices of any systematic or constructive meaning, rent* regulation *is designed to recreate a market in which the over-all pattern of prices responds to changes in supply and demand, while the local impact of severe and abnormal scarcities is kept within bounds* (Donnison, 1967, p266).

Crossman hoped that this new system would 'take rents out of politics'. But he also believed that it was too late to save the privately rented sector and that the future lay, on the one hand, with owner occupation and, on the other, with local authorities and housing associations (Banting, 1979). Perhaps it was because of this view that Crossman's Act re-imposed rent control on new construction, for it is difficult to find any other rationale for this measure. Either way, the effect was to make it almost inevitable that little new private housing to rent would be produced in the wake of the 1965 Act (Kemp, 1997).

House-building in this period was very largely confined to local authorities and the market for owner occupation. Both Labour and Conservative governments supported major local authority house building programmes from the Second World War through to the 1970s. The completion of new local authority dwellings in Britain increased rapidly after the war, reaching 190,000 by 1948; thereafter completions remained at over 100,000 a year for the next quarter of a century (Merrett, 1979). With the aid of subsidies from the Exchequer and from rate payers, local authorities were able to offer their tenants housing that was cheaper, more modern, built to higher standards, and – in practice if not in law – gave stronger security of tenure than that provided by private landlords.

Whitehead (1979) has shown that owner occupation can have substantial advantages over private renting for many households. It is not surprising therefore that the number of owner occupiers grew as real incomes increased. In addition, the growth of participation in the labour market by married women helped to increase the ability of moderate-income households to buy their home on a mortgage (Holmans, 1987). The 1950s and 1960s were for the most part years of relatively high economic growth, stable employment and low unemployment, which helped to underpin the growth in owner occupation.

The attractions of owner occupation for households that could afford to buy increased in the 1960s and 1970s, in part as a result of government policies, which further helped to shift demand away from private renting and towards owner occupation. During the 1960s the fiscal treatment of owner occupation changed from one of relative indifference to active support (Holmans, 1987). One such measure was the abolition of taxation on imputed rental income on owner occupied (but not on privately let) properties in 1963. Another was the introduction by the Labour government of the option mortgage scheme in 1967, which gave non-tax paying households a subsidy equivalent to that provided to taxpayers by mortgage interest tax relief. And when tax relief on the interest payments on consumer loans was abolished, it was kept in place on mortgages (though a £25,000 limit was introduced by the Labour government in 1974).

Thus, in the 1960s and 1970s Labour and Conservative governments introduced measures that increased the financial attractions of owner occupation. These tax concessions became gradually more important as an increasing proportion of working people became liable to pay income tax during this period.

The attractions of owner occupation over private renting were further enhanced by the rising trend of inflation in the 1960s and its acceleration after 1973. Inflation eroded the real value of mortgage repayments and outstanding debt, thereby allowing households to borrow larger multiples of their income than might otherwise have been feasible, safe in the knowledge that a few years' of inflation would reduce the real value of the repayments and outstanding debt to more manageable proportions. Moreover, for much of the 1970s the level of retail price inflation was greater than nominal interest rates, with the result that in real terms interest rates were negative. Building societies (or rather their investors) were virtually paying borrowers to buy a home with a mortgage (Ball, 1983; Merrett, 1982).

The failure of British economic policy to contain inflation was thus a contributory factor in accelerating the decline of private renting, by helping to make it more attractive to buy than to rent (Kemp, 1997). At the same time, the high rates of inflation prevalent during the 1970s had the effect of sharply reducing the rental yield on accommodation let on regulated tenancies with a fair rent (Holmans, 1987).

Since rents fell in real terms during the 1970s while vacant possession house values increased, landlords had a strong incentive to sell to owner occupiers and invest their money elsewhere, rather than re-let when a property became vacant (Holmans, 1987). Although private landlords could make capital gains from rising property values, the Rent Acts gave tenants relatively strong security of tenure (in law if not in practice), which made it difficult for landlords to repossess their properties. Because of the gap between vacant possession and tenanted investment values, it was economically rational for landlords to realise their investment by selling when the property became vacant and putting the proceeds in more profitable and less risky investments. This value gap was in large part a function of rent controls, security of tenure legislation, and the tax advantages of home-ownership (Doling and Davies, 1984; Hamnett and Randolph, 1988).

The gap between vacant possession and tenanted investment values created a space for property dealers to make large profits by purchasing tenanted property, 'encouraging' the tenant to leave and selling at vacant possession values (Hamnett and Randolph, 1988). In some cases, developers were able to obtain improvement grants to improve run-down privately rented houses, which they then sold at a substantial profit to owner occupiers (Williams, 1978). In this way, local authorities, perhaps unwittingly, subsidised developers to gentrify inner city neighbourhoods and to accelerate the decline of private renting and the growth of owner occupation (Crook and Bryant, 1982).

By the early 1970s, owner occupation had become the mainstream tenure to which a majority of households aspired (Holmans, 1987), while council housing had become the largest rental tenure. In contrast, private renting was now a minority sector and one that was continuing to shrink. It had also become much less central to policy debates. This was reflected in the legislation enacted, and in government papers published, in the 1970s. Although a number of measures were passed which dealt with the privately rented sector, the changes they introduced were mostly relatively marginal. The Conservative government under Prime Minister Edward Heath failed to address most of the problems facing the privately rented sector.

However, one measure that proved to be very important was the Housing Finance Act 1972, which introduced rent allowances for private and housing association tenants and rebates for council tenants (Cullingworth, 1979). The introduction of rent allowances was a significant turning point for the private rental sector. Up until 1972, rent control and subsequently rent regulation was seen as the principal means by which rents were to be made more affordable for low-income tenants. While the social security system provided help with housing expenditure for private tenants (and other householders), those who were not on benefit but nonetheless had a low-income were excluded from help. The new system of rent allowances extended income-related assistance with housing expenditure to low-income tenants who were not in receipt of supplementary benefit, the principal means-tested social security benefit (Deacon and Bradshaw, 1983). While rent control was a blanket mechanism, rent allowances were tailored to the individual needs and financial circumstances of the tenant.

More generally, rent allowances could be seen as a mechanism for facilitating the regular rent increases in the private market envisaged under rent regulation. And, as Holmans (1987) has pointed out, they also helped to protect low-income tenants from the rent increases that could be expected to result from the transfer of their lettings from old controlled to new regulated tenancies under the 1972 Housing Finance Act. In the vast majority of cases, the rent allowances were paid to the tenant.

In 1974, the Labour government introduced several changes to rent regulation, though ones affecting only a small part of the sector. Following the recommendations of the Francis Committee (1971) the 1974 Rent Act brought furnished accommodation within the regulated rent system. An important reason for this development was that some landlords were seeking to avoid rent regulation by letting their accommodation with a minimal amount of furniture included in the letting. At the same time, the 1974 Act excluded lettings made by resident landlords from the regulated tenancy framework.

The Housing Act 1974 included several measures that affected the privately rented sector. It introduced housing action areas (HAAs), which were intended to achieve rapid improvement in housing conditions in areas characterised by poor physical and social conditions. HAAs had more generous improvement grants than non-designated areas and local authorities had enhanced powers of compulsory purchase, which were used where landlords and owner occupiers were unable or unwilling to improve their properties within the designated area (Cullingworth, 1979; Thomas, 1986). In Scotland, where HAAs took a different form from England and Wales, the Housing Corporation was especially active in promoting the establishment of housing associations to take over from reluctant or recalcitrant owners and improve properties. This resulted in a significant transfer of inner city private rental dwellings to housing associations within HAAs, especially in Glasgow (Kemp, 1981; Maclennan, 1982).

In 1975 the Labour government set up a review of housing finance, which subsequently evolved into a review of housing policy more generally and became known as the *Housing Policy Review* (DoE, 1977). The Review focused very largely on the two main tenures of owner occupation and council housing and gave little consideration to private renting, which was instead relegated to a Review of the Rent Acts. As Cullingworth (1979) pointed out, the latter was concerned mainly with tidying up and rationalising the existing system of controls rather than with a fundamental appraisal of the role of the sector in the modern housing market. The 1977 Rent Act did little more than consolidate the legislation that was already in place and introduced no major innovations (Stafford and Doling, 1981).

By the time that Labour left office in 1979 the private rented sector had declined to 2.3 million dwellings or 11 per cent of the housing stock in Britain. The rate of decline during the 1970s was approximately 80,000 dwellings per annum. All the evidence seemed to suggest that the sector would continue to shrink in size for the foreseeable future.

Not only had the private sector declined considerably over the years, its role within the housing market had also changed. The decline had been concentrated in unfurnished lettings, so that a growing proportion of the sector comprised furnished accommodation. Increasingly, the sector was providing less long-term unfurnished housing and more short-term, immediate-access furnished accommodation. By this time, many private tenants were elderly, had low-incomes, rented unfurnished houses or flats, and had lived at their present address for many years often dating back to when private renting was the majority tenure. By contrast, a high proportion of private tenants, particularly in the furnished subsector where re-lettings were concentrated, were young, often single, usually without children, rented rooms or flats and had lived at their present address for at most only a year or two (Kemp, 1988a).

A survey of private tenants in England in 1978 found that just over two-thirds had a regulated tenancy under the Rent Act 1965, of whom one-third (or about one-fifth of all tenants) had a fair rent registered with the Rent Officer service. Seven per cent of private tenants had a controlled rent extant from the pre-1965 Rent Acts. Meanwhile, about one in twenty private tenants were renting from a resident landlord and one in six were either living in rent-free accommodation or otherwise renting tied accommodation (Todd et *al.*, 1982).

The 1978 survey also found that the ownership of privately rented housing was diverse and relatively small in scale. Over three-fifths of private lettings in 1978 were owned by individuals, and only a tenth by property companies. About a fifth was owned by employer landlords (Todd et *al.*, 1982). A survey of landlords in 'densely rented' areas of England and Wales in 1976 found that the median size of holding of non-resident individual landlords was only five to nine lettings, while for companies it was 50 to 99 lettings. Thus, private letting in Britain in the late 1970s (as had always been the case) was a fragmented, small-scale and largely un-modernised sector of the market economy (Kemp, 1988a).

Conclusions

The years from the Second World War until the late 1970s witnessed a sharp decline in the absolute and relative size of the privately rented housing sector in Britain. The decline was faster and more extensive in Britain than in most other advanced economies (Harloe, 1985). Despite attempts to pin the blame largely on government-imposed rent controls, this propitious decline was the result of a complex set of factors operating on both the demand and the supply sides. Although some commentators (mainly on the right of the political spectrum) thought that the gradual disappearance of the private landlord was both regrettable and to some extent reversible, for others (mainly on the political left) it was very welcome. Others again believed that the 'landlords' slow goodbye' (Eversley, 1975) was almost inevitable and called for a process of 'managed decline'. Either way, it seemed that the privately rented sector had become a 'stagnant backwater of the market economy' (Michael Hibbert cited in Kemp, 1980) and likely to stay that way for the foreseeable future.

CHAPTER 5:
Private renting since 1979:
towards a new consensus?

Introduction

This chapter looks at private renting since 1979. This period has witnessed major changes in housing and other aspects of social and economic policy, including significant developments in policy towards private renting. For reasons of space, the chapter focuses on the privately rented sector, but it is important to see developments in this part of the housing market in the context of other housing (Malpass and Murie, 1999) and social and economic changes that took place during this period.

Private renting under the Conservatives

With the election of a radical Conservative government in 1979 committed to dismantling the post-war settlement, rolling back the state, and releasing market forces, it was only to be expected that reviving the privately rented sector would become an important goal of housing policy when Mrs Thatcher came to power. In fact, although her first and second administrations were keen to halt the decline of the sector, it was never a central focus of their policy making. Instead, the emphasis – almost the obsession – of Conservative housing policy was on expanding home-ownership. Key secondary objectives were reducing public expenditure on housing and minimising the role of local housing authorities. The beauty of council house sales, so far as the Conservatives were concerned, was that they did all three things – expand owner occupation, reduce council housing and lower the public sector borrowing requirement – simultaneously (Kemp, 1992). Extending home-ownership had an evident priority for the Conservatives over reviving the private rented sector.

The Minister for Housing and Construction, John Stanley, set out the government's intentions and hopes for the private rented sector (quoted in Crook, 1986, pp1031-32):

> *We believe that the private rented sector has got a significant role to play in the provision particularly of accommodation which is required by those who are mobile, those who want accommodation for a relatively short period. There is an enormous demand amongst people who may be saving up to buy sooner, or later, who may have relatively low incomes at this particular time but can see income growth coming, for the availability of short term accommodation. All*

*the various changes that I have referred to in the 1980 Housing Act are meant
to try to increase the availability of that accommodation. As far as the other
wing of the private sector is concerned, the long stay accommodation, our
view is that we have to try and strike as equitable a balance as we can
between the landlord interest and the private tenant interest and we have no
further proposals to bring forward in that area at the moment.*

Thus, the Conservatives drew a distinction between long-stay and short-term
tenancies in the privately rented sector. The former, most of which were believed
to involve older and more longstanding tenants, were to be largely left alone. The
latter, which were to be the subject of changes enacted in the 1980 Housing Act,
were thought to be occupied by mobile households and people who needed to rent
prior to buying their home. Opposition to reform could be minimised by
restricting any radical changes to new lettings.

Housing Act 1980

The Housing Act 1980 included a package of measures aimed at stimulating the
privately rented sector (Crook, 1986). First, easier rules for regaining possession
were introduced for resident landlord lettings. Second, the remaining controlled
tenancies, extant from the pre-1965 years, were converted into regulated
tenancies. Third, the phasing in of increases in fair rents and the interval between
fair rent increases, were both reduced from three years to two. Fourth, a new form
of tenancy known as 'shorthold' ('short tenancies' in Scotland) was introduced.
These were regulated tenancies of from one to five years, which gave the
landlords the power to regain possession after the fixed term. Initially, all
shortholds had to have a fair rent registered, but this requirement ceased to apply
outside Greater London from December 1981 and in the capital from May 1987.

Finally, in England and Wales (but not in Scotland) a new form of tenancy known
as 'assured tenancies' was introduced. These were lettings by approved landlords
of newly built property at market rents. Thus, new privately rented construction –
which had been subject to rent regulation since 1965 – was deregulated in 1980,
provided the letting was an assured tenancy and the landlord was approved by the
Department of the Environment. The landlord approval scheme can be seen as an
attempt to shed the negative image that had dogged private landlordism for many
years (Kemp, 1988b).

The House of Commons Select Committee on the Environment (HCEC)
investigated the private rented housing sector in 1981/82. It doubted whether the
changes made by the 1980 Act would have more than a marginal impact on the
sector. The measures failed to address what it referred to as the 'central dilemma'
for the sector: the gap between the rate of return that investors required in order to
remain or invest in the sector and the level of rent that many tenants could afford
to pay. The committee argued that this gap could only be closed if there was a
significant redistribution of, or increase in, housing subsidies (HCEC, 1982).

In attempting to give landlords of property that was registered with the Rent Officer more regular rent increases, and thereby to raise rents nearer to market levels, the 1980 Housing Act initially had some effect. In the five years to 1980, the average registered rent increased by less than the retail prices index, average earnings, average house prices and the index of repair and maintenance costs. But in the five years following the 1980 Act, registered rents increased by more than all of these indices (Crook, 1986).

The introduction of shortholds was a response to the complaint that the inability of landlords to regain possession was a disincentive to investment in rental property. This was because of the gap between vacant and sitting tenant house values: in order to be able to maximise the selling price of a dwelling, they needed to be able to get vacant possession. The view of many people giving evidence to the House of Commons Select Committee in 1981/82 was that shortholds would have little impact (HCEC, 1982). This was partly because many landlords had already found ways to avoid or evade the security of tenure provisions of the Rent Act. For example, many landlords were using 'non-exclusive occupation agreements', which were licenses to occupy rather than tenancies and, consequently, exempt from the provisions of the Rent Acts (Crook, 1986). Doling and Davies (1982) pointed out that there were, in effect, two privately rented sectors: a smaller regulated sub-sector in which rents were set by the Rent Officer service; and a larger, unregulated sub-sector where rents were set by supply and demand. In some cases, they argued, the Rent Act was not so much evaded as simply ignored.

The attractiveness of shortholds to landlords appears to have increased after the House of Lords ruled in the case of *Street v. Mountford* (1985) that many non-exclusive occupation licences were in fact tenancies. This meant that many of these lettings, which previously had been thought to be outside the Rent Act, were in fact probably covered by it (Kemp, 1988a). While shorthold tenants had the right to get a fair rent registered, landlords at least had the right to regain possession at the end of a definite term of years. The evidence from a survey of private renters in 1988 was that about one in 20 lettings in England were shortholds by that date. Two-thirds of these had commenced in 1988 or the previous year (Dodd, 1990).

The most important feature of assured tenancies was that approved landlords could let them at market rents. From 1965 to 1980 newly built property had come within the regulated tenancy arrangements, and hence a fair rent could be registered on such property. The government believed that rent control on new privately rented construction was a major reason for the lack of new building within the sector. The validity of this assumption was put to the test via assured tenancies. When the Secretary of State for the Environment announced the approved landlord scheme, he made it clear that he had in mind as approved bodies the financial institutions such as the pension funds, insurance companies, and the building societies (who, because prior to 1986 they were not allowed to own houses or land, would operate through unregistered housing associations).

This list was subsequently widened to include other organisations that were 'suitably qualified to build and manage homes for renting' (DoE, 1984, p2).

In order to stimulate interest in assured tenancies, the Chancellor, Geoffrey Howe, introduced capital allowances in the 1982 budget for an experimental five-year period. Research on approved landlords found that the capital allowances were an important reason why many of the approved firms had become interested in the scheme (Kemp, 1988b). However, in the 1984 Budget, the next Chancellor, Nigel Lawson, unexpectedly phased out the allowances after only two years as part of a simplification of the tax system. According to the Minister for Housing, the Department of the Environment was not alerted to this abolition until it was too late to prevent it from happening (Young, 1989). Thus, the Chancellor's objective of simplifying the tax system conflicted with the objective of attracting private investment back into the rented sector. In fact, by April 1987 only 217 organisations had applied for and received approval, of which only a small minority were financial institutions of the type the Secretary of State had been particularly keen to attract (Kemp, 1988b). Moreover, only 742 assured tenancies had been built for letting by that date. A further 2,256 had been built as part of shared ownership and long leasehold schemes, almost all of them by McCarthy and Stone (Developments) Ltd, a builder of leasehold schemes for the elderly.

By the mid-1980s it was becoming clear that the measures introduced in the Housing Act 1980 were having only a limited impact on the sector and had failed to halt or reverse decline (Crook, 1986). Although registered rents had increased in real terms, they were still providing uncompetitive rates of return (Whitehead and Kleinman, 1986). While shorthold was having more impact than many commentators had anticipated, it tackled only the symptom and not the cause of the security of tenure problem for landlords. The real problem was that there was a gap between sitting tenant and vacant possession property values, which meant that landlords who wanted to sell needed to repossess the property in order to maximise their sale price. Finally, deregulation of new construction was clearly failing to have much impact at all.

Towards a new approach

During 1985 the Conservatives contemplated removing rent controls on new lettings but, in the event, shrank back from doing so. There seem to have been two main reasons for this retreat. The first was that it would have appeared to be giving succour to the unpopular private landlord. The second was that the Treasury was concerned about the cost implications for housing benefit of the rising rent levels that deregulation seemed to imply. Housing Minister, William Waldegrave (1987, p10) noted that the opposition to decontrol had come from a '...dubious alliance of those who absurdly believe that all private landlords are bound to be like Rachman and those who fear housing benefit costs rising if there are to be real market rents.' The responsibility for housing benefit lay with the Department of Health and Social Security – which was under pressure from the

Treasury to contain its rising budget – while housing was the responsibility of the Department of the Environment. Thus, inter-departmental conflict of objectives in government affected the prospects of reviving the private rented sector.

However, during 1986 the Conservatives introduced a range of initiatives aimed at paving the way for the introduction of new private investment into rented housing provision. These can be seen as precursors to the more fundamental changes announced in 1987 (Kemp, 1988c). First, the assured tenancy regime was extended to include refurbished property. Second, restriction on building societies owning houses and land was removed. Third, discussions were held with the building societies about the possibility of them taking over the ownership of council housing estates, though it soon became clear that this was not likely to develop in a significant way (DoE, 1987b). And, finally, the Local Government Act 1987 gave local authorities discretionary power to provide financial assistance to private landlords letting on assured tenancies. As well as these measures, the government also attempted to promote a new image for private landlordism. The Secretary of State for the Environment talked of the need to '...exorcise the ghost of Rachman', while the Minister for Housing, John Patten, spoke of wanting to create a new breed of 'model landlords' (1987 p24):

> *I can understand all the objections to old-style renting outside the council sector, but I'm trying to outflank that opposition by creating a form of 'new model renting' – assured tenancies...This isn't people with Alsatian dogs trying to kick down the front door and evict you. It's like motherhood and apple pie. After all who could possibly object to renting from organizations like the Halifax or the Woolwich?*

The 1987 housing white paper

Following their election for a third term of office, the Conservatives published their first housing policy white paper under Prime Minister Margaret Thatcher (DoE, 1987a). A separate version was published in Scotland (Scottish Office, 1987). The white paper was significant and not merely because it outlined an extensive array of policy innovations. For it also signalled a shift in the focus of attention in housing policy, away from the extension of home-ownership – although that was still the most important objective – and towards the 'demunicipalisation' of rented housing (Kemp, 1989).

The white paper set out four objectives for housing policy, the second of which was to 'put new life into the independent rented sector', by which it meant private rented and housing association accommodation (DoE, 1987a). The role that was envisaged for private renting in the white paper was very much to do with its immediate access characteristics and its ability to facilitate labour mobility (DoE, 1987a, p2):

> *...private renting offers a good option for people who need mobility or who do not wish to be tied by ownership...The private sector can offer greater*

flexibility and responsiveness to market demand. It can provide housing in a way that encourages labour mobility and meets changing needs of individuals and the economy as a whole. Restoring an active private rented sector will allow individuals to take advantage of improved prospects in different parts of the country. It will help progress towards a better match between supply and demand for labour.

Underlying the decontrol of private lettings was not only an ideological distaste for regulation but also an apparent belief that rent control and security of tenure legislation – in addition to the attractions of home-ownership – had been the main reason for the decline of private renting (DoE, 1987a). To further this objective of reviving the privately rented market, all new lettings by private landlords were to be deregulated. This, it was claimed, would mean that the letting of private property 'will again become an economic proposition'. Even so, the white paper (DoE, 1987a, p10) took care to explain that the government:

...does not propose to make any substantial changes in the regime for existing tenancies subject to the Rent Acts. It would not be right to disturb these existing tenancies, though minor amendments will be made to the succession rules. As and when such tenancies come to an end, landlords will be free to relet on the new basis.

Thus, once again, the government felt it necessary to stress that existing tenants would not be affected by the reform and that the changes would be largely confined to new lettings. That way, they hoped that political opposition to their proposals would be kept to a minimum. If the Conservatives had learned a lesson from the Rent Act 1957, this was it.

The Housing Act 1988

The proposals for private renting in the 1987 White Paper (and its Scottish equivalent) were included in the subsequent Housing Act 1988 and Housing (Scotland) Act 1988, which came into force on the 15th and 2nd January 1989 respectively. Under the 1988 Acts, all new private lettings were to be either new style, 'assured tenancies' or 'assured shorthold tenancies' (called 'short assured tenancies' in Scotland), both of which were modified versions of those introduced in 1980.

As well as strengthening landlords' grounds for possession, the approved landlord arrangement was abolished under the new style assured tenancies. Assured shorthold tenancies could no longer be referred to the Rent Officer for a fair rent to be registered and the minimum term was reduced from one year to six months. A second type of harassment offence was also introduced by the 1988 Act, largely to allay fears that deregulation would echo the alleged effect of the 1957 deregulation and herald a '...return of Rachmanism' (Kemp, 1988c).

Finally, in order to prevent private sector rents increasing on 'a sea of housing benefit subsidy' (Ivatts, 1988), Rent Officers were given a new role of policing housing benefit claims. From April 1989, local authorities had to refer new claims for housing benefit on deregulated tenancies to the Rent Officer to determine whether the rent was above a 'reasonable market rent' or the accommodation 'over large for the claimant's reasonable needs'. If the rent or the accommodation were unreasonable, the Rent Officer had to determine, for housing benefit purposes only, what a reasonable market rent would be for the property. The housing benefit paid on this reduced rent figure was to be used by the Department of Social Security (DSS) when it reimbursed local authorities for their housing benefit expenditure. Local authorities did not have to use the Rent Officer's figure to calculate housing benefit entitlement, but any benefit paid on rent above that amount would not be reimbursed by the DSS. In this way, the policy conflict between the DSS and Treasury on the one hand and the DoE on the other, over the housing benefit implications of deregulated rents, was resolved by using the Rent Officer as a form of backdoor rent regulation for private tenants on housing benefit (Kemp, 1990). These restrictions in eligible rents for housing benefit are considered in more detail in Chapter 10.

The Business Expansion Scheme

In the 1988 Budget statement, the Chancellor, Nigel Lawson, announced an extension of the Business Expansion Scheme (BES) to include companies letting on assured tenancies, for a limited period, until the end of 1993. It is clear from ministerial statements (e.g. Lamont, 1988; Young, 1991) that this was meant to act as a kick-start to investment in the private rented sector. It apparently did not reflect a view that the sector needed subsidies in order to make letting competitive. Rather, it was intended to be a demonstration project, showing that competitive returns could once again be made now that lettings had been decontrolled and the market set free (Crook *et al.*, 1991).

The BES was originally introduced in 1983 with the objective of encouraging small businesses as part of the 'enterprise culture' that the Conservatives were hoping to encourage. It provided tax relief to investors on the purchase of shares in BES firms and exemption from capital gains tax if the shares were held for at least five years. The generous tax relief provided under the scheme was intended to compensate for the high level of risk involved in investing in small and new firms (Mason *et al.*, 1988). The extension of BES to include residential property companies letting on assured tenancies had an immediate impact. In the first two years during which the scheme applied (1988/89 to 1989/90) £543 million was invested in assured tenancy BES companies. This produced approximately 10,000 dwellings, two-thirds of them newly built (Crook *et al.*, 1991).

While investment continued in the subsequent three years of the scheme, much of it was linked to housing associations and university halls of residence rather than to mainstream private renting. This development partly reflected a key feature of the BES, namely the fact that it, in effect, gave investors an incentive to disinvest after the minimum five-year holding period for the shares. Consequently, many companies sought to guarantee an 'exit route' for investors. Housing associations and universities – who saw the BES as a way of securing additional accommodation on cheaper terms than conventional loans – were able to 'guarantee' that they would buy back the property at an agreed uplift from the price at which they had originally sold them to the BES company. In several cases, the housing association schemes were linked to mortgage rescue packages aimed at preventing owner occupiers in arrears from being evicted. Other assured tenancy companies were sponsored by mortgage lenders with the aim of off-loading their stock of possessed dwellings, which had greatly increased during the early 1990s (see below). This was not a good time for lenders to sell possessed properties on the open market (Crook et al., 1995).

In total, approximately £3.4 billion was raised by around 900 public and private residential property companies within the BES, a substantial sum in a period of little more than five years. BES companies purchased an estimated 81,000 properties, but only about a quarter of them were acquired by what Crook et al. (1995) termed 'entrepreneurial' companies not linked to housing associations, universities or building societies (Table 5.1). An in-depth examination of the BES concluded that only a minority of the dwellings would remain in the open market lettings part of the privately rented sector. Most directors of BES companies reported that they would probably sell their dwellings as and when property prices picked up. The net yields on BES companies were uncompetitive compared with alternative investments and, consequently, even those directors who wished to keep their company going thought it unlikely that they would be able to continue in business (Crook et al., 1995).

Table 5.1: Estimated number of dwellings bought by BES companies in Britain, 1988/89 to 1993/94

Type of company	Dwellings	
	No.	%
Entrepreneurial	21,902	27
Building society	20,252	25
University	31,290	39
Housing association	7,701	10
Total	81,145	100

Source: Crook et al. (1995) Table 8.

An estimated £1.7 billion in tax relief was claimed by investors in BES rental housing companies, which at £21,000 per property acquired was equivalent to 44 per cent of the cost of the average BES property (Crook et al., 1995). The BES did bring a new generation of investors into the residential lettings market (Hughes,

1995) and brought the sector to the attention of the financial institutions. It also brought (albeit in many cases temporarily) what were often good quality dwellings into a rental market that, for much of the post-1945 period, had been associated in the public mind with sub-standard accommodation. But otherwise, it was a very expensive way to give a temporary boost to new investment in the private rental housing market (Crook *et al.*, 1995).

The end of decline

At the end of the 1980s, the long-term decline of private renting came to an end. The sector then proceeded to grow somewhat following rent deregulation (see Figure 5.1), a shift in trend that took the Department of the Environment's statisticians by surprise (Down *et al.*, 1994). Thus, between 1988 and 1995 the number of households renting privately in Britain rose from 2.1 to 2.4 million, an increase of 18 per cent or a sixth in seven years. The sector's share of the housing stock also increased slightly, from 9.2 to 10.3 per cent over the same period. This was an historically significant – if modest in scale – turning point in the development of the privately rented housing sector.

Figure 5.1: Privately rented dwellings in England, 1966 to 2003

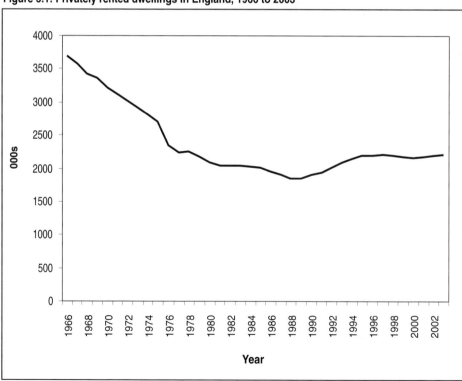

Source: ODPM, Housing Statistics online (www.odpm.gov.uk).
Note: From 1966 to 1990, the data relates to 31 December, thereafter 31 March.

The evidence suggests that this increase in supply cannot be wholly attributed to rent deregulation and the BES. In fact, despite deregulation, the yields on private lettings were still generally uncompetitive with alternative investments, taking into account relative liquidity and risk. And the 81,000 BES properties accounted for a very small share of the change in supply within the sector (Crook *et al.*, 1995). Moreover, at about the same time as rents were deregulated and the BES introduced, the owner occupied housing market south of the Scottish border entered into a slump that also seems to have boosted the private rental sector.

In the late 1980s and early 1990s, in the face of rising unemployment and increased interest rates, mortgage arrears and possessions increased to record levels. Meanwhile, property transactions declined sharply, house prices fell in nominal as well as in real terms, and around a million home-owners found themselves with negative equity in the sense that the value of their home was lower than the outstanding amount of their mortgage (Dorling and Cornford, 1995; Forrest and Murie, 1994). One result of this slump was that some owner occupiers who needed to move, but were unable to sell their property, opted to let it and rented somewhere else instead. Meanwhile, people who might have become first-time buyers delayed house purchase and rented their accommodation from a private landlord.

Hence, the housing market slump of the late 1980s and early 1990s in England increased both the demand for, and the supply of, privately rented accommodation. Crook *et al.* (1995) found that, in 1993/94, about one in ten of all privately rented addresses in Britain were owned by what they termed 'property slump landlords' who were unable or unwilling to sell because of the state of the owner occupied housing market. Crook and Kemp (1996a) estimated that these landlords accounted for around half of the increase in lettings since 1988.

Meanwhile, research indicated that there was little prospect of the financial institutions investing significant sums of money in the privately rented sector, either in the form of debt or equity. This was not only because of the low yields but also because of the lack of regular and detailed information about rents and yields compared with other investments, the poor image of private landlords, and what they perceived to be the relatively high degree of political risk attached to investment in the sector (Crook *et al.*, 1995; Property Research Unit, 1998).

The 1995 housing white paper

The Conservative government took further steps to encourage investment in the privately rented sector in the mid-1990s. A housing policy white paper published in 1995 proposed to make assured shortholds the default tenancy instead of assured tenancies (DoE, 1995). In other words, unless specified to the contrary, any lettings granted by private landlords would be fixed term shortholds rather than assured tenancies. It would therefore no longer be necessary for landlords to issue a notice with their tenancy agreement indicating that the letting was an assured shorthold. Part of the rationale for this move was the fact that some landlords were unintentionally creating assured tenancies instead of assured shortholds through failure to provide the written notice or to do so in the correct manner. Making shortholds the default tenancy in effect signalled a view that private renting was a short-term tenure rather than a long-term housing solution (Kemp, 1997). This change was put into effect in the Housing Act 1996.

The Conservatives' housing white paper also foreshadowed changes in the homelessness legislation in England and Wales, one aim of which was to encourage local authorities to make use of the private rental sector in discharging their re-housing obligations to homeless people. The relative size of the sector varied significantly between local authority areas and some councils were therefore better placed than others to make use of private lettings for homeless households (Bevan and Rhodes, 1997). Nevertheless, during this period an increasing number of councils began to engage more actively with the privately rented sector and to see private landlords as a potential resource to help tackle homelessness in their area.

The 1995 white paper also announced the government's intention of providing tax relief to a new vehicle to be called 'housing investment trusts' (HITs) in order to encourage the financial institutions in the sector. HITs were to be liable to pay only the small companies' rate of corporate taxation – which in 1996 was 24 per cent instead of the standard rate of 33 per cent – and were exempt from capital gains tax. Tax relief was thought to be necessary because the pension funds were exempt from paying tax on directly owned investments, but were thought unlikely to invest directly in residential lettings because of the management hassles and potential risk to their reputation that it would involve. Instead, the institutions would invest, if at all, indirectly via (tax-paying) property companies, but that would reduce the returns they could earn (Coopers and Lybrand, 1993, 1996; Crook and Kemp, 1999).

The Conservative government hoped that attracting financial institutions into the private rental housing market would help to modernise the ownership of the sector. The financial institutions would be able to bring a stain-free reputation to private landlordism and achieve economies of scale and more efficient management than existing landlords. Finally, because of the large sums for investment available to the financial institutions, it would be possible to increase the size of the privately rented sector in a way that would not be possible by relying on investment from private individuals (Crook and Kemp, 1999).

Statutory provision enabling the setting up of housing investment trusts was included in the 1996 Finance Act. As the name implies, HITs were a form investment trust, which are companies that in effect perform fund management on behalf of their shareholders. To qualify as a *housing* investment trust, companies had to invest in 'eligible residential property', which was defined as dwellings built or acquired by the company after April 1996. When acquired, the dwellings had to be vacant or let on assured shortholds and have a value not greater than £125,000 in Greater London and £85,000 elsewhere. The property value limits were intended to prevent HITs from using tax relief to invest in up-market properties. In fact, the limits – which were the same as those set for the BES in 1989 – were relatively low by comparison with average house prices, especially in London. HITs had to be public companies registered on the Stock Exchange, had to have net assets of at least £30 million and had to meet a number of other rules in order to qualify for the tax relief (Crook and Kemp, 1999).

Despite the tax relief on offer, HITs proved to be an experiment that failed. Crook and Kemp (2002) found that no HITs had been established five years after the legislation had been introduced. Estimates of the likely returns on HITs found that they were not competitive with alternative investments (Crook *et al.*, 1998a). The financial institutions considered both the quality and the cost of management and maintenance provided by managing agents to be too low and too high respectively. The tax relief was not sufficient to fully compensate pension funds compared with the returns on directly owned investments, a problem made worse by changes in advance corporation tax in the 1997 Budget. The rules governing HITs were considered to be onerous and also prevented them from operating like a normal property company. And the lack of sufficiently large and otherwise suitable portfolios available for purchase in the privately rented sector meant that they could not invest the amounts required in the short time scale specified by the rules governing HITs (Crook and Kemp, 1999). Thus, the dominance of the privately rented sector by small-scale landlords was itself an obstacle to investment in the sector by financial institutions (Crook and Kemp, 2002).

While the growth in private renting was relatively modest, there was a significant transformation *within* the sector. There was a marked reduction in regulated tenancies, a decrease in tied accommodation, and a very substantial increase in deregulated lettings (Bailey, 1999). In 1988, six out of ten private tenants in England had regulated tenancies, of which under half (44 per cent) had a registered rent set by the Rent Officer. Almost three out of ten private tenants were living in lettings that were not accessible to the general public, of which just over half (53 per cent) was rent-free. As well as other tied accommodation, lettings not accessible to the public included NHS accommodations, student residences and lettings made by relatives or friends at a low rent. Thus prior to deregulation, about nine out of ten lettings were either regulated or not part of the open market and half of these had a regulated rent or no rent at all.

By the mid-1990s, the situation had substantially changed. In 1996/97, for example, six out of ten private tenants in England had deregulated (assured or assured shorthold) tenancies, the rents of which are set by agreement between landlord and tenant. Only one in ten tenants had a regulated tenancy and only two in ten were living in accommodation that was not accessible to the general public. By this time, only one in ten tenants were living in rent-free accommodation and only one in 20 had a registered rent set by the Rent Officer. Similar developments occurred in Wales and in Scotland (Bailey, 1999). These trends continued under the New Labour government.

The legacy

By the time that the Conservatives left office in 1997, major changes had taken place in housing provision (Malpass and Murie, 1999). Indeed, housing was one of the few areas of the welfare state where the Conservative governments of 1979 to 1997 were able to effect significant retrenchment and restructuring. Unlike most other aspects of social policy, net public expenditure on housing was significantly reduced. The composition of government spending on housing had also changed (Hills, 1998). Assistance with housing costs in social housing was shifted from 'indiscriminate' bricks and mortar subsidies to means-tested housing benefit. The cost of mortgage interest relief rapidly escalated during the 1980s, but in the 1990s it was dramatically reduced as the rate of relief was cut back by the Major government. In addition, social housing rents rose over the period at a much faster rate that retail prices or average earnings (Hills, 1998; Wilcox, 1997). Local ceilings on the amount of rent to be taken into account in calculating private tenants' housing benefit entitlement had been introduced in 1996 (see Chapter 10).

The ownership of the housing stock was also transformed, with a shift from public to private during the Conservatives' period in office. Owner occupation increased from 56 per cent of the housing stock in Britain in 1981 to 67 per cent in 1996. Council housing declined from 30 per cent of the stock in 1981 to 19 per cent, and the housing association sector doubled in size, from 2 to 4 per cent of the stock, over the same period (Wilcox, 1997). Meanwhile, private renting ceased to decline after rent deregulation in 1988 and expanded marginally for the first time in seventy years. Just as important was the transformation within the sector and, in particular, the shift away from regulated and to deregulated lettings.

Private renting under New Labour

Throughout the Conservatives' 18 years in government, the Labour opposition was largely on the defensive, defending the old and accommodating itself to the new, rather than generating a radical, new alternative vision of its own. In government, New Labour appears to have accepted much of the analysis and many of the policy prescriptions of the Conservatives – in many ways, that is what was new about New Labour housing policy. They adopted a 'modified reprivatisation' discourse, one stripped of the ideological fundamentalism with which it was imbued by the previous government (Kemp, 1999). In place of the Conservatives' obsession with home-ownership and its mission to demunicipalise rented housing at all costs, New Labour dismissed ideology and self-consciously adopted the mantra, 'what matters is what works'.

Before the 1997 general election, New Labour made few housing policy commitments, though it did promise to allow the phased 'release' of capital receipts from the sale of council houses, to abolish the compulsion on local authorities to put housing management out to competitive tender, and to repeal the restrictions introduced by the Housing Act 1996 on the rights of homeless people to be re-housed in council accommodation (Malpass, 1998). Most importantly for the subject of this book, New Labour also promised *not* to reintroduce rent controls in the private rental market. The party also promised to introduce mandatory licensing of houses in multiple occupation.

After the general election it took some while for the new government's housing policy to become apparent. In Scotland a green paper on housing policy (Scottish Office, 1999) was published in February 1999 and it was not until the following year that an English housing green paper was published (DETR/DSS, 2000). In the meantime, a speech by the Minister for Housing and Local Government in England and Wales, Hilary Armstrong, indicated that an important goal was to 'make the market work' (Armstrong, 1998). While she accepted that market failure could make intervention necessary, this should be limited in scope.

Despite the pledge on rent control, more intervention was considered necessary in relation to 'fair rents' registered with the Rent Officer. Over the previous decade, registered fair rents had increased at a much faster rate than either the retail price index or average earnings. Some of the largest increases affected middle-class tenants living in mansion blocks in central London. It was in this context that limits were introduced on the rate at which fair rents could be increased on the remaining stock of (pre-1989) regulated private and housing association tenancies. New Labour made it very clear, however, that they had no intention of introducing rent controls in the deregulated privately rented market. A well-functioning, market rented sector aimed at younger and mobile households in particular was a central part of New Labour's housing policy (DETR/DSS, 2000).

The housing green paper

New Labour's English housing green paper presented the privately rented sector in a largely positive light. It argued that:

> A healthy private rented sector provides additional housing choices for people who do not want to, or are not ready to, buy their own homes. It is a particularly important resource for younger households. Through its flexibility and speed of access, it can also help to oil the wheels of the housing and labour markets. People moving for job reasons often need to rent a home at their new location, while homeowners whose work takes them away for a period can put their home to good use in the meantime by renting it out (DETR/DSS, 2000, p44).

Thus, New Labour set out a view of the private rental housing market that was similar to those sketched out in housing white papers by the previous Conservative governments in 1987 and 1995. It reflected the political consensus that had developed that the sector played several important, if small-scale, roles in housing provision (Best *et al.*, 1992). Perhaps the only difference between the view set out in Labour's green paper and that in the 1995 white paper, was that the Conservatives hoped to see local councils make greater use of the sector to discharge their homeless responsibilities, whereas Labour did not (Kemp, 1997).

The 2000 English housing green paper argued that the privately rented sector was '...performing below its true potential'. In part, this was because the condition and management of parts of the stock were not good enough. It was also because a small minority of landlords were exploiting their tenants. And, finally, it was because some landlords were failing to deal with their anti-social tenants, a problem that was '...compounded by the fact that such anti-social tenants are often dependent on Housing Benefit, paid directly to the landlord'. It was claimed that direct payments gave such landlords '...no incentive to enforce tenancy agreements or manage their property effectively.' New Labour's stated aim was '...to secure a larger, better-quality, better managed private rented sector' (DETR/DSS, 2000, pp44-45). It argued that most landlords wished to act responsibly and do a good job, though some did not. It was necessary, therefore, to improve or remove the worst landlords, to retain the best, and to attract reputable new ones.

In order to improve the standards of 'good and well-intentioned landlords', several actions were proposed. Local landlord accreditation schemes, which had begun to be developed by local authorities and universities, were to be encouraged and a good practice guide on the subject was published. In addition, the government pointed out that it had supported the development of a National Approved Lettings Scheme, the aim of which was to establish a recognised 'kitemark' for professional managing agents. A rent deposit scheme was introduced in England, the aim of which was to ensure that private landlords did not unfairly refuse to return tenant's deposits. Tenant and consumer groups had campaigned for measures to protect tenants, such as the introduction of a compulsory, independent rent deposit board along the lines of that developed in New South Wales, Australia (Phelps, 1998). However, in line with its more market friendly approach, New Labour introduced only a voluntary, pilot scheme (see Chapter 9). Compulsion would only be introduced, if at all, if voluntarism did not work. In practice, the pilot scheme had only limited success, in part precisely because it was voluntary. It was subsequently scrapped, and the government promised to replace it with a compulsory scheme.

New Labour's strategy to attract reputable investors, particularly financial institutions, into privately rented housing was to create 'certainty and confidence'. This was mainly to be achieved by retaining unchanged the legal framework of assured and assured shorthold tenancies introduced by the Conservatives. This approach was described by the Minister for Housing, Nick Raynsford, as a strategy of 'masterly inactivity'. Meanwhile, the reputation of the sector was to be enhanced by new safeguards against irresponsible or criminal behaviour by private landlords.

In order to make the worst landlords better, a mandatory system of licensing for houses in multiple occupation was promised, when parliamentary time allowed. The Scottish Executive had introduced a mandatory licensing system for HMOs in 2000 (see Chapter 6). The English green paper also proposed a permissive power for local authorities to introduce licensing in areas of declining housing demand. The aim would be to tackle criminal behaviour such as housing benefit fraud, drug dealing or prostitution that were thought to be destabilising local communities and accelerating neighbourhood decline. The green paper argued that an 'unholy alliance of bad landlords and bad tenants' in such areas was making life very difficult for respectable tenants, not least because some of these landlords were letting accommodation to anti-social tenants who had been evicted from social housing (DETR/DSS, 2000). In this way, licensing was to become, in effect, a tool for tackling a criminal justice problem.

The green paper also discussed at some length the idea of introducing conditions on the availability of housing benefit in order to encourage landlords to improve their property or to control anti-social behaviour on the part of their tenants. If introduced, this would mark a significant change in the nature of housing benefit, which is supposed to help tenants to afford their rent. Benefit conditionality would seek to restrict the ability of the tenant to claim this means-tested social security benefit, either because of the behaviour of their landlord *or* the condition and location of the property in which they were living. In the former case, the *tenant's* entitlement to housing benefit would be used as a tool of the criminal justice system for penalising (indirectly) their *landlord*; and in the latter as a tool of housing policy in order to limit the letting of sub-standard *property* in certain localities. It was left unsaid why tenants should be denied their right to a social security benefit in order to punish their landlord.

Housing benefit conditionality is one instance of New Labour's wider 'rights and responsibilities' agenda for welfare reform (Dwyer, 1998). Another example is the proposal to limit housing benefit where the tenant has been guilty of anti-social behaviour (DWP, 2003). A third is the idea of paying housing benefit direct to the landlord in areas of low housing demand only if they are meeting acceptable standards of provision and management (DETR/DSS, 2000). The underlying theme seemed to be a view that housing benefit should, and could effectively, be used as a means to achieve criminal justice ends. The practical and legal difficulties of using housing benefit in these ways to tackle what was a complex set of problems are considerable and the idea seems reluctantly to have been dropped, at least for the time being.

New Labour's Housing Bill

New Labour eventually published a draft Housing Bill in 2003, which was subject to consultation and modification before being introduced into the House of Commons later in the year. Among other measures, the Bill proposed the replacement of the housing fitness standard with a Housing Health and Safety Rating System. In addition, the Bill provided for the introduction in England and Wales of licensing of houses into multiple occupation and selective licensing of private landlords, as heralded by the housing green paper.

Under the Bill, local authorities would be required to implement a *mandatory licensing* scheme for larger HMOs, which were believed to have the worst management and conditions. The Office of the Deputy Prime Minister (ODPM) envisaged that this would encompass HMOs that had three or more storeys and were occupied by two or more households. The Housing Bill also included powers for local authorities to introduce a *discretionary licensing* scheme for other categories of HMO in its area or any part of it. Discretionary schemes would require the approval of the Secretary of State or the National Assembly for Wales. Before making such a scheme, local authorities would have to identify the problems arising from HMOs in the area, show that voluntary methods for dealing with those problems had not or would not be successful, and consider the representations of those likely to be affected by it.

The conditions for obtaining a licence under the mandatory and discretionary schemes were to be the same. Local authorities would be obliged to grant a licence if it was satisfied that the licence holder (and if applicable, the property manager) would be a 'fit and proper person', that the HMO was reasonably suitable for occupation, and that the proposed management arrangements were satisfactory. Licences would specify the maximum number of occupants for the HMO and *may* also include conditions relating to the condition of the house, its management and specify any works or actions that had to be undertaken within a certain time period. Operating without a licence or breaching its conditions would be a criminal offence. No rent would be payable for occupation of an HMO for which no licence was in force – a provision that made it unnecessary to restrict housing benefit on such properties.

The 2003 Housing Bill also included a discretionary power for local authorities to introduce a licensing scheme for private landlords in their area or any part of it. These *selective licensing* schemes were intended primarily for areas of low housing demand. In order to let or manage privately rented property in an area where such schemes existed, most landlords or their managing agents would be required to obtain a licence from the local council. Failure to do so would be a criminal offence and, again, no rent would be legally payable for the occupation of a property for which no licence was in force. The local authority would be obliged to grant a licence on payment of a fee if the proposed licence holder and proposed manager was a fit and proper person and the proposed management arrangements were deemed to be satisfactory. As with HMO licences, the local authority *may* include conditions to the licence concerning the management of the property, the condition of the property and its contents, and works or actions to be undertaken within a specified time.

In the selective licensing scheme – unlike HMO licensing – the Housing Bill proposed that licences must include requirements relating to: the provision to the local authority of documentation for the safety of gas and electrical appliances and furniture in the property; the provision of smoke alarms; a requirement to obtain references for new occupiers; and a requirement to supply new occupiers with a written statement of the terms of their occupation. These additional and mandatory requirements reflected the fact that the aims of selective licensing are different from those of HMO licensing. The latter was intended to protect the health and safety of tenants. In contrast, the principal objective of selective licensing was '...to tackle exploitative or criminal landlords and improve standards of tenancy (rather than property) management' (DETR, 2001, p12). Thus, selective licensing was not about improving unfit housing, but rather about criminal justice, including anti-social behaviour in areas of low housing demand. It aimed to enhance local council's ability in such areas to deal with the activities of disreputable landlords and anti-social tenants.

The 2003 Housing Bill also included new powers for local authorities to take enforcement action in respect of property that was licensable and on individual problematic HMOs that were not subject to the new licensing schemes. These actions included management orders, which were to enable the authority to take over the management of a property for a limited period in certain circumstances, for example, where a licensable property did not have a licence or where a licence had been revoked because the conditions of the licence had been breached and it was deemed necessary to make the order to protect the health, safety and welfare of the occupants or the people occupying or owning property in the vicinity.

The details of these new powers will doubtless be modified as the 2003 Housing Bill makes its way through parliament, but the main features are likely to remain in the subsequent Act. They are also likely to be criticised by private landlords and agents' associations as well as by those representing tenants. As Rugg and Rhodes (2003) have shown, while there is broad agreement across the various interest groups that the privately rented sector is 'performing below its potential', there is no consensus on how the problems of poor condition and management should be tackled. Pressure groups representing tenants tend to wish to expand the scope of regulation as far as possible, while those representing landlords and agents favour a much more limited approach.

Another matter altogether is what impact the measure will eventually have when put into practice. The level of resources made available to local authorities will undoubtedly be an important determinant of the success of the package of measures included in the Bill. Some authorities will pursue their new powers much more vigorously than others. Indeed, Crook (1989) found that many local authorities ignored their existing powers and often regarded HMOs as a low priority. Research on discretionary licensing in Scotland (see Chapter 6) also revealed that HMO work had low political and managerial priority in local government (Currie *et al.*, 1998). But even if they are effective, they may improve the condition of HMOs while at the same time reducing the number of such properties and increasing the rents of those that remain (Crook, 1989). However, the precise impacts are likely to vary according to the nature of the local rental housing market (Rugg and Rhodes, 2003). It is probably a truism of public policy implementation that the outcomes are rarely as beneficial as proponents hope or as pernicious as critics fear.

Housing benefit reform

The English housing green paper included a chapter with proposals for housing benefit in Britain as a whole. This itemised a whole series of failings of the scheme and debated a range of modest improvements that might be introduced. It also considered proposals for structural reform, but argued that these should wait until long-term changes to *social* housing rents had been introduced (DETR/DSS, 2000). Although unsaid, that still left open the possibility of structural reform for *private* tenants. Subsequently, New Labour's 2001 general election manifesto included a commitment to reform housing benefit for private tenants.

In November 2002, the Department for Work and Pensions (which had replaced the Department of Social Security) announced plans for a major reform of housing benefit for private tenants. The scheme was to be tested over two years in ten – in the event, there were only nine – 'pathfinder' local authority areas, before being rolled out nationally. The main aim was to simplify housing benefit in order to ease administration and improve transparency over benefit entitlement, and thereby to increase work incentives. Under this reform, housing benefit entitlement was to be calculated as a standard 'local housing allowance' for the locality. Within each locality, the housing allowance would vary only by household size and type. In the pathfinder areas, there would be no losers at the point of change; about half of all tenants would receive an increase in benefit, in some cases being paid more in housing benefit than they paid in rent to their landlord (DWP, 2002). Housing benefit and its reform is considered in more detail in Chapter 10.

Financial institutions and rented housing

Despite prolonged courtship from the Conservative governments of Margaret Thatcher and John Major, the financial institutions proved unwilling to invest significant sums in privately rented housing. The New Labour government was also keen to attract the financial institutions into rented housing. By the time that their housing green paper was published in 2000, it had become apparent that housing investment trusts had not provided sufficient tax stimulus to induce investment from pension funds and insurance companies into the sector (Property Research Unit, 1998; Crook and Kemp, 1999). The green paper noted that the government was considering the merits of tax incentives for the private rented sector (DETR/DSS, 2000), but it was another three years before anything more was heard. In the autumn 2003 Pre-Budget Report, the Chancellor of the Exchequer, Gordon Brown, announced that he was considering the introduction of new tax rules to allow the setting up of property investment trusts along the lines of US real estate investment trusts (REITs). This announcement was prompted by the recommendation of the Barker inquiry into housing supply that measures be taken to encourage institutional investment in privately rented housing in order to increase the size of the sector (Barker, 2003).

REITs are investment vehicles that pay dividends to investors out of the pre-tax profits, thus ensuring that the returns are taxed only once. They are required to pay at least 90 per cent of taxable income in dividends each year (Adams, 2003). A similar vehicle in Britain could potentially provide the tax transparency that pension funds require from indirect residential property investment. How effective such a vehicle would be in Britain will depend upon the exact tax provisions in the legislation and any rules affecting the operation that are introduced by the government – and by the Stock Exchange if they are to be public companies. One of the lessons from the HIT experience is that these trusts are unlikely to attract institutional investment unless they are allowed to operate more or less like a normal property company and do not have unduly onerous investment restrictions (Crook and Kemp, 2002).

As part of the 2004 Budget, the government published a consultation document on the possibility of introducing a new vehicle for indirect property investment (HM Treasury and Inland Revenue, 2004). Provisionally referred to as Property Investment Funds (PIFs), the vehicle would apply both to commercial investment (such as offices and retail properties) as well as residential investment. PIFs would be listed on the Stock Exchange and probably required to distribute a high proportion of their earnings to share holders. The latter would then pay tax according to their individual tax liability. Many of the details and rules governing PIFs have yet to be decided but they could potentially provide the tax transparent vehicle that financial institutions require in order to invest in residential lettings.

An alternative route for financial institutions to invest in the privately rented sector is via lending money to housing associations developing so-called 'market renting' schemes. These are schemes that have been developed by private subsidiaries of housing associations, which use the surplus generated by them to cross-subsidise their not-for-profit activities. Such housing is typically targeted at moderate-income, young professionals and 'key workers' (such as nurses and teachers). The rents are often a little below market levels and are set to provide a margin of profit rather than to maximise returns. It has been estimated that less than 5,000 homes have been produced in this way so far, but it has the potential to become more substantial (Goodchild and Syms, 2003). The pioneers in this housing are the Joseph Rowntree Foundation, which developed what it called 'city-centre apartments for single people at affordable rents' in Birmingham and Leeds.

Buy to let

If the financial institutions were proving circumspect about investing in housing to let, that was not true about private individuals. Perhaps the most striking development on the supply side of the privately rented sector at the turn of the century was the re-emergence of leveraged investment in the privately rented sector – referred to as 'buy to let' – by private individuals. This was an industry initiative rather than one promoted by government.

Originally, Buy to Let was a scheme introduced by the Association of Residential Letting Agents (ARLA) and a panel of mortgage lenders in September 1996. It involved the provision of loan finance to moderate and high net-worth individuals wishing to invest in housing to let. Previously, the mortgage lending criteria and products available to landlords were '…strictly limited, relatively expensive and quite inflexible' (Heron and Stevens, 1999, p30). For example, private landlords typically had to pay a premium of around two per cent over the mortgage rates charged to owner occupiers. Under the approved Buy to Let scheme, landlords were charged mortgage rates that were closer to those paid by owner occupiers. One condition of the scheme was that the borrower had to agree to the property being managed by a member of ARLA, thereby providing the lender with the comfort that the security for the loan was being professionally managed. The advantage for ARLA was that its members would gain extra business, which was particularly important now that house prices were beginning to recover and property slump landlords were at last able to sell their unwanted properties.

In due course, other mortgage lenders that were not part of the official Buy to Let panel of lenders began marketing loans under a 'buy to let' label (distinguished here by lower case letters). If these other mortgage lenders also required borrowers to use a managing agent, it was not a condition that was enforced in practice, since some of these buy to let landlords did without them. In the end, buy to let became simply a catchy marketing term that meant mortgaged investment in privately rented housing. It helped to normalise the image of private landlordism and make it respectable to invest in this market (Rhodes and Bevan, 2003).

Buy to let proved to be highly successful for mortgage lenders. In the first half of 1999, only three years after the ARLA scheme was launched, mortgage lenders had a total of £3.6 billion in outstanding buy to let loans. By the first half of 2003, 334,800 buy to let loans were outstanding, worth £31.2 billion or 4.3 per cent of the total mortgage market (Council of Mortgage Lenders, 2003). Thus, in only four years the value of buy to let loans had expanded eightfold. The Council of Mortgage Lenders estimated that, in the year to June 2001 alone, as many as 50,000 individuals invested in private rental housing for the first time using buy to let mortgages (Pannell and Heron, 2001).

Why did buy to let develop into such a significant market? Firstly, market conditions within the privately rented sector had significantly improved. The 1988

Housing Act had deregulated rents. It had also introduced assured shorthold tenancies, which meant that landlords could be sure of regaining vacant possession, as could lenders in the event of the landlord defaulting on the mortgage (Rhodes and Bevan, 2003). The New Labour government had kept its promise to leave the letting framework introduced by the Conservatives in place, thereby almost eliminating political risk. From the mid-1990s, interest rates fell to historically low levels, making it financially viable to borrow money to invest in rental housing for the first time in decades. Low interest rates also meant that the returns available on building society and bank deposit accounts were low, thereby increasing the relative attractiveness of property as an investment. At the turn of the century, the stock market fell for three years in a row, reducing the attractiveness of investment in shares. In a related development, the performance of pension funds deteriorated. Meanwhile, many companies were beginning to switch from final salary schemes into defined contribution schemes, which carried much more risk for their employees. This made property seem like a safer bet to some people. Rhodes and Bevan (2003) found that many buy to let sideline landlords viewed their property as their pension. At the same time, the demand for good quality privately rented accommodation seems to have increased from young single people and older divorced and separated adults.

For their part, lenders began to see the attractions of lending to private landlords when previously they had been relatively circumspect about it and largely focused on lending to owner occupiers. During the housing market slump of the late 1980s and early 1990s, lenders gained experience of the landlord market. This occurred both when some of their borrowers let their home when they could not sell it, and when lenders took possession of properties of borrowers in arrears and let them for the duration. This revealed that arrears and possessions were often lower than on owner occupied property and, therefore, that lending to landlords was not as risky as they previously thought. Meanwhile, the decline in first-time buyers meant that lenders had to find new outlets for their loans. Competition among lenders (facilitated by financial market deregulation in the mid-1980s) forced them to provide new products in order to attract borrowers. One result was the emergence of a wider range of loan types and the emergence of mortgage products geared specifically at the needs of private landlords (Rhodes and Bevan, 2003).

Borrowing money to buy rental property enabled landlords to gear up their investments and thereby purchase more properties than would otherwise have been possible (Rhodes and Bevan, 2003) and to achieve a higher rate of return. Typically, the properties purchased were new or modern flats and to a lesser extent houses, which were seen as having low maintenance costs and the maximum potential for sale (if necessary) to the owner occupied market. However, some full-time or 'business' landlords invested in older property in need of refurbishment (Rhodes and Bevan, 2003), thereby doubling up as developers in order to maximise the opportunity for capital gain. Rhodes and Bevan (2003) found that buy to let landlords targeted two main types of tenant: young professionals and students. Many buy to let lenders prohibited the borrower from letting to tenants on housing benefit. Landlords typically hoped to hold on to their 'good tenants', a strategy that minimised void periods and the costs and risks associated with re-letting.

Buy to let appears to have made a modest but important difference to the public image of housing to let as an investment and increased the supply of modern properties in good condition within the private rental market. Concerns have been raised about whether some of the new breed of property investors are naïve or have been mislead into thinking that landlordism is easy money or do not realise that housing to let should be viewed as a long-term investment. However, Rhodes and Bevan (2003) found that buy to let investors did have a long-term perspective, either seeing it as a business (and hence their livelihood) or as their future pension. Concerns have also been raised about the impact of buy to let on house prices in some high demand localities and about rents falling in some areas due to over-supply by buy to let landlords. In fact, so far, mortgage lenders have experienced relatively few problems with buy to let, with low levels of default and possessions (Pannell and Heron, 2001). In the first half of 2003, only 0.45 per cent of buy to let loans were more than three months in arrears, a proportion that was less than half the figure for the mortgage market as a whole (CML, 2003).

There are several reasons why lending to landlords may be less risky than lending to owner occupiers. Firstly, if the tenant cannot afford the rent, the landlord can repossess the property and re-let it to someone else, a process that is almost certainly easier and quicker for landlords than taking possession from a defaulting owner occupier is for lenders. Second, the social security safety net for tenants has fewer holes than that for low-income owner occupiers struggling to afford the mortgage. Third, unlike lending to owner occupiers, lenders do not need to gain vacant possession in order to realise their security in the event of mortgage default. Indeed, '...a lender's position is usually improved by the presence of tenants, as there is usually a rental stream which will normally exceed the mortgage payments. A lender can therefore sell the property with tenants *in-situ* to another landlord investor' (Pannell and Heron, 2001, p33).

Conclusions

The last two decades of the twentieth century and the early years of the twenty-first witnessed major social, political and economic changes in Britain. The housing sector, including private renting, was not divorced from these developments but instead was closely tied up in them. Although the privately rented housing market was not transformed, at the margin there were some significant changes. The long decline of private renting came to an end and, far from having finally disappeared as some hoped and others feared, the sector experienced a modest revival in size and in fortunes. The deregulation of lettings in 1989 helped foster this growth and prompted a new confidence in the sector on the part of private landlords. The owner occupied housing recession of the late

1980s and early 1990s, also helped fuel growth in the rental market, as did the increase in single person households and the expansion of higher education.

By the turn of the century, private renting was no longer seen as an historical anachronism (Cowan and Marsh, 2001) whose decline had to be managed. Instead, it was widely seen as a tenure that could make a potentially important, if limited, contribution to housing provision. Debates about private landlordism were much less polarised than had been the case for many decades. Buy to let had paved the way for an influx of a new wave of highly geared, investment-oriented landlords. It seemed that the private rental housing market had entered a new phase.

Part II
Private renting today

CHAPTER 6:
The stock of dwellings

Introduction

The history and development of the privately rented sector is reflected in the housing stock. In particular, the age and type of dwellings within the sector reflect the legacy of the house-building booms of the nineteenth century; the lack of new building for much of the twentieth century; the history of rent controls and their impact on repair and maintenance over the same period; and the more recent, modest revival of fortunes. This chapter looks at the privately rented housing stock today. It examines recent trends in the size of the sector, as well as the location and nature of the stock and its condition. It also looks at houses in multiple occupation, their incidence, condition and occupants.

Recent trends

From around the First World War until the late 1980s, the *proportion* of the housing stock in Britain that was rented from private landlords gradually declined. It was not until the Second World War that the *number* of such dwellings also began to decline, which thereafter it did year on year until the late 1980s. The reasons for this decline and the mechanisms by which it took place were discussed earlier in this book. The net result of this long-term decline was that, by the late 1980s, only about one in ten dwellings in Britain were rented privately (Table 6.1).

However, since the late 1980s the number, and to a lesser extent the proportion, of privately rented homes has increased. Thus, between 1989 and 2002 the number of dwellings in the sector in Britain expanded by around a sixth, rising from 2.1 to around 2.4 million. As a proportion of the total stock, the sector increased by about half a percentage point, rising from 9.2 per cent to 9.8 per cent, over this period. This increase occurred in the early to mid-1990s, since when the sector has more or less stabilised in size.

Table 6.1: The size of the private rented sector in Britain, 1951 to 2001

Year	000's	% of total stock
1951	7,130	52
1961	4,952	31
1971	3,673	20
1981	2,354	11
1991	2,177	10
2001	2,434	10

Source: ODPM, Housing Statistics On-line (www.odpm.gov.uk).

While the private rental sector remains a relatively small part of the overall housing system, the increase since the late 1980s is significant, for it came after seven decades of more or less continuous decline. It is noteworthy, however, that the increase has been more prominent in England and Wales than in Scotland. Indeed, although the number of private rental dwellings has increased in Scotland, as a proportion of the stock the sector has remained stagnant (Table 6.2). The reasons for this differential recovery are unclear, but may in part relate to the fact that England but not Scotland experienced a slump in the owner occupied housing market from the late 1980s to the mid-1990s. This was the period when most of the growth in lettings took place, during which there was a marginal shift of both dwellings and households from owner occupation to private renting.

Table 6.2: Change in the size of private rented sector dwelling stock in Britain, 1988 to 2001

Year[1]	England	Wales	Scotland	Britain
	000s	000s	000s	000s
1988	1,848	90	139	2,077
2001	2,168	111	156	2,434
	(+17%)	(+23%)	(+12%)	(+17%)
	%	%	%	%
1988	9.6	7.8	6.7	9.2
2001	10.2	8.7	6.7	9.8

Source: ODPM, Housing Statistics (www.odpm.gov.uk).
Note: 1. December 1988 and April 2001.

During the late 1980s and early 1990s, house prices in England fell in nominal as well as real terms, leaving perhaps a million dwellings in 'negative equity', that is, the market value of the dwelling was less than the amount of the outstanding mortgage (Forrest and Murie, 1994). Unable or unwilling to sell, substantial numbers of owner occupiers who needed to move opted to let their property while renting another somewhere else. Thus, the property slump created both additional demand as well as supply within the sector from existing owner occupiers. Meanwhile, people who might otherwise have been first-time buyers chose to rent accommodation and defer purchase for the short-term. Indeed, the age of first-time buyers increased in this period.

Since the mid-1990s, house prices have recovered and the growth in private renting has tailed off, but this episode reinforces the point that the privately rented sector is not an isolated market, but rather is connected to the wider housing system. What happens in one part of the housing market can affect other parts. There is considerable movement of *households* into the sector from other tenures as well as vice versa (Kemp and Keoghan, 2001). This inter-tenure movement of households is considered in more detail in Chapter 8. There is also considerable movement of *properties* between private renting and other tenures, especially owner occupation (Kemp, 1998). Consequently, the privately rented sector is relatively fluid (DETR, 1998a). About a third of properties move into or out of the private rental market in a five-year period (ODPM, 2003a). This is illustrated in Table 6.3, which shows the components of change in the privately rented stock in England between 1991 and 1996. By far the biggest component of change was the movement of properties between owner occupation and private renting. The flow between these two tenures accounted for six out of ten losses from the privately rented sector and seven out of ten gains to it. All of the other components of change, including new construction, were small by comparison. Thus it is the net flow of properties between owner occupation and private renting that is the most important factor determining change in the size of the sector.

Table 6.3: Gains and losses to and from the private rented sector from 1991 to 1996, England (000's of dwellings)

1991 Stock			1,626
	Gains	**Losses**	**Net change**
Owner occupation	+ 469	- 312	+ 157
Local authority	+ 24	- 6	+ 18
Housing association	+ 20	- 22	- 2
Vacant	+ 111	- 159	- 48
New build	+ 30		+ 30
Demolition, conversions and changes of use	+ 12	- 16	- 4
Total	+ 666	- 515	+ 151
1996 Stock			**1,777**

Source: DETR (1998a) Table 1-2.

Although there is considerable movement of properties between private renting and owner occupation, at the margin the overall size of the sector appears not to be very responsive to changes in rent levels or rates of return. Surveys of private landlords suggest that the majority of *existing* landlords would not increase or reduce the size of their property portfolio in response to changes in the real level of rents or house prices (Kemp and Rhodes, 1994b; Crook and Kemp, 1996b). Potential investor landlords, of course, may be more responsive to market signals than existing landlords. However, Bramley *et al.* (1999) estimated that the stock transfer elasticity from owner occupied to privately rented housing was less than 0.1. In other words, a ten per cent rise in rents would stimulate an increase of less than one per cent in the size of the privately rented sector.

The geography of private renting

The location of the private rental housing market is not uniform but varies from one place to another (Kleinman and Whitehead, 1985; Allen and McDowell, 1989). Furthermore, the geography of private renting varies according to sub-sector, such that the spatial distribution of furnished lettings is different from that of unfurnished lettings and from employment-related lettings (tied accommodation).

One of the most obvious spatial differences is that there are variations in the relative size of the privately rented sector between the three nations that comprise Great Britain. At 6.7 per cent, privately rented housing in Scotland is only three-fifths of the size of the sector in England. Meanwhile, the Welsh privately rented housing market is only three-quarters of the size of the English sector in relative terms. The reasons for these differences in the extent of private renting are not clear. In all three nations, however, the sector is small by comparison with most other OECD countries (Harloe, 1985; Maclennan, 1988).

Analysis of the geography of private renting in England by Kleinman and Whitehead (1985) found that furnished renting was concentrated in London (especially inner London) and in a number of ports, coastal towns and university cities mainly in the south. The unfurnished sub-sector was much more evenly dispersed, but high concentrations existed in London, coastal towns, some northern areas and a number of rural localities. The spatial distribution of tied accommodation was closely linked to the location of the armed forces and agricultural employment, as well as several other occupations (such as policing, caretaking, nursing) that are more evenly spread across the country.

Private renting is over-represented in inner and outer London and in seaside and spa towns. Indeed, London accounts for a fifth of all privately rented dwellings but only an eighth of the total housing stock in England. The reasons for the greater size of the sector in London are examined by Whitehead and Kleinman (1987). There is also a modest over-representation of the sector in rural districts. By contrast, the sector is under-represented in industrial towns of the midlands and north, southern industrial towns and new towns (DETR, 1998a). In Wales, the proportion of households renting privately varies from about two per cent in Torfaen to 13 per cent in Powys (Houston *et al.*, 2002a). In Scotland, private renting is over-represented in rural areas and in the four cities but under-represented in other urban areas (Table 6.4).

Table 6.4: Proportion of households renting privately in urban and rural areas in Scotland

Type of area	% of households
Large urban areas	9.4
Other urban areas	3.2
Accessible small towns	3.1
Remote small towns	8.0
Accessible rural areas	6.9
Remote rural areas	8.3
All	5.9

Source: *Scottish Household Survey, 2001* (own analysis).

The dwelling stock

The characteristics of the dwelling stock vary considerably between the different housing tenures. This is true, for example, of the age and type of dwellings in each housing tenure and their physical condition. The housing stock in Britain is old compared with many of the other advanced economies, such as France, Germany, Sweden and the USA (DETR, 1998a). The private rental stock in Britain is also old by comparison with the owner occupied sector and social housing. For instance, six out of ten privately rented dwellings in England were built before 1945 compared with only four out of ten dwellings in the stock as a whole. Two-fifths of privately rented dwellings were constructed before 1919 compared with only a fifth of the entire housing stock (Table 6.5).

Table 6.5: Age of the PRS dwelling stock in England, 2001

Date of construction	Private renting		All tenures
	000s	%	%
Pre-1919	952	43	21
1919 to 1944	352	16	18
1945 to 1964	243	11	21
1965 to 1980	307	14	22
Post-1980	337	15	19
Total	100	100	100

Source: ODPM (2003) *English House Condition Survey 2001: Corrections Page* (www.odpm.gov.uk).

Despite substantial transfers to owner occupation since the First World War, the private rental sector still contains a fifth of all dwellings built before 1900. However, the proportion of pre-1919 dwellings in the sector is declining (down from 54 per cent in 1996 to 43 per cent in 2001 in England). Meanwhile, the proportion of post-1980 dwellings is increasing (up from 8 per cent in 1996 to 15 per cent in 2001). These trends probably reflect the continuing outflow of older dwellings to owner occupation and the inflow of modern houses from owner occupation and from new construction, processes that have helped to improve the quality of accommodation within the privately rented sector in recent years (see below).

To a great extent, the aged nature of the private rental stock reflects both its domination of the housing market prior to the First World War and the relative lack of new construction since then and particularly since the Second World War. The age of the privately rented sector has considerable implications for the *condition* of the dwellings, a subject that is discussed later in the chapter. The age structure of the stock is also reflected in the *types* of dwellings that comprise the sector. In relative terms, the sector has a very high proportion of flats, especially converted flats. One in six privately rented dwellings are converted flats compared with less than one in twenty in the housing stock as a whole. There are also relatively more purpose-built flats and terraced houses in the sector than in the housing stock as a whole. By contrast, detached and semi-detached houses are under-represented within private renting, as are bungalows (Table 6.6).

Table 6.6: Dwelling types within the PRS in England, 2001

Type of dwelling	Privately rented		All tenures
	000s	%	%
Purpose-built flat	478	22	15
Converted flat	340	16	3
Bungalow	112	5	10
Detached house	138	6	15
Semi-detached house	356	16	28
Terraced house	767	35	28
Total	2191	100	100

Source: ODPM (2003a) *English House Condition Survey 2001: Building the Picture,* London: Office of the Deputy Prime Minister.

The historical pattern of new construction for private renting, and of transfers to and from the sector over time, has produced a distinctive age structure for each of these different types of dwellings. Thus, nine out of ten converted flats within the sector were constructed before 1919. Meanwhile, eight out of ten terraced houses rented from private landlords were built before 1945. By contrast, eight out of ten purpose-built flats were built after 1944. The proportion of the sector that comprises purpose-built flats has increased over time, such that six out of ten dwellings within the sector built since 1980 are now of this type (DETR, 1998a). In fact, over time there has been a shift from houses to flats within the sector, which reflects the shift of private renting from a mainstream tenure housing families as well as single people, to one much more focused on the latter type of tenant (see Chapter 8).

The condition of the stock

The condition of the housing stock, including privately rented dwellings, has improved considerably in recent decades. However, the privately rented sector still accounts for a disproportionate share of sub-standard and un-modernised housing. The condition of the sector nevertheless varies significantly according to the age and type of dwelling. The condition of bedsit accommodation is especially poor.

In the past, an important indicator of dwelling condition was the presence or absence of the five 'basic amenities' of a kitchen sink, bath or shower, a wash hand basin, hot and cold water, and a WC (DETR, 1998a). The importance of this indicator reflected the fact that many dwellings (most of which were originally privately rented) had been constructed without them prior to the introduction of more stringent building and public health legislation in the nineteenth century. Since then, the construction of dwellings with these amenities, together with slum clearance by local authorities and improvement work by owners of homes built without them, has resulted in a rapid decline in the number of dwellings lacking one or more of these amenities. In 1981, 13.5 per cent of privately rented dwellings lacked one or more of the basic amenities, but by 1996 the figure was only 1.8 per cent (DoE, 1982; DETR, 1998b).

Because of this progress in respect of the five basic amenities, the official government indicator of the facilities that should be contained in a modern home has been revised. The report of the *1996 English House Condition Survey* defined a 'modern dwelling' as '…one that has kitchen and bathroom installed after 1964, PVC wiring, modern sockets and modern lighting fittings and a central or programmable heating system which is 30 years old or less' (DETR, 1998a: para 4.33). In effect, this replaced an absolute definition of a modern dwelling with a relative one. On this measure, privately rented and local authority dwellings were less likely to have all modern facilities than those owned by their occupier or housing associations (registered social landlords). The facility most likely to be missing in the privately rented sector was central heating, a feature lacking from a quarter of all dwellings in the sector in England (DETR, 1998a).

The current statutory minimum standard for housing in England and Wales is the 'fitness standard'. Legally, a dwelling is unfit for habitation if it fails to meet one or more of nine requirements laid down in section 604 of the Local Government and Housing Act 1989. Among other things, the dwelling must be free from disrepair, structurally stable, free from dampness prejudicial to the health of the occupants, and have adequate provision for lighting, heating and ventilation. As with the other key indicators of stock condition, the privately rented sector has a higher rate of unfitness than other housing tenures (Table 6.7). The rate of unfitness in the sector is highest among terraced houses and converted flats.

Table 6.7: Rate of unfitness by tenure in England, 1991 to 2001 (% of households)

Tenure	1991	1996	2001
Owner occupied	5.4	5.4	2.9
Housing association	7.1	3.8	3.0
Local authority	6.8	6.8	4.1
Private rented	24.7	17.9	10.3

Sources: DETR (1998b) *English House Condition Survey 1996: Supporting Tabulations* (www.odpm.gov.uk) and ODPM (2003a) *English House Condition Survey 2001: Building the Picture*, London: Office of the Deputy Prime Minister.

The number of privately renting households living in unfit dwellings has fallen considerably in recent years. In 1986, 31 per cent of privately renting households were living in unfit dwellings, compared with 25 per cent in 1991, 18 per cent in 1996, and 10 per cent in 2001 (DETR, 1998a; ODPM, 2003a). However, this improvement was due more to the changing composition of the sector – for example, older, unimproved dwellings with regulated tenancies being sold into owner occupation when tenants leave – than to improvement activity by landlords of individual dwellings (Crook *et al.*, 2000; DETR, 1998a).

In Scotland, the statutory minimum standard for housing is the 'tolerable standard'. To comply with this standard, dwellings must meet ten items, which include: being structurally stable; being substantially free from rising or penetrating damp; having satisfactory provision for ventilation, heating and natural and artificial light; and having both a bath or shower and wash hand basin with a satisfactory supply of hot and cold water suitably located within the house. The *2002 Scottish House Condition Survey* found that only one per cent of occupied dwellings were below the tolerable standard (BTS), the same proportion as in 1996. The main reason for failure in 2002 was absence of adequate heating, lighting or ventilation. BTS dwellings were disproportionately located in the privately rented sector, which accounted for a fifth of them (21 per cent). Between two and three per cent of privately rented dwellings in Scotland were BTS in 2002 (Communities Scotland, 2003).

The amount of repairs outstanding is also a key indicator of stock condition and, again, on this measure the privately rented sector does relatively badly. The sector has higher levels of disrepair than the other housing tenures. For example, the *2001 English House Condition Survey* found that the mean 'basic standardised repair cost' was £38.62 per square metre for the privately rented sector compared with £18.66 for the stock as a whole. On average, privately rented dwellings required £2,500 urgent repair work compared with £1,300 for the housing stock as a whole (ODPM, 2003b). Meanwhile, the *1998 Welsh House Condition Survey* found that the average total repair cost for privately rented dwellings was twice that for the dwelling stock as a whole (Houston *et al.*, 2002a). The *2002 Scottish House Condition Survey* also found a high level of disrepair in the sector. Seven out of ten privately rented dwellings in Scotland showed evidence of 'critical disrepair', defined as disrepair covering elements that are critical to the wind and weather proofing of a dwelling or to its structural integrity (Communities Scotland, 2003).

Average outstanding repair costs increases according to the age of dwelling. This is hardly surprising, as the state of repair of dwellings can be expected to deteriorate over time. The incidence of disrepair is higher among tenants with regulated tenancies than those with deregulated tenancies. Accommodation that is not accessible to the general public has a lower incidence of disrepair than other privately rented dwellings (DETR, 1998a).

As with the provision of standard amenities and modern facilities, the level of disrepair in the privately rented sector is improving. Indeed, between 1991 and 1996 the condition of the sector in terms of disrepair improved, whereas for the stock as a whole there was little or no improvement over this period. Again, the main reason for this improvement was the transfer into the sector of better quality dwellings from the owner occupied sector, rather than because landlords were carrying out more repair work (DETR, 1998a; Crook *et al.*, 2000).

As well as these individual indicators of stock condition, it is important to consider overall measures. The *1996 English House Condition Survey* developed an indicator of 'poor housing' based on unfitness, substantial levels of disrepair, and the need for essential modernisation. On this composite measure, it was found that the privately rented sector had a disproportionate share of poor housing, accounting for a fifth of all households living in poor housing in England. Tenants with regulated tenancies were the most likely to be living in poor housing, while those in accommodation not accessible to the general public (such as tied housing) were the least likely to do so. The private tenants most likely to be living in poor housing were: housing benefit recipients, the unemployed, older people, and young people (DETR, 1998a). These groups are of course more likely than other types of private tenant to be living on a low income and to have relatively weak bargaining power within the marketplace.

The New Labour government introduced the concept of a 'decent home', by which they meant one that satisfied the four following criteria (DETR, 2002; ODPM, 2003a):

1. Meets the statutory minimum standard for housing.
2. Is in a reasonable state of repair.
3. Has reasonably modern facilities and services.
4. Provides a reasonable degree of thermal comfort.

The *2001 English House Condition Survey* found that the incidence of 'non-decent' dwellings was much higher in the privately rented sector than in the other main housing tenures. About half of all privately rented dwellings were non-decent compared with a third of dwellings in the stock as a whole. However, the proportion of the privately rented housing stock that was non-decent in 2001 (49 per cent) was substantially lower than in 1996 (63 per cent). The extent of failure to meet the Decent Homes Standard varied according to each of the four criteria. In 2001, one in ten privately rented dwellings failed the Decent Homes Standard for housing. One in six were not in a reasonable state of repair, about one in twenty did not have reasonably modern facilities or services, and two out of five failed to provide a reasonable degree of thermal comfort to the occupiers (ODPM, 2003b).

The incidence of non-decent dwellings varied across the privately rented sector. About half of all dwellings containing unregulated tenancies were found to be non-decent in 2001, the same as for the sector as a whole. Meanwhile, just over a third of dwellings not accessible to the general public were non-decent. By contrast, three-quarters of all dwellings with a regulated tenancy were found to be unfit by the surveyors (Table 6.8). The very high incidence of non-decent regulated tenancies reflects the old age of many of the dwellings within this part of the privately rented sector, the long history of rent controls that have made it uneconomic for landlords to repair or maintain them properly, and the weak bargaining position of many regulated tenants.

Table 6.8: Privately renting households living in non-decent housing in England, 2001

Sub-sector	% living in non-decent housing
Regulated	74
Non-regulated	49
Not accessible to public	37
All private tenants	49

Source: ODPM (2003b) *English House Condition Survey 2001: Supporting Tables* (www.odpm.gov.uk).

Single person households aged under 60 and couples aged 60 and over are over-represented in non-decent dwellings, as are unemployed people and economically inactive households (excluding students in full-time education), and people in the lowest two income quintiles. Asian households are also considerably over-represented in non-decent housing, but black households are under-represented. The proportion of white households in non-decent privately rented housing is the same as for the sector as a whole. Households in which the oldest person is aged 85 or more are considerably over-represented in non-decent privately rented housing: in 2001, eight out of ten of these households were living in non-decent housing. Three-quarters of privately rented households that have been in their present accommodation for between 20 and 29 years are living in non-decent homes, as are nine out of ten households that have been resident for 30 or more years (ODPM, 2003b).

Thus, non-decent homes are disproportionately occupied by low-income and economically inactive households and especially by older, regulated tenants that have been living in their accommodation for several decades or more. These are among the more vulnerable households in the sector. One of the New Labour government's targets is to reduce the number of vulnerable households living in non-decent homes. For this purpose, 'vulnerable' households are defined to mean those in receipt of income-related or disability social security benefits. On this measure, the percentage of vulnerable households in the privately rented sector living in non-decent housing fell from 73 per cent in 1996 to 55 per cent in 2001 (ODPM, 2003a), a decline of a quarter in just six years.

Houses in multiple occupation

One of the characteristics of private renting is that it can provide flexible forms of living arrangements, including sharing of accommodation by unrelated people and by more than one household. One particular form of dwelling that involves sharing of accommodation or facilities within a dwelling is houses in multiple occupation (HMOs). This form of dwelling forms an important part of the private rental sector.

There are various definitions and classifications of HMOs, including legal definitions such as that set out in the Housing Act 1985 in England. For research purposes, the government (DETR, 1999) developed a six-fold classification as follows:

1. Traditional HMOs (bedsits).
2. Shared houses.
3. Households with lodgers.
4. Purpose-built HMOs with shared facilities.
5. Hostels, guesthouses, boarding houses and 'bed and breakfast' (B&B) establishments.
6. Self-contained converted flats.

Not all HMOs are privately rented or even residential dwellings. Guesthouses and B&Bs are commercial rather than residential premises, though in practice some long-stay residents may regard them as their home. Most purpose-built HMOs are owned by social housing landlords. Many hostels are owned and managed by housing associations and local authorities, though a minority are run by the private sector. Private hostels and board and lodging accommodation occupied by homeless people could be regarded as comprising the bottom end of the private rental market, one step below HMOs (Kemp and Rhodes, 1994a).

The government includes self-contained converted flats as one of their categories of HMO on the grounds that they were originally constructed as one house. However, it is not clear what policy or practical benefit is gained from including self-contained flats in converted dwellings within the HMO category. While they usually involve the sharing of a common entrance and stairs, this is also true of purpose-built, self-contained flats. In North America and the Netherlands houses converted into self-contained flats are referred to as condominiums (van Weesep, 1987).

In this chapter HMOs are taken to mean complete, self-contained dwellings that are occupied by more than one household or by two or more unrelated adults who are not partners. This definition excludes buildings comprising self-contained converted flats. The main focus here is upon bedsits, shared houses, and households with lodgers (categories 1 to 3 in the government's definition above).

The *English House Condition Survey* has provided some basic information about the first three types of HMO listed above, that is, bedsits, shared houses and flats, and households with lodgers. (There is relatively little information available about HMOs in Wales and Scotland.) It has been estimated that there are approximately 450,000 of these HMO dwellings in the private rental sector in England, in which live around 550,000 households containing about a million people (DETR, 1999). Around half of these residents live in shared houses and flats, with the remainder more or less evenly divided between traditional HMOs (bedsits) and lodgers living with other households (Table 6.9).

Table 6.9: Houses in multiple occupation in the PRS in England, 1996 (000s)

	Bedsits	Shared flats and houses	Households with lodgers[2]	Total[1]
Dwellings	56	189	202	447
Households	165	188	202	555
People	267	547	253	1,067

Source: DETR (1999) *Houses in Multiple Occupation in the Private Rented Sector*, Tables 2.2 and 2.3.
Notes: 1. Excludes 8,000 purpose-built HMOs as well as hostels and B&Bs.
        2. The number of people is the number of lodgers and excludes members of the landlord's household.

Traditional HMOs or *bedsits* comprise the smallest part of the HMO sub-sector of the private rental housing market in terms of dwellings, but account for a disproportionate share of households. On average, there are four bedsits in each of these HMOs, of which one is unoccupied. Hence there are three times as many households as dwellings in this part of the HMO market (Table 6.9). On average, each dwelling accommodates five people. The high vacancy rate probably reflects a high level of tenant turnover and the related fact that bedsit accommodation is often of very poor quality (see below). Although many bedsit residents live in traditional HMOs because they have little alternative, not everyone does. For a minority of people, bedsits may meet their personal or lifestyle needs, such as convenient location, anonymity, or freedom from onerous householder responsibilities (Currie and Miller, 1987).

Traditional HMOs are typically pre-1919 houses. They may have originally been built for middle-class households but have since been converted into bedsits. The number of traditional HMOs in England fell by about 10,000 between 1991 and 1996. However, the proportion of bedsits moving into or out of the sector was small by comparison with shared houses and households with lodgers. Two-thirds of traditional HMOs in 1996 were in the same category in 1991 (DETR, 1999).

The number of *shared houses* was relatively stable between 1991 and 1996, but only two-fifths of the shared houses or flats at the latter date had also been shared at the beginning of this period. There is, therefore, considerable movement of dwellings into and out of the shared housing market, with many staying in this sub-sector for only a few years at a time. It is not clear to what extent these shifts into and out of the shared housing market reflected movements between tenures or landlords switching between the self-contained and shared accommodation markets. Shared houses are typically terraced dwellings. More than half of them were built between the wars. On average, they contain three people per dwelling. In total, about half a million people live in shared houses or flats (DETR, 1999). The shared housing market is discussed further in Chapter 8.

Lodgers tend to live in dwellings that were built before 1919 and in flats more than houses. In total, there are about a quarter of a million lodgers in England. While all lodgers are private renters, more often than not their landlord is an owner occupier. In 1996, 68 per cent of households with lodgers were in the owner occupied sector, six per cent were in social housing, and 26 per cent were in the private rental sector. The number of households containing lodgers was stable between 1991 and 1996, but only a third of the 1996 total had also contained lodgers in 1991 (DETR, 1999). This suggests that householders tend to let out a room in their home for only short periods of their lives rather than more permanently. The lodging market thus tends to involve relatively transient tenants and landlords.

HMOs have a reputation for being in poor condition. Research carried out for the Department of the Environment in the mid-1980s found that four out of every five HMOs surveyed were unsatisfactory. They were deemed to be unsatisfactory either because of (1) lack of amenities, (2) inadequate management by the landlord or agent, or (3) overcrowding (excessive number of occupiers to rooms) or over-occupation (excessive number of people to facilities). In addition, (4) one half had disrepair costs in excess of £10,000 (in 1985 prices). Altogether, one in six HMOs were found to be unsatisfactory on all four measures (Thomas with Hedges, 1987).

The physical standard of HMOs appears to have improved since the mid-1980s, but many dwellings within the sector remain in poor condition. Little is known about the condition of HMOs in Wales or Scotland, but the *English House Condition Survey 1996* found that conditions varied across the three sub-sectors of bedsits, shared housing, and households with lodgers. Shared housing was generally in a similar condition to the sector more generally, while dwellings containing households with lodgers was in a better condition. Bedsits generally exhibited the worst conditions (DETR, 1999).

Bedsits have a slightly higher rate of unfitness than the privately rented sector as a whole, but are more likely to be unfit for more than one reason. Two-fifths of bedsits are unfit because they fail to meet certain additional legal requirements on HMOs in respect of unfitness, which relate to considerations such as means of escape from fire, cooking and food preparation, and washing and WC facilities. In total, two-thirds of traditional HMOs are unfit, either because they do not meet the standards required of all dwellings or because they fail to meet those required of HMOs (DETR, 1999).

What to do about the condition of HMOs is an unresolved and highly intractable problem. Licensing is often seen as one route to tackling the poor conditions and inadequate management of many HMOs. Local authorities in Scotland were given discretionary power to introduce HMO licensing in 1991, but by the end of the decade only seven of the 32 unitary authorities north of the border had done so and with only limited success (Currie *et al.*, 1998; Currie, 2002). The Scottish Executive replaced this discretionary scheme with a mandatory one in 2000. The Housing Bill 2003 includes provision for a mandatory HMO licensing scheme in England and Wales (see Chapter 5) as a way to improve conditions within this sub-sector of the market. To some extent, there is a trade-off between property condition, homelessness and affordability (Crook, 1989). Closing down the worst HMOs could lead to more homelessness if the displaced tenants are not re-housed or cannot find alternative accommodation. This might be more of a problem in high demand areas such as London than in low demand localities. Reduced supply may result in higher rents (albeit mediated by the rules governing housing benefit in the case of low income tenants: see Chapter 10). In turn, higher rents might eventually prompt an increase in the supply of decent HMOs, provided landlords can obtain sufficiently high returns. However, the evidence from a study of the Scottish cities suggests that the supply of shared rooms has not increased since rents were deregulated in 1989 (Bailey, 1999).

Experience of the discretionary licensing system in Scotland found that the success of the scheme was limited by, among other things, insufficient staff and financial resources to support its implementation; low priority within councils for HMO work; lack of effective corporate working across local authority departments (housing, environmental health, and planning); and inconsistencies between licensing powers and other statutory powers, such as policing and building control (Currie *et al.*, 1998). These practical difficulties are also likely to affect the success of mandatory licensing both north and south of the border. Moreover, as Currie (2002, p152) has observed of the Scottish system: '…it continues a historical culture towards HMOs of enforcement and control and is replete with sanctions but lacks tangible incentives that would be attractive to landlords.' Given the poor conditions that exist, unless HMO landlords are provided with financial assistance or incentives to improve their properties, the practical success of mandatory licensing is likely to be limited.

Why is private rental housing in worse condition than other tenures?

The fact that the privately rented sector is in worse condition compared with owner occupation, local authority housing and housing association dwellings, raises the question of why that is the case. One obvious cause of the relatively poor condition of the sector is the fact that much of the stock is old. Many privately rented dwellings were constructed at a time when building standards were lower. Moreover, dwellings decline in condition over time and require repairs or, eventually, remedial work to put them back into good condition. However, the willingness and ability of private landlords to undertake repair and improvement work was inhibited for much of the twentieth century by the existence of relatively inflexible forms of rent control in the sector. Additionally, Nevitt (1966) argued that the way in which landlords were taxed, and especially the fact that they were not allowed to offset depreciation against their rental income, made it uneconomic for them to carry out improvement work.

Meanwhile, the excess demand that (partly because of rent control) characterised the sector over this period meant that landlords had little difficulty letting properties that were in poor condition (DoE, 1977). Thus, because private renting was a seller's market, there were few competitive pressures on landlords to keep their properties in good condition or improve them to modern standards; but in any case, rent controls, the tax system, and the low incomes of many private tenants, made it uneconomic for them to do so. There is also evidence that some tenants preferred low rents and poor condition property to higher rents and better conditions (Cullingworth, 1963). To some extent, this rent/quality trade-off will have reflected the low incomes of many private tenants.

Since 1989 landlords have been able to charge market rents and excess demand is no longer a universal feature of the privately rented sector. In theory, rent deregulation should have made it possible for landlords to charge a rent that gives them an economic return and keep the property in good condition (Crook *et al.*, 2000; Crook, 2002a). However, this assumes that rents reflect property conditions such that an improvement in the condition of a property will result in a commensurate increase in the market rent. In fact, research has found that rents reflect the condition of the property only in the regulated sub-sector, where many are set by Rent Officers. In the deregulated sub-sector, statistical analysis has found little relationship between the condition of properties as judged by trained surveyors and the rent being paid by the tenants living in them (Crook and Hughes, 2001; Crook et *al.*, 2000). In other words, it appears that many tenants are unwilling to pay higher rents for better quality property. This may be because they have little knowledge of building technology and hence little awareness of the structural condition of the property. It may also be because they are more interested in the more superficial aspects of dwelling condition than the structural condition. As Crook *et al.* (2000, p82) have suggested, tenants:

> *...may be more interested in decorations and white goods, for example, than the state of the roof. That may not be an entirely irrational approach for tenants to take because so many of them stay at their current accommodation for only short periods. Hence, there is arguably less need for them to care about more structural aspects of the condition of their accommodation.*

The post-deregulation shift towards six month assured shorthold tenancies, combined with the shift towards younger and more mobile tenants, may have reinforced this poor relationship between the underlying condition of property and the rent that landlords are able to charge. If, once in residence, tenants become aware of problems with the condition of the property, they can always move on after the six month tenancy has come to an end. Meanwhile, restrictions in eligible rents for housing benefit (see Chapter 10) may have reduced landlords' ability to carry out repairs in some cases. Whatever the reason, the end result is that landlords appear to have relatively little incentive to improve conditions at the lower end of the market (Crook and Hughes, 2001; Crook *et al.*, 2000).

Conclusions

A substantial minority of privately rented dwellings are in poor condition along a range of different measures. This is particularly true of properties within the regulated part of the sector. Although conditions are improving, this reflects largely the transfer of better condition properties into the sector from owner occupation rather than because of landlords improving the existing stock of rented homes. It is likely that the surge of buy to let investment in new build flats and houses in recent years will also help to improve the overall condition of the stock to a modest extent. But while many dwellings let by private landlords are of poor quality, it is important not to lose sight of the fact that most are in fact in good condition. HMOs, however, are generally not in good condition, are often poorly managed, and accommodate some of the most vulnerable private tenants.

CHAPTER 7:
Private landlords

Introduction

Private landlords are important actors within the housing market. While they no longer own the majority of homes in Britain, private landlords still account for one in every ten of them. Until recently, relatively little was known about them. They were an under-researched topic and little information was available about who they were, why they had become landlords, and their motivations and attitudes to letting.

In the past, debates about private landlordism have often been based on stereotypical images and myths, rather than an understanding based on research. On the one hand, the ghost of Rachman has often hung heavy over popular images of the private landlord (Kemp, 1987b). Thus, landlords have often been portrayed as rather seedy, if not criminal characters, charging exorbitant rents for slum property. On the other hand, landlords have sometimes been presented as oppressed by decades of rent control, reluctantly burdened with tenanted and unprofitable property let to tenants who are often better off than they are. While these two contrasting images have undoubtedly faded, Rachman imagery still sometimes features in contemporary debates about the private rental housing market.

Meanwhile, in the absence of up-to-date information, public policy has until recently been formulated on the basis of implicit assumptions about landlords' motivations and behaviour. Policy makers have tended to assume that private landlords, if not perfectly informed and economically rational investors, are at least fairly knowledgeable and reasonably rational economic agents who will respond to market signals, economic incentives and changes in tenancy legislation. However, research indicates that a substantial minority of landlords scarcely conforms to this 'reasonably rational investor' image (Kemp and Rhodes, 1997).

Fortunately, in recent years, a considerable amount of research has been conducted on the privately rented sector, including private landlords, which has begun to shed much more light on the people and organisations that own private housing to let. A growing evidence base about private landlords is emerging on which more realistic policies can be formulated. This chapter draws on this recent research to present an overview of private landlords in Britain today. It looks at who they are, when they became landlords and why they did so, the size of their property holdings, how they regard their properties, what they think about being landlords, and how they think others perceive them.

Who becomes a private landlord?

Private landlords do not form a homogeneous group. On the contrary, 'The term *private landlord* encompasses a wide range of types of individuals and organisations and includes some who would not recognise that term as a description of themselves' (Crook and Kemp, 1996b, p16). People providing accommodation for relatives or employees seem to be especially likely not to regard themselves as landlords at all (Kemp and Rhodes, 1997).

Table 7.1: Types of private landlords in Britain

Type of landlord	% of lettings
Private individual/couple	57
Partnership	6
Private company	16
Public company	5
Charity or charitable trust	5
Church or Crown Commissioners	1
Government department	3
Educational establishments	2
Other	7
Total	100

Source: Crook *et al.* (1995) p6.

There are an estimated 700,000 private landlords in England alone (ODPM, 2003c). Table 7.1 presents a simple classification of landlords by the percentage of privately rented dwellings owned by each of them in Britain. It shows that private individuals (including couples) are by far the most common form of landlord. Companies (including employers) account for only a minority of dwellings. The importance of different types of landlord varies between the three nations of the country. Private individuals are particularly dominant in the private rental sector in Wales, where around nine out of ten tenants rent from this type of landlord (Houston *et al.*, 2002a). In England, the proportion of private tenants renting from a private individual has increased in recent years and is now about two out of three (Table 7.2). In Scotland, about half of all private tenants rent from an individual and the remainder from a company of one sort or another (Kemp and Rhodes, 1994b). Despite these differences, it is clear that the ownership of privately rented housing – unlike most other sectors of the economy – is not dominated by companies (Kemp, 1988a).

Most private individual landlords are middle aged or elderly. Crook *et al.* (1995) found that, among lettings held by private individuals in Britain, 70 per cent were owned by people aged between 25 and 59 years, and 28 per cent by people aged 60 or more. The same survey found that about three-quarters of private individual

Table 7.2: Trends in type of landlord in England

Type of landlord	% of lettings		
	1994	1998	2001
Private individual/couple	47	61	65
Partnerships	3	4	5
Companies	25	22	13
Other organisations	25	14	17
Total	100	100	100

Sources: Crook *et al.* (2000) Table 2.1; ODPM (2003c) Table 1.

landlords were men. Although the overwhelming majority of private individual landlords are white, black and Asian people are over-represented among landlords (Crook and Martin, 1988).

There are relatively few full-time private individual landlords. Crook *et al.* (1995) found that full-time landlords accounted for only 15 per cent of lettings owned by private individuals in Britain. In fact, most individual landlords are in full-time paid employment, though a substantial minority are retired (Table 7.3). Thus, for the most part, private individual landlordism is a part-time activity or sideline (Thomas and Snape, 1995). Letting property is something that these people do in their spare time, rather than as a full-time occupation.

Table 7.3: Employment status of private individual landlords in England

Employment status	% of lettings
Full-time landlord	15
Paid employment 30+ hours per week	51
Paid employment less than 30 hours/hours vary	12
Looking for work	1
Sick or disabled[1]	1
Wholly retired	16
Looking after home/family	3
Other	1
Total	100

Source: Crook and Kemp (1996b) p19.
Notes: 1. Including temporarily sick.
Total may not sum exactly 100 due to rounding.

A minority of individual landlords are involved in the building trade or in one of the property professions such as surveying. For these people, owning rental property represents an extension of their work skills and expertise into a cognate area. Perhaps not surprisingly, they are more likely to manage their property themselves than to contract it out to a managing agent. They are also more likely to do their own minor repair and maintenance work (Crook and Kemp, 1996b).

As with private individuals, letting residential property is not the core business of most corporate landlords. Crook and Kemp (1996b) found that companies owned one in five lettings in England, but only three-fifths of these were property companies. Three-quarters of property companies were mainly residential property companies. In total, property companies owned only one in ten of all lettings. A more recent survey by the ODPM (2003c) found that the proportion of private lettings owned by companies had fallen to only one in eight in 2001. Meanwhile, Kemp and Rhodes (1994b) found that, in Scotland, about three out of ten lettings was owned by property companies. Of these, seven out of ten were owned by residential property companies.

In their qualitative study of private landlords, Thomas and Snape (1995) identified three broad types of landlord: business landlords, sideline landlords, and organisational landlords. Bevan *et al.* (1995) subsequently extended this three-fold classification into a four-fold one in which sideline landlords were divided into *formal* landlords and *informal* landlords. Formal sideline landlords were typically non-resident individuals who had lettings at one or two properties. Some of them were letting because they were unable to sell their properties because the housing market was at that time in slump. But most viewed their property as security for the future and especially for when they retired; the property was therefore ultimately their pension. In due course the importance of the rental income would switch from paying off the mortgage and covering the other outgoings, to providing either an income or a capital sum with which to purchase an annuity. Informal sideline landlords were usually letting out a room in their own property and often did not regard themselves as landlords at all. In some cases, they had not actively sought to let the room, but were simply helping out a relative or friend who needed accommodation. Those who had sought to become a resident landlord wanted the rental income in order to help with their mortgage costs. Either way, informal sideline landlords tended to see letting as just a temporary phase in their lives (Bevan *et al.*, 1995).

Crook *et al.* (2000) also distinguished between four different types of landlord:

- *Business landlords*, who get most of their income from private letting and view their properties as an investment for rental income and/or capital growth;
- *Sideline investor landlords*, who get a minority of their income from letting but also view their properties as an investment;
- *Sideline non-investor landlords*, who also get a minority of their income from letting but do not view their properties primarily as an investment; and
- *Institutional landlords*, that are corporate organisations rather than individuals, get a minority of their income from letting and do not regard their properties primarily as investments.

Crook *et al.* (2000) found that three out of five lettings was owned by sideline landlords, with business and institutional landlords accounting for roughly equal numbers of the remainder. Business and sideline investor landlords together accounted for just over half of all lettings in England in 1998 (Table 7.4). By 2001, there had been a decline in business and sideline non-investors and an increase in lettings owned by sideline investor landlords (ODPM, 2003c).

Table 7.4: Classification of private landlords in England

Type of landlord	% of lettings	
	1998	2001
Business landlord	22	15
Sideline investor landlord	32	45
Sideline non-investment landlord	27	18
Institution	19	22
All	100	100

Sources: Crook *et al.* (2000) p95; ODPM (2003c) Table 9.

Another way of looking at the importance which private rental property has for landlords is according to the proportion of their income that is derived from housing rents. In general, the rent received from letting residential accommodation accounts for a relatively small component of landlord income. In England, three-fifths of lettings in England in 2001 had landlords for whom residential rents represented a quarter or less of their income. Only about one in six lettings had landlords for whom rent accounted for more than three-quarters of their total income (ODPM, 2003c). Kemp and Rhodes (1994b) found that, in Scotland, three-quarters of lettings were owned by landlords for whom rents represented a quarter or less of them income, while about one in eight were owned by landlords for whom residential rents accounted for three-quarters or more of their total income.

This relatively small share of rent in landlords' incomes is not only due to the fact that letting residential property tends to be a sideline rather than a full-time activity. It also reflects the relatively small scale of private landlordism. Most landlords own relatively small letting portfolios (Table 7.5). In Scotland, the median portfolio in 1992/93 was ten lettings (Kemp and Rhodes, 1994b). The median in England was even smaller at seven lettings at about the same time (Crook and Kemp, 1996b) and by 2001 had fallen to only four lettings (ODPM, 2003c).

Not surprisingly, private individual landlords tend to have smaller portfolios of residential lettings than corporate landlords. The great majority of private individual landlords own less than 25 lettings. Hardly any individual landlords own 100 or more lettings, but a substantial minority of corporate landlords have portfolios of that size (Crook *et al.*, 1995; Kemp and Rhodes, 1994b; ODPM, 2003c).

Table 7.5: Size of landlords' letting portfolios

No. of lettings	% of lettings	
	England	Scotland
1	30	23
2 to 4	23	15
5 to 9	13	12
10 to 24	11	12
25 to 49	5	11
50 to 99	5	5
100 to 249	7	11
250+	6	11
All	100	100

Sources: ODPM (2003c) Table 2; Kemp and Rhodes (1997) Table 3.

Becoming a landlord

We have already noted that private landlordism has often had a poor image, though that is slowly beginning to change. It is also an activity that often brings with it many hassles and anxieties that are not shared by other types of investment, such as bank deposit accounts and equities. Given these problems, why do people become landlords? Are they volunteers or conscripts? Do they see letting property as a source of current income or a nest egg for the future?

Information on how and why landlords acquired their properties can provide important insights into the nature of private landlordism. For example, properties may be actively acquired in order for the landlord to let them with the objective of making a competitive return on the investment. Alternatively, they may be acquired incidentally, as part of a wider transaction – such as the purchase of a shop or farm – which has been undertaken for reasons that may have had little to do with the letting of residential property. Or the property may have been inherited from a relative.

Perhaps not surprisingly, the single most common method of acquiring property among landlords currently letting accommodation is by purchase. However, inheritance is much more common in the privately rented housing sector in Scotland than it is in England. Surveys of private landlords found that 40 per cent of privately rented addresses in Scotland had been inherited compared with 15 per cent in England. Far more addresses had been purchased in England than was the case in Scotland (Crook and Kemp, 1996b; Kemp and Rhodes, 1994b). This supports the suggestion made in Chapter 8 that the sector is less dynamic in Scotland than in England. In both countries, though, a significant minority of addresses had been acquired neither through purchase nor inheritance (Table 7.6).

Table 7.6: How landlords acquired their lettings

How acquired	% of lettings	
	England	Scotland
Bought with cash	49	34
Bought with a loan	13	11
Inherited	15	40
Received as a gift	6	3
Acquired it some other way	17	12
Total	100	100

Sources: Crook and Kemp (1996b), p30; Kemp and Rhodes (1997) Table 4.

Kemp and Rhodes (1997) found that privately rented addresses located in urban areas in Scotland were much more likely than those in rural areas to have been purchased (61 per cent compared with 39 per cent) and much less likely to have been inherited (27 per cent compared with 47 per cent). This emphasises the significant differences that exist between the privately rented sector in urban and rural housing markets.

While many landlords have purchased rather than inherited their properties, this does not necessarily imply that they originally did so in order to let them to tenants. Instead, they might have acquired them in order to live in the accommodation themselves. Alternatively, they might have bought them for speculative purposes; with the aim of selling-on the properties with a capital gain (see the discussion of 'property dealers' later in the chapter). In fact, the evidence shows that most addresses that have been purchased or built were acquired in order for the landlord to let the accommodation (Crook and Kemp, 1996b; Rhodes and Kemp, 1997). In other words, most landlords entered the market as volunteers, not as conscripts.

A related issue is whether or not landlords acquired their properties with sitting tenants or with vacant possession. Other things being equal, it is clear that owners have more options available to them on properties that they have acquired vacant than those which have tenants already living in them (Whitehead, 1978). In fact, the evidence shows that about half of privately rented addresses in England and three-fifths in Scotland had either been acquired without sitting tenants or had been built by the landlord. In other words, more often than not, landlords had acquired a vacant property, which they had then let to new tenants.

While most addresses have been acquired with vacant possession and then subsequently been let to tenants, this does not necessarily mean that landlords first began letting the property for investment reasons. In fact, there are a great variety of reasons why landlords begin letting. Surveys of private landlords in England and in Scotland conducted in the 1990s found that less than one half of privately rented addresses were first let by the landlord in order to provide an income or a return on the investment. Other motivations for first letting accommodation were to provide accommodation for an employee, to help pay the mortgage or running costs, to utilise spare space in the accommodation, and to help a friend or relative. Motives varied according to the type of landlord. Investment motives were by far the most important reason why business landlords first let their properties, but for institutional landlords the aim was more often to provide accommodation for an employee (Crook and Kemp, 1996b; Kemp and Rhodes, 1994b, 1997). More recent survey evidence indicates that investment motives have become more important reasons among landlords (ODPM, 2003c).

Not surprisingly, properties where rent is being charged are much more likely to have been acquired for investment reasons than properties which are rent-free or tied accommodation. In Scotland at least, there are also significant differences between urban and rural landlords. In particular, urban landlords are very much more likely than rural ones to have originally acquired and let their property for either rental income or capital gain. Rural landlords are more likely than urban ones to have acquired and let them in order to house an employee or as an incidental part of another transaction. An example of the latter would be where a farmer had acquired a farm or additional land that happened to include cottage property (Kemp and Rhodes, 1997).

How do landlords perceive their property?

Leaving aside why they originally acquired and first let their properties, it is important to know how landlords *currently* view them (Crook and Kemp, 1996b; Kemp and Rhodes, 1997). The original reason for acquisition might have ceased to be relevant or the experience of letting may have altered their motivations. For example, the day-to-day management hassles or experience of difficult tenants may cause landlords to become disillusioned with letting property. There again, landlords may feel satisfaction with having a tangible asset under their control or with the income and capital gains they are earning on their investment. Either way, this may have implications for the nature of the rental housing market, including the experience of renting for the tenant.

About two-fifths of privately rented addresses in Scotland in 1992/93 – the most recent data available north of the border – and seven out of ten in England in 2001 were regarded by the landlord as an investment, either for rental income, capital growth or both (Kemp and Rhodes, 1997; ODPM, 2003c). A significant minority of properties – though about twice as many in Scotland as in England – were currently regarded as somewhere to house an employee. Other properties were seen as somewhere for the landlord to live, either now in the case of resident landlords, or in the future in respect of some non-resident landlords. For a very small proportion of private individual landlords, the property was their current or former home, which they were unable or unwilling to sell (Table 7.7).

Table 7.7: How landlords regard their lettings

	% of lettings	
	England	Scotland
Investment for capital growth	4	15
Investment for rental income	14	11
Investment for capital growth and rental income	39	17
To live in (at some time)	2	6
To help someone out	5	4
Unwilling/unable to sell former home	6	2
To house employee(s)	9	27
Incidental to another activity	3	7
Other/don't know	18	12
All	100	100

Sources: Crook *et al.* (2000) p94; Kemp and Rhodes (1997) Table 5.

Not surprisingly, there are significant differences in how properties are regarded between those that are rent-free and those for which rent is paid. For example, Kemp and Rhodes (1997) found that 60 per cent of properties in Scotland where rent was being charged were regarded as an investment compared with only seven per cent where nil, or only a nominal, rent was being asked for. In contrast, the great majority of addresses that were rent-free were regarded as somewhere to house an employee (74 per cent). Likewise, almost three-fifths of urban properties were regarded as an investment, compared with only a third of rural ones. Rural landlords were more likely than urban landlords to regard their property as somewhere to house an employee (cf. Satsangi, 2002).

Further insight into the nature of private landlordism can be gleaned from knowledge of what landlords (of properties that are not rent-free) expect the rent to cover. Surveys show that most landlords expect the rent to cover the cost of providing the accommodation and related outgoings. Thus, most expect the rent to cover repairs as well as wear and tear. However, less than one half of landlords say that they expect the rent to give them a return on the initial purchase price or the open market vacant possession value of the property. These data confirm that a significant – if shrinking – minority of landlords do not see their properties as a commercial investment on which they wish to obtain an economic return (Crook *et al.*, 2000; Kemp and Rhodes, 1997).

Attitudes to letting accommodation

Knowing whether or not landlords regard their property as an investment or in some other way, does not necessarily tell us whether they have positive or negative views about letting residential accommodation. For instance, landlords might have bought an address as an investment and still regard it as such, but nevertheless feel that letting property is a burden they could now do without. In fact, surveys of landlords have shown that most are generally quite positive about what it is like to let accommodation nowadays.

Crook and Kemp (1996b) found that private landlords and their managing agents in England were largely positive about what it is like to let accommodation. Their research found that a clear majority of landlords agreed with the statements that tenants generally look after their property, that tenants are generally good at paying the rent on time, and that the law allows them to charge a reasonable level of rent these days. Most landlords also disagreed with the view that landlords only let if they cannot sell the property. The managing agents tended to be even more positive about letting than the landlords. They also found that landlords who had inherited the property were as positive about letting accommodation as those who had acquired it in some other way. In other words, inheritor landlords '…were not disenchanted or reluctant owners of housing to let' (Crook and Kemp, 1996b, p47). However, they also noted that this did not necessarily apply to all people who inherit property because reluctant inheritors may have already sold the property.

Crook and Kemp (1996b) also asked landlords what were the best and worst things about being a landlord. It is notable that one in six landlords replied 'nothing' when asked this question. Among other responses, the most frequently mentioned *best things* were: the rental income, the prospect of capital growth, and providing a service to the local community. Managing agents especially highlighted the rental income, investment for capital growth, and security as the best things about being a landlord in their view. Thus, while the main attractions are the financial returns (rental income and capital growth), a non-financial attraction (providing a service) is also seen as important by a significant minority of private landlords.

According to the landlords, the *worst things* about being a landlord were troublesome tenants, the time taken up with management, the cost of repairs, and rent arrears. Managing agents also highlighted these three aspects of management and also re-possessions. This suggests that the 'hassles and anxieties' of property management are what landlords least like about being a landlord. It is noticeable that very few landlords or agents mentioned housing benefit, low returns, or tax on rental income. While a significant minority of business landlords mentioned 'bad image' as one of the worst things about being a landlord, hardly any other landlords did so (Crook and Kemp, 1996b).

Classifying landlords

Landlords are a heterogeneous group of individuals and organisations, and exhibit a variety of motives for letting accommodation. In consequence there are dangers in discussing them as a whole, for almost all they have in common is that they provide accommodation for other people to live in. Not surprisingly, therefore, researchers have sought to group landlords into different categories in order to make more sensible generalisations about them. Earlier in the chapter we presented data on the four-fold classification of private landlords devised by Crook *et al.* (2000), which was based on a large-scale survey of landlords. However, there are limits to the sophistication or richness of typology that can be employed in a quantitative survey of private landlords, especially where the study has broader objectives.

Of the various *qualitative* classifications of private landlords, perhaps the most interesting is that devised by Allen and McDowell (1989). They produced a six-fold classification based on a range of factors including landlords' historical and ideological attachment to property and their different economic resources and investment practices. However, their classification was based on a study of landlords in just two London boroughs and the fieldwork was conducted two decades ago. What follows is an attempt to update and extend that classification and make it more generally applicable. In doing so, it draws on more recent, in-depth qualitative studies as well as large-scale, quantitative surveys.

Stewardship landlords

This group of landlords include the old London estates such as Grosvenor, the Church Commissioners, the Crown Estate, and charitable trusts. Allen and McDowell (1989) described them as 'traditional landlords'. The role and operations of these organisations is governed by an often-conflicting combination of commercial and social imperatives. As Allen and McDowell (1989, p49) put it, 'The activity of letting residential property for this group does not amount to a straightforward commercial activity; it is modified by a service ideology, and a set of obligations and requirements that stem from their historical role in the rented market.' Such landlords are required to make a profitable return on their activities. But they also tend to operate with a sense of stewardship and long-term commitment to maintain the estate rather than simply to maximise their returns (Crook *et al.*, 1998b). For this or other reasons, some of these landlords may also feel under an obligation to house poorer tenants at rents that may be less than the market level and not just those who have the ability to pay commercial rates.

Employer landlords

Although they have declined in importance, employer landlords still perform a quantitatively important role within the privately rented sector. In general, tied housing today is provided by employers because of a need to employ workers outside of the normal working day (Allen and McDowell, 1989); because they need an employee to be on hand at short notice; or because of the remote location of the work (Bevan and Sanderling, 1996). In the past much more than in the present, tied housing has also been provided where employers have had difficulty in recruiting workers because of a shortage, or the cost, of housing. In the past, employer landlords have included farmers and agricultural enterprises, utility companies, breweries, hospital trusts, police forces, educational institutions and the armed services.

Employer landlords let accommodation essentially for employment reasons rather than as a property investment. Indeed, many employer landlords provide the accommodation at nil or only a nominal rent, though some do seek to charge the full market rent. In the agricultural sector, farmer workers' low wages have often been combined with the provision of rent-free accommodation and, indeed, the latter has been necessary because of former (Bevan and Sanderling, 1996). Employer landlords are unlikely to respond to housing market signals and increase or decrease supply as returns rise or fall. However, the low level of rents (or lack of them) on tied accommodation does constrain some landlords in terms of investing in the refurbishment or even the maintenance of their accommodation.

The number of employer landlords and of tied tenants has fallen over recent decades, not only in agriculture but also in other trades. The nineteenth century coal companies (and later, British Coal) owned large stocks of rented accommodation, but these have largely been sold off. Over recent decades, mechanisation of farm work has drastically reduced the number of agricultural workers and, with them, the number of tied cottages. The trend in recent years has been for farmers to sell off surplus dwellings or let them on the open market to private tenants or as holiday homes (Bevan and Sanderling, 1996).

Prior to the First World War, the most common form of employer landlord was people who employed live-in, domestic servants. At that time, very large numbers of households employed live-in domestic servants and the design of more expensive dwellings reflected this fact. In his pioneering study of poverty in York, Seebohm Rowntree (1901) distinguished between middle and working-class households according to whether or not they employed a domestic servant. What was unique about this type of employer landlord is that they were also resident landlords. Looked at from the tenant's perspective, their employer was not only their landlord, but also lived in the same dwelling as them; the tenant's home was part of their workplace. Domestic service was one of the most important sources of employment for single women before 1914. The number of households employing domestic, live-in servants declined rapidly after the First World War as it became increasingly difficult to find people who were prepared to enter domestic service. The modern equivalent of this type of landlord is families employing a live-in nanny to look after their children but this is much less common than domestic service before the First World War.

Informal landlords

A substantial share of the lettings market is owned by the highly diverse category of informal landlords. Informal landlords let accommodation as a sideline to their main source of income, usually full-time employment (see Bevan *et al.*, 1995;

Thomas and Snape, 1995). Informal landlords operate for a variety of reasons, many of them not strictly commercial. While some let in order to supplement their income, others wish merely to cover their costs. Many, but by no means all, informal landlords are resident in the same building as the accommodation they let. Some have spare space in their home that they want to utilise, while others may be lonely and want companionship. Some of these informal landlords need or want help with paying off their mortgage. Others may want to help someone out, such as a friend or relative or homeless people (Thomas and Snape, 1995). In other words, many informal landlords are not commercial operators motivated mainly, or in some cases even at all, by a desire for profits. They bear little resemblance to the Rachman image that has often pervaded debates about private landlordism.

Most informal landlords have only one or at most a few lettings. They often let accommodation for only a temporary period of their lives, expecting either to sell the accommodation when the tenant leaves or not re-let the room when the lodger moves on, though some let for many years and even decades. Many informal landlords operate in ignorance of the law of landlord and tenant, and some are not aware of even basic market information such as prevailing rent levels (Bevan *et al.*, 1995).

A central characteristic of informal landlords, particularly those letting rooms to lodgers in their own homes, is that the control and possession of their property is very important. They are hiring out part of 'their' house and hence the ability to regain possession, and – especially in the case of those letting to lodgers – to *control* how the tenant uses it, is often as important as the financial benefit they gain from letting the accommodation. As Allen and McDowell (1989) point out, informal landlords embody the conflict between the economic and the social roles of privately rented property in its sharpest form.

Investor landlords

Along with informal landlords, investor landlords own a substantial share of the lettings market. They include a wide range of individuals and organisations, some of which let accommodation as a sideline and others of whom are full-time business landlords. Their prime motive for letting accommodation is the rental income or the prospect of capital gain (or both). While some investor landlords have been in the residential lettings market for many years, others are more recent entrants to the business. Among the latter are many landlords who have invested in the so-called 'buy to let' market. However, some buy to let landlords already had a track record of letting property and re-mortgaged their properties or expanded their business on the back of the more attractive lending terms now available to them (Rhodes and Bevan, 2003). Some investor landlords specialise in the student lettings market.

Some *sideline investor* landlords see the property as their 'pension' in the sense that they have let it in order to provide an income or (if they sell) as a way of securing a lump sum for when they retire. This is true of many buy to let landlords (Rhodes and Bevan, 2003). Others have invested in the accommodation because it provided what they saw as a good investment opportunity. For some it is a tangible investment over which they have some control, unlike shares or bank and building society deposit accounts (Bevan et al., 1995; Rhodes and Bevan, 2003). These were typical motives for private landlords in Victorian Britain (Damer, 1976; Gauldie, 1974; Kemp, 1982a).

For the small minority of individuals who are full-time *business* landlords, residential property is often seen as a good way to earn a living or at least one about which they feel knowledgeable. Typically, these individual business landlords usually have more lettings than sideline investor or informal landlords (and need to, in order to live on the proceeds). They are often fairly knowledgeable about landlord and tenant law and about the lettings market more generally. They are often more interested in rental income than capital gains. It is not untypical for full-time business landlords to have '...built up their portfolio over a period of years through a process of reinvestment, sometimes having been originally involved on a part-time basis whilst in other employment' (Bevan et al., 1995, p13). Thus, some business landlords began as sideline investors. Some buy to let landlords are full-time operators who obtain their livelihood from the lettings market (Rhodes and Bevan, 2003).

Investor landlords are not only individuals; some are partnerships and private firms. Their holdings range from a handful of properties to several hundreds, but most operate on a fairly modest scale. Very often, the small private firms are property companies that have been in operation since a time when private renting was the majority tenure. Sometimes trapped in the market because of the security of tenure provisions of the Rent Acts, often letting poor quality accommodation on low rents to elderly people, such landlords have been disinvesting from the market as and when their properties become vacant. The continued existence of regulated tenancies on pre-1989 lettings has meant that such landlords have not all benefited from the sea change in the residential lettings market during the 1990s; but it has, nonetheless, provided them with a new set of opportunities when they do gain vacant possession.

Commercial landlords

Commercial landlords are a relatively rare breed in the residential lettings market. They comprise large private and public residential property companies and commercial property companies with significant portfolios of residential lettings. Examples include @home.nationwide (formerly known as Quality Street), BPT (formerly the Bradford Property Trust), Dorrington, and the Freshwater group. Another is the Unite Group, which specialises in providing accommodation for students and NHS workers. The company leases properties to universities and the NHS, which in turn let out the rooms (Bowers, 2002).

Commercial landlords tend to own several thousand lettings and operate on a fully commercial basis, buying and selling properties on the basis of commercial judgements about the returns that can be obtained or how particular investments fit into their portfolio. Property (residential or commercial as the case may be) is their core business, though some also have investments in other sectors of the economy.

Some of these landlords have been operating in the residential lettings market for many years – in the case of the BPT, since 1928 (Hamnett and Randolph, 1988). But others – such as the Unite Group and @home.nationwide – are relative newcomers, seeking to benefit from the new opportunities presented by the deregulated rental market. @home.nationwide also operates as a managing agent for other landlords. Many of the more long-standing property companies had downsized the scale of their operations over the years, but some of them began to re-let more actively following the implementation of the changes made by the 1998 Housing Act (Crook and Kemp, 1999). Table 7.8 shows some of the larger listed companies and their market capitalisation. Two of these companies – City North and Artesian – were BES companies, so it is clear that the scheme has had an afterlife to some extent.

Table 7.8: Residential property companies and their market capitalisation, 1999

Company	Market capitalisation £m
Bradford Property Trust	348.6
Mountview	105.5
Grainger	100.2
Gander	32.3
City North	52.7
Pathfinder	8.1
Artesian	4.9

Source: Wood (1999) Table 1.

Financial institutions

Even rarer than commercial landlords are the financial institutions that are private landlords. These comprise the small number of financial institutions – pension funds, insurance companies, life assurance companies and mortgage lenders – who own residential housing to let (see Crook and Kemp, 1999).

Financial institutions were major investors in residential property in the nineteenth century and, to a lesser extent, in the 1930s when they acquired substantial portfolios of middle-class blocks of flats (Kemp, 1984; Hamnett and Randolph, 1988). Between the 1950s and the 1970s, though, financial institutions withdrew from residential lettings and invested their money elsewhere (such as in commercial property and equities). They had been frightened off by, among other things, rent control, the unfavourable fiscal regime for private landlords, and political controversy over private landlordism. In some cases, they sold individual properties to owner occupiers, including sometimes to the sitting tenants. In other cases, they sold entire portfolios or blocks of flats to intermediaries – flat break-up merchants – who then sold them on individually to owner occupiers, sometimes after making improvements to the property (Hamnett and Randolph, 1988).

The result is that today less than one per cent of the assets of the financial institutions remains in residential lettings. This is a much smaller share than in some other countries, such as Canada, Germany, the Netherlands and Switzerland (Priemus and Maclennan, 1998). As discussed in Chapter 5, recent governments have sought to entice the financial institutions back into the residential lettings market through mechanisms such as housing investment trusts, but without much success.

For the financial institutions, residential property is simply one of a range of possible investment outlets with different investments characteristics such as liquidity and risk. Investments are made on strictly commercial criteria – often based on fine judgements about relative rates of return – within a diversified portfolio of investments. Unlike commercial landlords, they have no particular attachment to property as such (it is not their core business). Investments are made in property in order to provide a match between their often long-term liabilities and their assets and as a means of portfolio diversification (Crook and Kemp, 1999).

Property dealers

Surprisingly, property dealers or 'trading landlords' were not included in Allen and McDowell's typology, even though they were probably more prevalent in the late 1970s when their research was carried out than they are today. Property dealers seek to make profits through the capital gains that may be made from buying and selling residential properties. Many of these property dealers are landlords only incidentally. This is not only because it is capital gain rather than rental income that they seek (though that is indeed their aim), but rather because they seek to hold on to properties only for just so long as is necessary to make that capital gain. Rents may provide a useful income stream during the holding period while landlords wait to sell (Crook and Martin, 1988).

Property dealers seek to capitalise on a number of features of rental housing and the property market. First, the existence of a property market cycle makes it possible to 'buy cheap and sell dear'. The incentive to deal in property is obviously much greater when upwards movements in property prices are sharp rather than gentle. House price booms (and slumps) thus provide opportunities for short-term property dealing.

Second, the scope for property dealing has been facilitated by the existence of rent-controlling legislation. In restricting the rent that may be charged, rent control also reduces the *tenanted* market value of controlled property, since this will approximate to the capitalised value of the future stream of rental income that it can be expected to generate. However, because there exists scope to sell suitable *vacant* properties in the owner occupier market, under rent control the tenanted value of a house will generally be less than its value with vacant possession (Hamnett and Randolph, 1988).

The existence of this 'value gap' for much of the twentieth century provided opportunities for property dealers to make profits from buying and selling rental housing (Hamnett and Randolph, 1988). On the one hand, the depressed rental income and value of tenanted property gave landlords an incentive to sell rent-controlled property. On the other, the possibility of buying up cheap, rent-controlled property and subsequently obtaining vacant possession, and then selling onto the owner occupier market at enhanced prices, presented dealers with opportunities to make capital gains (Crook and Martin, 1988).

Property slump landlords

During the economic recession in the late 1980s and early 1990s, mortgage lenders possessed thousands of homes from their borrowers, as mortgage arrears increased with the growth in unemployment and the rise in interest rates. In this way, building societies and banks became private landlords by default. Because the recession was accompanied by a fall in property transactions and in real house prices, mortgage lenders tended not sell all of the homes they possessed but hung onto some while waiting for the housing market to recover from the slump.

More generally, Crook and Kemp (1996a) have referred to the emergence of 'property slump landlords' at this time. These were home-owners who, because they could not sell their homes or did not want to do so because of the fall in house prices and growth of negative equity, choose to let them out instead. Letting the property helped to ensure that they received some income from their former homes, even if it did not always fully cover all of their mortgage payments and other costs. Some of these property slump landlords themselves became tenants of other landlords, particularly in cases where they had to move elsewhere to take up a job. Although many regions of England were affected by this phenomenon, property slump landlords appear to have been especially concentrated in the south, where falling house prices and negative equity were more severe, and among those who bought the property after 1988.

A more localised version of property slump landlords now exists in low demand housing markets, mainly located in parts of the north of England. A spiral of decline in demand and in house values, has led to some owners letting their property or selling to landlords seeking to take advantage of very low capital values. Since rents, often under-pinned by housing benefit, appear to have remained more robust than capital values, incoming landlords can obtain very high rental yields provided that tenants can be found for the properties. Where tenants cannot be found, the owners may simply abandon the properties.

Rates of return

As an investment, two types of return are potentially available on private rental property: the rental income and capital gain. The rent can provide a regular source of income, while the capital gain (or loss, if house prices fall) is only a nominal one unless the property is sold and the increase (or decrease) in value is realised. However, landlords can benefit from increases in capital value even if they do not sell. This is because properties can be used as security on loans and hence higher values enable landlords to borrow more than would otherwise be possible.

The income or yield on rental housing can be defined and measured in a variety of more or less sophisticated ways (see Crook *et al.*, 2002). One of the most widely used methods to measure the rental yield is to compute the annual rental as a percentage of the capital value of the property. For this purpose, the capital value is the price at which the property could be sold on the open market with vacant possession. This measure gives the gross rental yield. However, landlords incur expenses in letting their property including both management costs and repair and maintenance expenditures. Therefore, it is common to deduct management and maintenance expenditure from the gross yield to calculate the net rental yield.

Landlords may not always be able to collect all of the rent on their property, either because there are periods when the property is unlet or because the tenant has fallen into arrears. If the arrears of rent cannot ultimately be collected from the tenant, they may have to be written off as a bad debt. Deducting any rent lost due to void periods or bad debts gives an alternative, lower calculation for the net yield. This is sometimes referred to as the 'net, net yield'. Except where specified to the contrary, references to the net yield here do not take account of rent lost due to voids and bad debts.

Most landlords have to pay tax on their rental income (after allowance is made for mortgage interest payments and certain management expenses and repair expenditure). However, landlords' tax liability will vary according to the type of landlord and other factors. Consequently, the post-tax return on a particular letting will also vary depending upon the landlord. For this reason, comparisons of the income from property are usually based on the pre-tax return.

Although there is a significant minority whose motives for letting are not strictly commercial, the majority of landlords see their property as an investment on which they expect to get a return. If they do not obtain an adequate return, they may seek to disinvest from the sector or not invest in more properties. Survey evidence suggests that many existing landlords are not responsive to marginal changes in rates of return on their properties (Crook and Martin, 1988; Kemp and Rhodes, 1994b; Crook and Kemp, 1996b). Nevertheless, over time the willingness of new investors to enter the market, and of existing landlords to purchase additional properties or continue letting their current ones, is likely to reflect the rates of return available in the sector.

One of the underlying factors behind the decline of the privately rented sector in twentieth century Britain was that rates of return were not competitive with alternative investments. As a report on investment returns published by the British Property Federation noted:

> *Historically, rates of return on private rented investments have not been competitive. Survey evidence prior to deregulation [in 1989] suggested that returns were below landlords' requirements and that rental returns did not cover all their costs, let alone give a return on investment...* (Crook *et al.*, 2002, p15).

In evidence put before the House of Commons Environment Committee's investigation into the private rented housing sector in 1982, the British Property Federation (BPF) argued that a *net* rental of six per cent (equivalent to a gross yield of about nine per cent) was necessary to maintain the supply of private rental housing at its current level (House of Commons Environment Committee, 1982).

Evidence from the then Department of the Environment's regular survey of returns on regulated tenancies let at registered rents indicated that the mean gross rental yield being obtained in the mid-1980s was in the region of two to three per cent in London and three to five per cent elsewhere in England and Wales (Whitehead and Kleinman, 1986). Although rental yields were somewhat higher on properties with rents set outside the Rent Act, they were still generally below the level considered by the BPF to be sufficient simply to maintain the current level of supply. However, estimates by Whitehead and Kleinman (1988) suggested that, on certain types of letting in London, it was possible to obtain gross returns at, or even above, nine per cent on unregistered rents.

Rental yields increased after rent deregulation in 1989. A survey of a representative sample of privately rented addresses in Britain in 1993 found that, on average, landlords were obtaining a gross rental yield of 7.6 per cent. The mean net rental yield – that is, the gross yield less management and maintenance expenses – was 5.6 per cent. The gross rental yield on lettings taken out since rent deregulation (9.2 per cent) was about double that for lettings taken out before 1989 (4.4 per cent). There was considerable variation around these averages, between different types of lettings, different types of properties, and different types of landlords (Crook *et al.*, 1995).

In addition to rental income, the returns from private letting can include capital gains. Crook and Kemp (1996b) found that the mean annual rate of real (that is, inflation-adjusted) capital gain since time of purchase of the property was 1.6 per cent. Once again, there was considerable variation around this average, with more recently purchased properties having a lower mean capital gain than those purchased earlier. Indeed, one in twenty properties, almost all purchased since 1988, had made a capital loss since they were purchased (Crook et al., 1995).

These capital losses reflect the housing market slump of the late 1980s and early 1990s. Since that survey was carried out, the housing market has recovered from the slump and entered a boom, with annual price rises in double figures by the turn of the century. Although rents continued to rise during the second half of the 1990s and beyond, they did so at a slower rate than house prices. The result was that rental yields declined over the same period (Rhodes and Kemp, 2002). However, these lower rental yields have to be balanced against higher rates of capital gain.

Crook et al. (2002) undertook an in-depth examination of rates of return in England. They found that the mean gross rental yield was 9.3 per cent, while the net yield was 6.8 per cent. The mean, inflation-adjusted capital growth since date of purchase was 3.8 per cent. The total return was 10.9 per cent. The figure for the mean net yield included deductions not only for management and maintenance expenditure, but also for losses due to bad debts and voids. Management and maintenance expenditure reduced the rental yield by 1.7 per cent age points, equivalent to 18 per cent of the gross yield. Meanwhile, losses due to bad debts and voids accounted for a further 0.8 percentage points or nine per cent of the gross yield. Altogether these deductions reduced the gross rental yield by 2.5 percentage points or 27 per cent of the gross return.

Crook et al. (2002) also found that rental yields on deregulated tenancies open to the general public varied according to the type of landlord, with investment oriented landlords achieving higher returns than other types of investor. Business landlords were on average obtaining a net rental yield of 8.0 per cent, while sideline investor landlords were obtaining 8.2 per cent. Meanwhile, sideline non-investor landlords were getting only 4.7 per cent.

The same study found that the mean net yield on deregulated lettings open to the general public where rent was being charged was 7.3 per cent. This is higher than the six per cent net yield cited by the BPF as being necessary to maintain the supply of privately rented properties at its current level in the early 1980s (see above). Rent deregulation has made rental housing more profitable and to that extent it is not surprising that new investment is once again flowing in the sector, even if at a relatively modest level. However, the profitability of rental housing needs to be considered in the context of the returns that are available on alternative investments, taking into account the relative degree of risk and liquidity associated with them.

Crook et al. (2002) compared the net rental yield and total *nominal* return on deregulated lettings with the returns being earned on commercial property and other types of investment in the same year. This revealed that the net rental yield on deregulated residential lettings was higher than the equivalent return on retail premises but lower than on offices and industrial property. Total returns were lower on residential than on all three types of commercial property. Although rental yields were much higher than on equities, total returns were considerably lower. However, the returns from different investments may change from one year to the next. For example, at the turn of the century, share prices on the stock market fell sharply for several years, making the returns from equities poor compared with rental housing (Table 7.9). Rental yields are arguably less volatile than stock market returns, making them more secure if less spectacular (cf. Damer, 1976).

Table 7.9: Rates of return on deregulated lettings compared with other investments, GB, 2000 (%)

Type of investment	Net rental yield	Capital growth	Total Return
Residential lettings[1]	5.7	8.1	13.8
Commercial property[2]			
Retail	6.2	0.4	6.6
Office	7.4	8.1	15.5
Industrial	8.4	5.4	13.8
All	6.9	3.5	10.4
Other assets			
Equities (all share index)	2.1	- 8.0	- 5.9
Gilts (long dated)	5.2	4.0	9.2
Cash (Treasury bills)	6.2	–	6.2

Source: Rhodes and Kemp (2002) p51.
Notes: 1. University of York Index (GB valuations).
            2. IPD UK annual index.

In summary, post-deregulation returns are much more competitive with alternative investments than before 1989, even if they are not necessarily better than those on commercial property. The turn of the century falls in the stock market reminded some investors that shares really could go down as well as up. Moreover, the associated problems with private and occupational pension funds also drew attention once again to private rental housing as an investment. And, as noted in Chapter 5, the shift towards lower inflation and, with it, lower interest rates, has meant that the returns on rental property are much more attractive than building society and bank deposit accounts. At the same time, lower interest rates have made it attractive once again to borrow money in order to invest in rental housing. Gearing the investment in this way not only allows landlords to purchase more housing than they would otherwise have been able to do, but also raises the rental yield on the equity invested. Meanwhile, the reduction in the interest rate premium paid by landlords over that paid by owner occupiers fell in the late 1990s and remains small. These developments have underpinned the surge of investment in buy to let mortgages, whereas in the more recent past borrowing money to invest in rental housing was not an economic proposition.

Conclusions

The stereotypes about landlords that have often pervaded debates and clouded understanding of the sector do not adequately reflect the varied nature of contemporary private landlordism. Private landlords are a diverse group of individuals and organisations, encompassing a wide range of attitudes and motivations for letting. Many landlords are not fully informed, rational economic actors who respond directly to market signals or changes in government legislation, though some of them are and do. While many *existing* landlords appear not to be very responsive to rates of return, the decisions of *potential* landlords are likely to be much more influenced by what they can earn in the sector compared with alternative investment opportunities. For private individuals, the alternatives are likely to be building society and bank deposit accounts, equities and private pension schemes. For financial institutions the range of alternatives is much larger and includes commercial property, equities and the bond market. The performance of private rental housing relative to these alternatives has improved since rent deregulation, especially in respect of the investments open to private individuals. The rise of the buy to let market has to be seen in that context and represents a return of landlords with the sorts of motives that were common before the First World War.

CHAPTER 8:
Private tenants: who rents privately?

Introduction

This chapter looks at who rents their accommodation privately and at the roles that the sector performs for such households. The focus is upon tenants in the privately rented market today. However, it is important not to lose sight of the fact that the sector is a dynamic and changing part of the housing market and that, in consequence, the types of household that rent privately have changed over time. Indeed, the decline of private renting from being the mainstream housing tenure to only a minority one was accompanied by significant changes in the types of household in the sector and the roles it performed in the housing market.

The chapter begins by setting out the demographic, social, and economic circumstances of private renters. It then moves on to discuss the main roles that the sector performs in the current housing market. It subsequently examines residential mobility, including moves into and out of the sector. Finally, it looks at private tenants' attitudes to renting privately and their tenure preferences and intentions.

A profile of private tenants

The different types of household are not evenly spread across the various housing tenures. Instead, there is a distinct socio-economic and demographic patterning by tenure, with a different distribution of household types in each of the main tenures of owner occupation, social housing and privately rented housing. These patterns reflect the different attributes of each tenure as well as the needs, preferences, and circumstances of different households and the constraints facing them. In other words, private renting has a distinctive tenant profile compared with the other main tenures. Moreover, there are important differences between unfurnished and furnished tenancies within the privately rented housing sector.

The distinctiveness of private renting compared with other tenures is particularly evident in the age structure of tenants living in the sector. Private tenants tend to be much younger than other heads of household (Table 8.1). Compared with other tenures, a far higher proportion of heads of household in the privately rented sector are young people aged under 25. Thus, one in six heads of privately rented households are aged under 25, compared with about one in twenty social tenants and one in a hundred owner occupiers. A higher than average proportion of privately renting households is also headed by younger middle-aged people (25 to 44 years). By contrast, older middle-aged people (45 to 64 years) are under-represented in the privately rented sector as are, to a lesser extent, older people (aged 65 and above).

Table 8.1: Age of household head[1]

Age	Private renters			All tenures
	Unfurnished %	Furnished %	All %	%
Under 25	12	30	18	4
25 to 44	53	55	53	38
45 to 64	20	11	17	33
65 to 79	9	3	7	18
80 and over	6	1	4	7
Total	100	100	100	100

Source: H. Green et al. (1999), Housing in England 1997/1998, London: The Stationery Office.
Notes: 1. 'Household reference person' see Walker et al. (2003) p166.

There are also age distinctions between unfurnished and furnished privately renting households. Furnished renting is overwhelmingly a young person's tenure. Thus, three out of ten heads of household in the furnished sub-sector are aged under 25 and another five out of ten are aged from 25 to 44 years. Although the age profile of unfurnished renters is younger than owner occupation or social renting, there are less young people and considerably more older people among unfurnished private renters than among furnished renters (Table 8.1).

The ethnicity of heads of privately rented households also differs from that of the two main housing tenures. Private renting accommodates a higher proportion of people from minority ethnic groups than do owner occupation and social housing. There are, however, important differences in tenure between the different minority groups. Pakistani and, to a lesser extent, Indian heads of household are over-represented in private renting. There are fewer Black Caribbean and Bangladeshi heads of household in the privately rented sector than in social housing but more than in owner occupation.

The distribution of household types in the privately rented sector is very different from those in the owner occupied sector, but less so from those in social rented housing. Single people living alone account for about a third of private tenants and a similar proportion of social housing tenants, compared with only about a quarter of owner occupiers. About one in eight privately rented households comprises adults sharing with others, which is about double the proportion found in the other two tenures. Couples with children are under-represented in private renting, but lone parents are slightly over-represented. Childless couples are also under-represented among privately rented households, as they are among social housing tenants, compared with all tenures together.

A comparison of furnished and unfurnished private renting households again shows up some important differences in household types (Table 8.2). About a quarter of furnished tenants, but only one in ten unfurnished tenants, comprises single people sharing their accommodation with other adults. There are very few lone parents or couples with children renting furnished accommodation, but about a quarter of unfurnished households fall into one or other of these categories. Childless couples are also more likely to rent unfurnished than furnished accommodation from private landlords. In total, seven out of ten furnished tenants are people living on their own or sharing with other adults.

Table 8.2: Household type

Household type	Private renters			All tenures
	Unfurnished %	Furnished %	All %	%
Couple, no children	29	19	26	38
Couple, dependent children	17	9	15	21
Lone parent	12	4	10	7
Large adult household	8	32	15	6
Single person	34	36	34	28
Total	100	100	100	100

Source: ODPM (2003d) 'Summary of English Housing Provisional Results: 2002-03', *Housing Statistics Summary*, Number 18, Table 5.

The age and household structure of private tenants is reflected in their marital status. About one in three private tenants comprises single people who have never married, a much higher proportion than in social housing (one in five) or owner occupation (one in ten). Married people are very under-represented in private renting, as they are in social housing, but cohabiting is over-represented. It appears that many people in work who are cohabiting tend to rent privately until they decide to marry and buy a house together, not wishing to make the latter commitment until they have also made the former one (Oakes and McKee, 1997). Divorced and separated people are over-represented in the sector but less so than in social housing. In fact, whereas marriage tends to be associated with moves *out* of private renting and into owner occupation, divorce is often linked with a move back the other way or into social housing, for one of the former partners (Kemp and Keoghan, 2001).

Comparing unfurnished with furnished renting also reveals significant differences in marital status. Single, never married people are considerably over-represented

among furnished tenants, nearly three-fifths of whom are in this category. A far
higher proportion of unfurnished tenants than furnished tenants is married or
widowed. But divorced and separated people are found in equal proportions in the
two sub-sectors. Thus, for some separated and divorced people, especially men,
the loss of the marital or cohabiting home is often associated with loss of furniture
and other household goods that couples accumulate over time, leaving them
forced to rent furnished rather than unfurnished accommodation.

When it comes to economic status, it is social housing, rather than private renting,
that is out of line. Most private tenants and owner occupiers are in full-time paid
employment, but this is true of only a quarter of social housing tenants. Where
private renting differs from owner occupation (as well as social housing) is in
accommodating a below average proportion of retired heads of household and an
above average proportion of students.

Table 8.3: Economic status

Economic status	Private renters			All tenures
	Unfurnished %	Furnished %	All %	%
Working full-time	58	57	58	53
Working part-time	9	10	9	7
Unemployed	3	4	3	2
Retired	16	3	12	28
Other inactive	14	26	17	10
Total	100	100	100	100

Source: ODPM (2003d) 'Survey of English Housing Provisional Results: 2002-03', *Housing Statistics Summary*, Number 18,
Table 9.
Note: Students are included in the 'other inactive' category.

The main differences in economic status *within* the private rented sector are in the
proportion of retired or other inactive households. The unfurnished sub-sector has
three times as many retired heads of household as the furnished sub-sector. There
are more 'other inactive' heads of household in the furnished sub-sector than in
unfurnished accommodation (Table 8.3). However, whereas inactive heads of
household in furnished rental accommodation are more likely to be students, in
unfurnished lettings they are more likely to be lone parents.

Length of residence

One respect in which the privately rented sector is very distinct is length of
residence. In Britain, much more so than in other advanced economies, the
privately rented sector is now very largely a short-term or transitional tenure. Most

private tenants have lived at their current address for only a short period and very few have lived there for a long time; whereas with social housing and owner occupation, it is the other way around.

As Table 8.4 shows, a third of heads of privately rented households in Britain have lived at their current address for less than 12 months. Altogether, three-fifths of private tenants have lived at their current address for less than three years, compared with only one in six owner occupiers and a quarter of social housing tenants. Looking at it from the other end of the scale, only one in six privately rented heads of household have lived at their present address for ten or more years, compared with two-fifths of social housing tenants and over half of owner occupiers. Thus there is considerable turnover within the privately rented housing sector; far more so than in the other tenures.

Table 8.4: Length of residence of household head[1]

Length of residence	Private renters			All tenures
	Unfurnished %	Furnished %	All %	%
Less than 1 year	27	52	35	10
1 year but less than 2 years	16	17	16	7
2 years but less than 3 years	12	9	11	7
3 years but less than 5 years	12	8	10	12
5 years but less than 10 years	13	8	12	17
10 years or more	20	6	16	47
Total	100	100	100	100

Source: Walker *et al.* (2003) *Living in Britain: Results from the 2001 General Household Survey.*
Notes: 1. 'Household reference person'.

Although both unfurnished and furnished private renting are largely short-term sub-tenures, this is especially true of the latter. About half of household heads renting furnished tenancies in Britain have lived at their present address for less than 12 months, compared with a quarter renting unfurnished tenancies. Eight out of ten household heads in the furnished sub-sector have lived at their current address for less than three years, compared with six out of ten in the unfurnished sub-sector. The unfurnished sub-sector has rather more long-stay households than the furnished sub-sector, which to some extent reflects the age and household differences between them (see Table 8.4).

Although some of the high turnover is a consequence of movement into and out of private renting, there is also a high level of household moves within the sector. In 2001/02, 445,000 private tenants in England alone moved from one privately rented dwelling to another. This raises the question of whether private tenants are moving from choice or because they have been forced or persuaded to leave by their landlord. This is an important question, not least because many contributors to policy debates on private renting implicitly seem to assume that tenants are forced to move at the end of a six month assured shorthold tenancy. The dividing line between being forced to move and choosing to do so is not clear cut. For example, suppose a tenant decides to leave when their shorthold tenancy comes to an end because the landlord has been unpleasant or refused to carry out repairs: is that a voluntary move or a forced one? Bearing this caveat in mind, as well as the inevitable limitations of structured questionnaire surveys, the evidence suggests that most moves by private tenants are voluntary, but there are nonetheless a significant number of moves that are involuntary.

The *2000/01 Survey of English Housing* asked heads of privately rented tenancy groups who had been resident for less than 12 months the *main* reason for moving from their last address given. Confining the answers just to those who moved within the privately rented sector, the single most important reason for moving, given by 25 per cent of movers, was a change of job or to move nearer to their place of work. Another 14 per cent moved for personal reasons including divorce or separation and marriage or cohabitation. Meanwhile, four per cent had wanted to live independently. A further 26 per cent said they moved because they wanted bigger or smaller accommodation or to live in a better area. Some 13 per cent moved because the accommodation was no longer available and two per cent because they could not afford the rent or mortgage. Although a minority, the latter two reasons accounted for around 80,000 unwanted moves (Bates *et al.*, 2002).

The role of private renting

It is clear from the very distinctive characteristics of private tenants that the sector performs a different set of roles within the housing market from those performed by social rented housing and owner occupation. A seminal article published in 1985 argued that the privately rented sector performed four main roles in the housing market (Boviard, Harloe and Whitehead, 1985; see also Whitehead and Kleinman, 1986). They called these roles:

- The traditional role.
- The tied housing role.
- The easy access role.
- The residual role.

The traditional role

The 'traditional role' referred to the fact that the privately rented sector accommodated a large number of households who had lived in the sector for many years, often stretching back to the era when the sector was the main housing tenure. They had entered the sector as young households and had remained there ever since, not moving out like other households. This role was exemplified by the high proportion of elderly tenants who had lived in the sector for thirty of more years. As Holmans (1996, p12) has put it, 'They are for the most part survivors from earlier times when private sector renting was a more common tenure for mainstream family housing.'

To some extent the continued existence of this traditional role was something of an anomaly. Why did these households remain in the sector during the 1960s and 1970s and not, like many others, leave for owner occupation or social housing, given the relative advantages of these latter tenures over the former? It might be that these private tenants were more or less satisfied with their accommodation and saw little reason to leave. Their rents were relatively low (often well below market levels) and they had strong security of tenure under the Rent Acts. Although the condition of their accommodation – in terms of the provision of the standard amenities, dwelling fitness, and disrepair – was often poor, they may have got used to these defects and possibly did not notice them very much. Certainly, house condition surveys show that elderly people are often more satisfied with their accommodation than younger people, are less likely to be aware of the deficiencies of their accommodation, and less willing to accept the disruption that often goes with undertaking major repairs and improvements (Thomas, 1986).

While some of these long-stay tenants may have remained in the privately rented sector because they were satisfied with their housing situation (or not sufficiently dissatisfied to move to the growing tenures of owner occupation and council housing), others may have been trapped. Many of these traditional tenants had low incomes and may not have been able to afford owner occupation or may have been unwilling to commit the increased expenditure on housing that buying a home would have entailed. Moreover, the older they became, the less viable it would have been for them to take out a mortgage. Others, who might have hoped to be re-housed by social landlords, may not have been a priority, perhaps because they were regarded as adequately enough housed as it was.

The traditional role has declined considerably since Boviard *et al*'s article was published in the mid-1980s. At that time, a very high proportion of private tenants were elderly and many had lived in the sector for several decades or more. According to the *1983 General Household Survey*, for example, three out of ten private tenants in Britain were aged 65 or over and four in ten unfurnished tenants had lived at their current address for over twenty years. Most of these tenants had low incomes, were renting houses rather than flats, had regulated tenancies, were renting unfurnished accommodation, and were paying 'fair rents' under the 1977 Rent Act (Kemp, 1988a).

Table 8.5: Trends in elderly private tenants[1]

Year	000's	% of all tenancy groups
1988[2]	565	33
1990[2]	460	27
1993/94	377	18
2000/01	271	12

Source: Calculated from Bates *et al.* (2002) *Housing in England 2000/1*, London: The Stationery Office, Table A5.4.

Notes: 1. Tenancy groups where at least one adult was aged 60 or over.

2. Excludes tenancies in non-privately renting households.

Since the mid-1980s, the composition of the private rented sector has changed considerably. As we have seen, elderly households are now under-represented in private renting, not over-represented. Table 8.5 shows the absolute and percentage decline in elderly private tenants in England since the late 1980s. Over this period, the number of privately rented households containing at least one adult aged over 60 halved. Thus, many of the elderly private renters identified by Boviard *et al.* (1985) have left the sector, probably because they have died or moved into residential care or the homes of relatives. Because the role of the sector has changed since these households first moved into it, younger age cohorts of households did not age within the sector but tended to move into social housing or owner occupation in middle age. Hence, as elderly people died or moved out of the privately rented sector, they were increasingly not replaced by new cohorts of ageing private tenants. The traditional role of the sector, in the sense outlined by Boviard *et al.* (1985), has become much less important.

Tied accommodation

The 'tied accommodation' role refers to people whose home comes with their rented business premises as well as those renting their home from their employer. An example of the former is people who are renting a flat with a shop, while the latter would include agricultural workers in tied housing, people in the armed forces, and caretakers living in houses owned by schools. Although not often discussed as such, tied accommodation also includes students living in halls of residence and other types of accommodation owned or leased by universities and colleges, as well as hospital trust accommodation occupied by nurses and doctors. Tied housing is not usually accessible to the general public.

Very often, tied accommodation is occupied rent-free or at nominal, or below market, rents. In the nineteenth century, company housing was common in single industry towns or where one main employer dominated the job market. In the South Wales coal field areas, for example, company housing was very common (Daunton, 1977). Tied housing also tended to be common where workers needed to be close to their place of work or could be called out at short notice. It also tended to be common in employment sectors where wages rates were very low, as in agriculture, or where there were labour shortages (which themselves may have been due to low wages), or where housing was particularly scarce.

For a variety of reasons, the need for tied accommodation has declined considerably since the nineteenth century. In the first place, many of the industries that provided company housing, such as coal mining and agriculture, have since declined considerably in terms of employment. Secondly, improved transport and communication links meant that it was less necessary for essential workers to live close to their place of work. Thirdly, the emergence of social rented housing in the twentieth century meant that employers had much less need to provide low-rent accommodation. Finally, rising real incomes and easier access to mortgage credit meant that far more people than previously could afford to buy their own homes and therefore had less need to rent them. And as noted in Chapter 7, the decline of domestic service also reduced the number of people living in tied accommodation.

The easy access role

Unlike the traditional role, the easy access role remains an important function of the contemporary privately rented sector. Private rental housing, and particularly the furnished sub-sector, has a number of important attributes that make it an important source of 'easy access' accommodation in the housing market (Crook, 1992; Whitehead, 1999):

- Private tenants can move quickly and frequently.
- Entry and exit costs are relatively low.
- Private tenants can rent furnished accommodation.
- Living arrangements can be more flexible than in other tenures.

Firstly, moving home is relatively quick and easy in the privately rented market compared with either social housing or owner occupation. Unlike owner occupation, it is not necessary to sell one's current home before acquiring a new one (though it will usually be necessary to see out the remainder of the tenancy). Unlike social housing, it is not necessary to join a transfer waiting list or meet needs-based qualifying criteria. Private tenants can move when and where they wish, subject of course to their budget constraints and preferences and the availability of vacant accommodation to let. Landlords are willing to provide short-term tenancies of six months (even less in some cases), so that tenants can move relatively frequently if they so wish – which, as we have seen, many of them do.

Secondly, unlike owner occupation, private renting entails relatively low entry and exit costs (though as Chapter 9 points out, entry costs such as deposits and rent in advance can still be difficult for some low-income tenants to afford). Owners typically have to pay legal costs, estate agency fees, Stamp Duty, and other incidental expenses when buying one house and selling another. Although it is possible to get 100 per cent mortgages, deposits running into several thousand pounds are commonly paid by first-time buyers. While social housing tenants do not normally have to pay a deposit to a get a house or flat, they usually have to join a waiting list and queue for accommodation, often for several years.

Thirdly, in the private rental market it is possible to rent furnished accommodation, which is especially important for new households (Forrest and Kemeny, 1980). Although some social landlords do provide some furnished accommodation, this generally accounts for a very small proportion of their lettings (Rooney, 1997). The number of furnished private lettings has been fairly constant at about 2-3 per cent of the total housing stock for at least the last three decades. The twentieth century decline of privately rented housing was largely among unfurnished lettings (Kemp, 1988a).

Finally, private renting can provide flexible living arrangements so that, for example, tenants can share accommodation with other households and rent only part of a dwelling, unlike other tenures. As noted in Chapter 6, there has been a significant increase in the number of people sharing their accommodation. This reflects the growth in single person households as well as the rising number of university students. As Heath and Kenyon (2001, p87) have pointed out,

The expansion of higher education is...having a significant impact on changing patterns of leaving home and household formation; with increasing numbers of young adults being exposed to forms of shared living as students, many are continuing to share after graduation.

Sharing can have disadvantages, such as lack of security for personal property or even safety, especially for lower-income people living in large HMOs and at the bottom end of the market (Kemp and Rugg, 1998). But sharing accommodation also has many benefits for some people. It allows them to minimise their rental payments, something that can be especially important to young people who wish to spend a high proportion of their budget on entertainment. It can also provide access to a higher standard of accommodation than would otherwise be possible (Heath and Kenyon, 2001). For young people especially, sharing can provide companionship (Jones, 1995) and access to a ready-made social life, which is why some better off people in their twenties choose to live in such accommodation rather than rent on their own (Kenyon and Heath, 2001).

For these reasons, private renting is important for households that are new, young, or relatively mobile, and for those who need accommodation in a hurry or for only a very short period. This part of the market is buoyant and can be expected to remain so. Divorce and relationship breakdown, the growth in single person households, the increase in the number of students in higher education, the need for students to repay loans and tuition fees, the growth of the flexible labour market, and the emergence of a low inflation economy, are all factors that are likely to help keep this role buoyant for the near future.

Newly formed households are disproportionately likely to make use of privately rented housing. Thus, in Scotland, the private rental sector provides the first independent home for about three out of ten households (Pieda, 1996). Similarly, in England, while the sector accounts for one in ten of all households, it provides the first home for around four in ten newly formed households. The corollary is that new households account for a substantial share of households moving into the private rental sector (Figure 8.1). Kemp and Keoghan (2001) found that almost half (48 per cent) of households moving into the sector in England were new households, with the remainder comprising ex-owner occupiers (36 per cent) and former social housing tenants (16 per cent).

Figure 8.1: The movement of households into and out of the PRS (000's)[1]

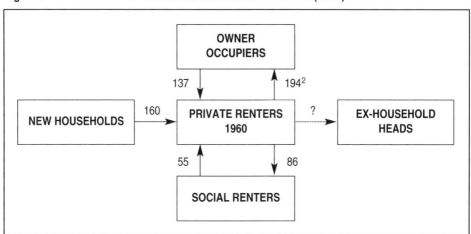

Source: Bates *et al.* (2002), *Survey of English Housing 2001/02.*
Notes: 1. Household heads, resident less than 12 months. + In addition, an estimated 10,000 private renters became sitting tenant purchasers.
2. The number of ex-household heads leaving the sector is unknown. This refers mainly to people dying or moved into residential care etc.

One important group within these newly formed households is students. They constitute an important demand group within the private rental housing market. In some university towns, they dominate particular neighbourhoods and in effect constitute a separate sub-market (Rhodes, 1999; Rugg *et al.*, 2000, 2002). The expansion of student numbers since the early 1990s has meant that they account for an increased share of the total stock of private rental tenancies. Even before this increase, McDowell (1978) had pointed out that students are to some extent in competition with low-income families at the lower end of the private rental market. A group of three or four students can usually outbid a low-income family in terms of the rent they could afford to pay for a house assuming the property is available to either type of tenant. However, for the landlord the alternative to letting a house to students might be to sell it into owner occupation rather than to let it to a low-income family.

After graduation, many students go onto become young, urban professionals, living in the private rental housing market prior to buying a home of their own. Since the late 1980s, there has been a shift away from owner occupation and to private renting among young people in England (Holmans, 1996). The economic recession and fall in house prices in the late 1980s and early 1990s in England may have been important, initial causes of this shift. Meanwhile, the growth of private renting, including good quality accommodation indistinguishable from owner occupied housing, helped to make private renting an attractive alternative. The need to pay off student loans, along with later child rearing and marriage than previously, also may be among the factors accounting for the switch between owner occupation and private renting among young people.

Single people and childless couples on 'middle incomes' see city centre private renting as offering greater flexibility and freedom than owner occupation and allowing them to spend their income on other things, according to a study in Leeds by Oakes and McKee (1997). The young adults in their study had some reservations about renting: rent was seen as 'dead money' and, compared with ownership, private renting involved less control and fewer rights. But although owner occupation was seen as the ultimate goal, at this stage of their lives private renting had important benefits, not least of which was that it enabled them to be mobile and able to relocate for employment reasons. Moreover:

> *Renting was seen as bringing a limited commitment, with no substantial deposit or liabilities for repairs or maintenance; it allows freedom to focus on other activities like work and leisure; and it allows investment in other priorities like one's own business, or greater leisure spending on holidays, etc. This tenure was also seen as ideal for sharing where the partnership is not necessarily permanent* (Oakes and McKee, 1997, p2).

Similar sentiments were found in focus groups among young urban professionals in the private rented sector in Scotland carried out by Pieda (1996).

The residual role

By the residual role, Boviard *et al.* (1985) meant low-income tenants who could not, at least in the short-term, gain access to their preferred tenures of social housing or owner occupation. These households are often unwilling private renters, trapped in the sector, at least for the short-term (see below). They include middle-aged couples and families more typically seen in social housing or owner occupation. They tend to rent unfurnished rather than furnished accommodation. They may have previously lived in the two main tenures but had to leave because of relationship breakdown or eviction. They tend to have low-incomes – either because they have low earnings if in work or because they are unemployed or economically inactive – and to be reliant on housing benefit. This role is also likely to remain important, especially in areas of high housing demand, such as London and the South-east of England.

It is sometimes argued that these economically inactive and low-income households would be more appropriately housed in social housing rather than the private rented sector (Maclennan, 1982; Kemp, 1988a). There is certainly evidence to suggest that some of them at least would prefer to rent from a social housing landlord rather than a private one (see 'Attitudes to private renting' below). Houston *et al.* (2002a) found that 12 per cent of private tenants in Wales were on a social housing waiting list. Similarly, Carey (1995) found that 13 per cent of private tenants in England were registered on a waiting list for local authority or housing association accommodation. Unemployed and economically inactive tenants were especially likely to be on a waiting list. Lone parents, and to a lesser extent couples with dependent children and elderly people, were more likely than other types of household to have their names down for a council or housing association place (Carey, 1995).

Why should such households prefer, or be better off, living in social housing than renting privately? In the first place, social housing generally offers the prospect of long-term accommodation with strong security of tenure, in contrast to the short-term and insecure tenancies that are commonly available in the private rental market. Secondly, because of the way that they have been subsidised and are financed, social landlords provide accommodation at rents that are generally well-below market levels. In contrast, most private tenants pay market rents for their accommodation. Thirdly, although conditions vary greatly within both tenures, social housing is often better quality than that which is available to low-income households in the private rental market (Holmans, 1996). Generally speaking, *low-income* tenants tend to live in the poorer quality housing within the private rented sector (Crook *et al.*, 1998, 2000). In summary, social housing often provides better quality and lower rent accommodation, as well as more security of tenure, than private rental housing.

In recent years there has been considerable debate about the extent to which the production of new social housing is sufficient to meet the scale of housing needs that exists. The scale of housing need is a matter of some debate and estimates vary considerably. However, an authoritative study by Holmans (1995) estimated that approximately 90,000 new social housing dwellings were needed per annum in England during the 1990s. This compared with an average new supply of 65,000 social housing dwellings during that decade, which suggests there was an annual shortfall of 25,000 dwellings. Meanwhile, the number of homeless households accepted for re-housing by local authorities fell for much of this period. A subsequent study by Holmans (1996) suggested that the number of households in 'housing need' whose accommodation was being provided in the private rented sector, rather than in social housing, increased by a total of 150,000 between 1988 and 1994/95. As well as unemployed people, this figure included 45,000 additional lone parents and 42,000 economically inactive tenants below retirement age (many of whom will have been long-term sick and disabled people). The majority of these households rely on housing benefit to pay all or part of their rent. More recently, the Barker review of housing supply has confirmed that there remains a substantial shortfall in social housing construction (Barker, 2004).

Thus, at the margin, the residual role of the private rental sector is significantly influenced by the supply of social housing dwellings relative to the demand for that accommodation, as well as by the rules governing access to it. A further factor of considerable importance is the availability of housing benefit to enable these low-income tenants to afford market rents within the private rented sector. Housing benefit is examined in more detail in Chapter 10.

A new role: an escape route from social housing?

In recent years, and certainly since Boviard *et al.* (1985) published their article, the private rental market seems to have taken on a new – but, as yet, small-scale – role as an escape route from unsatisfactory social rented housing (Kemp and Keoghan, 2001). The private rental sector is often seen in life-course terms as a transitional tenure. It is often characterised as providing a 'stepping stone' to owner occupation and social housing (Murie *et al.*, 1976). In this view, new households will spend some time in private renting while they save up enough money for a deposit to buy a house, or wait their turn (or accumulate enough 'points') to be allocated a social housing tenancy. Short-term accommodation in the private rented sector is viewed as a precursor to permanent accommodation in either owner occupation or social housing.

This 'waiting room' perspective on private renting is implicitly based on the notion of a housing ladder in which there is a hierarchy of tenures, up which households move over time. Owner occupation is seen as forming the top rung, social housing the middle, and private renting the bottom rung. New households that move into the private rented sector for their first home will stay there for a temporary phase in their lives before moving on to better things. Thus, low-income households will move from private renting into social housing and remain there or eventually move into owner occupation (perhaps by taking up their Right to Buy). Other households will move from private renting into owner occupation and thereafter trade up to bigger, better or more expensive homes within that tenure. Meanwhile, some better-off new households will by-pass the private rental sector altogether and move directly into owner occupation, while mainly low-income households will go directly into social housing.

However, recent years have witnessed a small but significant flow of households out of social housing and into private renting (Figure 8.1). While some of this 'reverse flow' is the result of forced moves due to factors such as relationship and family breakdown, most of it is the result of social tenants moving into the private rental sector from choice. The evidence suggests that these tenants are moving into the private rental sector in order to obtain a better house or move into a better neighbourhood than they could get in social housing (Gibb *et al.*, 1997; Kemp and Keoghan, 2001).

The movement of households by choice from social housing to private renting reflects the fact that the accommodation and the neighbourhood within which it is located are diverse within both tenures. Both social housing and private renting include accommodation of poor quality as well as of high quality; in popular and high demand areas as well as in unpopular and low demand areas. Unlike social housing, however, the private rental sector is not largely located on housing estates but is much more scattered spatially. Moreover, many privately rented dwellings were previously in the owner occupied sector or built since 1980 (see Chapter 6). Hence private renting now offers positive dwelling and neighbourhood characteristics for tenants wishing to exit from unattractive dwellings on unpopular social housing estates (Kemp and Keoghan, 2001).

Meanwhile, prevailing images of these two tenures are also in the process of change. To some extent, the social construction of private renting has been rehabilitated (in England at least) over the past decade. The traditional image of private renting as invariably offering only poor quality accommodation let by exploitative landlords has, to some extent, dissolved and more positive images, both of private landlords and of private renting, are now more commonplace in the property pages of the newspapers and elsewhere in the mass media. Meanwhile, the prevailing image of social housing has deteriorated as the sector has become increasingly residualised and as parts of the stock have become increasingly difficult for landlords to let and for tenants to live in (Power, 1997).

The opportunity for social housing tenants living in poor quality accommodation or on unpopular housing estates to transfer to more attractive places *within* the sector are limited. While social housing offers lower rents and much stronger security of tenure than private renting, it also provides tenants with relatively little choice or scope for exercising their preferences. Some local authorities, especially those with low-demand housing on their books, are experimenting with more 'choice-based lettings', but most social housing tenants have to accept what they are offered. Social housing tenants may find themselves stuck in their present accommodation for many years while waiting for a transfer to be offered to them and, even then, it might prove to be to a house or flat (or a neighbourhood) in which they would prefer not to live. In these circumstances, it is hardly surprising that some households are choosing to exit from the sector. Private rents are generally higher than social housing rents, but for claimants housing benefit currently covers all of the extra rent provided it is within the local rent ceiling and the accommodation is not larger than the household is deemed to need. Hence the cost – in terms of higher rent – of moving from social to private rented housing is borne by the taxpayer through the housing benefit scheme and not by the tenant (Kemp and Keoghan, 2001). While this is set to change from 2006 or 2007 with the national roll-out of the local housing allowance (see Chapter 10), it will remain the case that the scheme will cover much if not all of the higher rent.

However, households that choose to leave social housing for private renting may not necessarily be intending to do so permanently. Evidence from Scotland suggests that some of these households hope eventually to move back into social housing. Gibb *et al.* (1997) found that many of the former social housing tenants who had moved into new or rehabilitated private rented housing thought they would go back into social housing when they next moved home. It appears that, unable to transfer to accommodation or neighbourhoods of their liking, they had taken what Hirschman (1970) called the 'exit' option, but perhaps only temporarily. They had left social housing in the hope that they would ultimately be able to move into more attractive housing in that sector at some stage in the future. Hence they were seeking to exit from a particular dwelling or neighbourhood rather than from the tenure of social housing as such.

From this perspective, for the tenants surveyed by Gibb *et al.* (1997), private rented accommodation was providing both an escape route from unsatisfactory social housing and ultimately an opportunity to re-position themselves for re-entry into better social housing (though whether they achieve the latter goal is another matter). However, the image and perhaps the reality of private renting and social housing are different in Scotland from in England. North of the border, social housing has remained more important and images of private renting appear to be more negative than in England. The Scottish findings may not therefore carry over directly to England. What is clear, though, is that the private rental market is beginning to perform a new role as dissatisfied social housing tenants seek to exercise choice over the housing and neighbourhoods in which they live (Kemp and Keoghan, 2001).

Attitudes to private renting

Surveys consistently find that the majority of households, including most private tenants, say that owner occupation is their preferred tenure, if not now then at some time in the future (Ford and Burrows, 1999). The great majority of private tenants say they intend to buy a home one day. This is of course an important reason why young people dominate the private rented sector, for by middle age many people have indeed become owner occupiers.

The fact that the majority of private tenants intend or would like to buy their own home in the future raises the question of why they have not done so already. Life-course factors help to explain why many young private tenants have not yet bought their home, for as we have seen renting privately has important attractions for people during their early housing careers. Financial factors are the most important in explaining why many private tenants have not bought a home of their own. Not being able to afford a deposit, belief that they would not be able to get a mortgage, difficulty of affording the repayments, and not being able to afford the properties that they might want to buy, were the four main reasons why private tenants had bought somewhere, according to one survey of housing attitudes in Britain (Hedges and Clemens, 1994). Other factors included not wanting to be in debt, not having a secure enough job, the cost of repairs and maintenance, and not wanting the responsibility that goes with being an owner occupier.

Thus for financial and other reasons, some households have little option but to rent their home, either in the short-term or permanently. But whether it is for a short or a long period, many people rent at some point during their lives, including accommodation in the private rental sector. This raises the question of whether people who are renting from private landlords are doing so from choice or from constraint. Is the private landlord their preferred type of landlord or would they rather rent from a council or a housing association?

The *British Social Attitudes Survey* shows that the majority of private tenants are renting from their preferred type of landlord (Kemp, 2000a). However, a significant minority of private tenants say they would prefer to rent from a social landlord rather than a private one. Couples, and people who were either divorced or separated, were more likely to say they preferred a social housing landlord, while those who were single were more likely to say they preferred to rent from a private landlord. Meanwhile, only a small minority of social housing tenants would prefer to rent from a private landlord (Table 8.6). About a quarter of private tenants say they would like to live in council housing if they could get it, but twice as many (just over half) say they would not. Thus it would appear that, while most private tenants are volunteers in the sense that they are renting from their preferred landlord type, a significant minority would rather live in social housing.

Table 8.6: Preferred landlord by current landlord in Britain, 1999

Tenure	Council tenants %	Housing association tenants %	Private tenants %
Private landlord	7	9	56
Housing association	14	63	22
Council	78	27	16
Don't know	1	1	6
Total	100	100	100
(base)	(500)	(204)	(222)

Source: Kemp (2000a), p141.

Private and social landlords are seen as having different sets of relative advantages and disadvantages. A majority of private tenants believe that private landlords are generally better than councils at providing good quality housing and housing in good neighbourhoods. However, a majority of them also think that councils are better than private landlords at giving tenants good long-term security, doing repairs and maintenance, charging reasonable rents, and providing value for money (Kemp, 2000a). Clearly, therefore, private landlords have a somewhat mixed reputation among private tenants and the general population.

Table 8.7: Preferred landlord by nation (according to people in all tenures)

Tenure	England %	Wales %	Scotland %	Britain %
Private landlord	27	34	17	26
Housing association	32	27	26	31
Council	35	30	50	36
Don't know	5	7	5	5
Total	100	100	100	100
(Base)	(2,723)	(160)	(261)	(3,144)

Source: *British Social Attitudes Survey 1999* (own analysis).

However, attitudes to private renting also appear to differ between the three nations of Britain. This was clearly revealed, for example, by the *British Social Attitudes Survey*, which asked respondents what type of landlord they would choose if they preferred, or had, to rent their home. People living in Scotland were significantly less likely than those living in England and Wales to say they would choose a private landlord (Table 8.7) and much more likely to say they would prefer a local authority landlord.

Conclusions

The relative importance of the various roles that the private rental housing market now performs is very different from what it was in the nineteenth century and in the first half of the twentieth century. As the sector declined in quantitative importance during the twentieth century, its position within the wider housing market changed. Towards the end of the twentieth and into the twenty-first century, its roles have continued to develop.

Private renting still performs important and distinctive roles within the housing market. But in recent years, the role of the sector in housing young people early in their housing careers has become increasingly important, a trend that is likely to continue in the immediate future. However, we have also seen that a new, if modest, role is emerging for the sector as a refuge from the less attractive housing and neighbourhoods in the social housing sector. To that extent, private renting is very much a modern form of housing provision, in tune with the emerging shift towards what commentators such as Giddens (1994) have referred to as a post-traditional society.

CHAPTER 9:
Access to accommodation

Introduction

This chapter looks at access to accommodation in the privately rented sector. It begins by examining the nature of access to this part of the housing market. It then looks at how tenants find their accommodation. After that it explores the issue of deposits and rent in advance, which many tenants are obliged to pay when taking a private tenancy. Finally, it looks at landlords' letting strategies and the implications these have for access to the housing market.

Access to accommodation

The Labour government's *1977 Housing Policy Review* (DoE, 1977) argued that the privately rented sector performed an important safety value function in the housing market. When demand exceeded supply, it was the privately rented sector that soaked up the extra demand for accommodation. While this is to some extent an over-simplification of how the housing system might react to excess demand, nonetheless it does highlight one of the important roles that the sector can perform. Housing shortage creates considerable pressure on the private rental market, with implications for rent levels and ease of access to the sector. High rents and keen competition for accommodation can make it especially difficult for low-income tenants to obtain a private tenancy.

The terms and conditions of access to each of the three main tenures of owner occupation, social rented housing and privately rented housing, differ significantly. Although private renting is part of the private housing market, the nature of access to it is somewhat different from access to the owner occupied sector. Equally, while private renting is part of the rental housing market, access to this tenure is again different from access to local authority and housing association accommodation. It is worth exploring these differences in more detail as this will help to identify the unique features of access to the private rental sector.

Social housing is largely an administered housing system in which tenants queue for accommodation and, once at the top of the queue, are allocated tenancies on particular dwellings. Although prospective social housing tenants may be allowed some choice in the area to which they are allocated tenancies, and may be allowed to refuse one or two offers of accommodation, they generally have relatively little say over which particular dwelling is offered to them. Although social landlords have begun to experiment with more choice-based lettings, especially in areas of low housing demand, the majority of their tenancies are still allocated to people on what is, in effect, a take-it-or-leave it basis.

By contrast, private tenants generally do have some degree of choice over which areas, and among which types of property, they search for accommodation. That is one reason why some low-income tenants opt for private renting over social housing (Houston *et al.*, 2002b). Tenants' degree of choice is of course constrained by their income and wealth, often severely so in the case of low-income tenants looking for accommodation in areas of housing pressure. Even so, private tenants are not allocated to a pre-determined property by some invisible bureaucratic hand. Instead, they look for somewhere to live within their budget from among a more or less limited number of properties in a more or less limited number of areas.

Compared with owner occupation and social housing, access to privately rented accommodation is relatively quick and, compared with owner occupation, relatively cheap. It is not usually necessary for prospective private tenants to join a housing waiting list; instead they are generally able to secure vacant accommodation on demand, subject to a number of important constraints discussed below. Obtaining a private tenancy can be relatively quick – indeed, in areas of high demand, tenants have to be very quick. The whole process may even be completed inside a day (Rugg, 1999); but as letting agents and landlords increasingly make use of credit and identity checks, it will usually take longer for the tenancy agreement to be finalised.

Nor do private tenants have to meet the 'housing need' criteria commonly employed by social housing managers. Unlike owner occupiers, private tenants do not have to obtain a mortgage or invest their own equity before gaining access to accommodation. However, they often need to put down a deposit and pay the first month's rent in advance in order to cross the threshold of their new home (see below). Consequently, most people who are unable to obtain or afford a mortgage, and who are unable or unwilling to rent from a social housing landlord, can usually obtain accommodation in the private rental market. Those who are unable to obtain access to private rental housing may have to resort to 'non-tenured' forms of accommodation (Conway and Kemp, 1985; Whitehead and Kleinman, 1986) such as bed and breakfast establishments and hostels, or even sleep rough. At the lower end of the housing market, the margin between multi-occupied dwellings, boarding houses and commercial hostels can be slim (see Kemp and Rhodes, 1994a). As Whitehead and Kleinman (1987, p331) have remarked, '...at the bottom of the market both households and dwellings undoubtedly move back and forth' between bedsit accommodation and bed and breakfast hotels. It may depend upon the state of the local housing market and the rules governing the housing benefit scheme as much as anything else (Whitehead and Kleinman, 1986, 1987).

Finding accommodation

Tenants use a range of methods to find accommodation in the private rental housing market. These include: word of mouth methods such as contact with friends, relatives and work colleagues; responding to advertisements in newspapers or newsagents' windows and on notice boards; and using letting agents. Carey (1995) found that, among tenants as a whole, the most common way of finding accommodation was informal, word of mouth methods. These accounted for two out of five rent-paying tenants who had moved into accommodation within the previous five years. Meanwhile, three out of ten had responded to an advertisement and one in six used a letting agent. These figures include tenants living in dwellings that were not on the open market, such as student housing and NHS accommodation, where rent was being paid. Tenants living in resident landlord lettings were much more likely to have found their accommodation via informal, word of mouth methods than tenants with assured and assured shorthold tenancies. The greater importance of informal methods among tenants of resident landlords than among other types of tenant reflects the high degree of personal contact that is usually involved in such lettings and the considerable importance attached to getting on well with the landlord (and vice versa). Knowing the landlord already, or being put in touch via an acquaintance, can help to reduce the risk of making a bad decision in such cases. Meanwhile, assured and assured shorthold tenants were more likely to have responded to an advert and very much more likely to have used a letting agent (Carey, 1995).

Research evidence suggests that the majority of tenants find their accommodation fairly easily. However, a substantial minority do experience difficulties of one sort or another, but the extent of these difficulties varies according to the type of tenancy. Thus, Green *et al.* (1998) found that, among tenants who had moved into their accommodation within the previous five years, a quarter of tenants of resident landlords had experienced difficulties, compared with a third of assured tenants and two-fifths of assured shorthold tenants (Table 9.1).

Table 9.1: The ease with which accommodation was found by type of letting[1]

	Assured %	Assured shorthold %	Resident landlords and no security lettings %	All lettings %
Found with difficulty	32	41	24	38
Found easily	68	59	75	62
Total	100	100	100	100

Source: Green *et al.* (1998) Table A5.42, p187.

Note: 1. Tenants who have lived at their present address for five years or less.

The extent to which tenants experience difficulty also varies according to the rent level of the accommodation they have taken on. The lower the rent, the less likely tenants are to report difficulty in finding accommodation. Among tenants whose weekly rent (net of services) was less than £30, only about one in ten reported having experienced any problems finding their present place. Among those with a rent of between £50 and £60 per week, about a third had problems, while among those with a rent of £100 or more per week, half said they had difficulty finding somewhere to live (Green *et al.*, 1998).

To some extent, these differences reflect the fact that resident landlord lettings (among which, tenants report less difficulty in finding accommodation) tend to have lower rents than assured and assured shorthold tenancies. Even so, this cannot account for all of the effect. Tenants finding it difficult to obtain accommodation may end up having to pay a higher rent than those who have no difficulty. In addition, higher income tenants (who, other things being equal, tend to pay a higher rent) may perhaps be more choosey and, in consequence, report having more difficulty finding somewhere that they consider suitable. Partial support for the latter hypothesis is found in the evidence about the number of places tenants looked at in addition to the one they eventually took.

There is considerable variation in the number of properties that different tenants view before they take somewhere. Among tenants who have lived at their present address for five or less years, four out of ten viewed only the place in which they were living. A similar proportion looked at between one and three other places. Finally, two out of ten viewed four or more places – of whom about a third looked at nine of more other places – before taking their present accommodation (Table 9.2). Tenants living in lower rent accommodation were much more likely to have viewed only the place they took than those living in more expensive properties. For instance, two-thirds of tenants living in accommodation on which the rent was less than £30 per week (net of services) at the time of the *1996/97 Survey of English Housing* looked only at their current accommodation when they moved. By contrast, about half of tenants whose rent was between £50 and £60 per week looked only at their present place. This compares with just over a quarter of tenants paying £100 or more in rent per week (see Green *et al.*, 1998). Thus, on average, the higher the rent, the more places they had viewed before choosing their present accommodation. To the extent that rent levels reflect incomes, this indicates that lower-income tenants have less choice than better off tenants.

The problem that tenants most commonly encounter when they are looking for accommodation is finding somewhere they feel they can afford. Green *et al.* (1998) found that three-quarters of tenants who experienced difficulty said that they had problems finding somewhere affordable. However, only about one in twenty mentioned finding somewhere that took housing benefit recipients as one of the problems they experienced. About a quarter said they experienced difficulty finding accommodation in the right area, and a sixth had problems finding somewhere in good condition. One in ten had difficulty finding accommodation that was large enough for their needs, while a similar proportion had trouble finding somewhere quickly.

Table 9.2: Number of places looked at in addition to present accommodation[1]

No. of places	%
Present place only	41
1	10
2 to 3	28
4 to 8	13
9 or more	8
Total	100

Source: Green *et al.* (1998) Table A5.43, p187.

Note: 1. Tenants who had lived at their present address for five years or less.

There is relatively little information available about how long tenants take to find their accommodation in the private rental housing market. Kemp and Rhodes (1994a) reported that a quarter of tenants living in houses in multiple occupation (HMOs) in Glasgow found their accommodation in less than a week. Most HMO tenants took more than a week but less than a month. However, a significant minority of HMO tenants – three out of ten housing benefit recipients and two out of ten non-recipients – took more than a month to find their accommodation.

Rent in advance and deposits

Although the privately rented sector provides accommodation to which it is relatively easy to gain access by comparison with social rented housing and owner occupation, it is not costless. Quite apart from the time and money spent in searching for new accommodation, removal expenses have commonly to be paid, which are of course likely to be much higher for unfurnished than for furnished tenants. Moreover, most landlords and letting agents require new tenants to pay a deposit (sometimes called a bond) or rent in advance or both. In addition, if a tenant makes use of a letting agent to find the accommodation, they (if not the landlord) are often required to pay a fee for the service. The Housing Act 1988 made it legal for landlords to charge 'key money' – a non-returnable payment – but in practice very few tenants make such a payment.

The evidence suggests that the majority of private tenants are required to pay a deposit when signing up for a tenancy. The *Survey of English Housing* indicates that around seven out of ten tenants pay a deposit. Even on poorer quality accommodation, a majority of tenants are required to make these payments to the landlord or letting agent. For example, a study of the lower end of the privately rented sector in six local authority areas in England and Wales found that half of the tenants had paid a deposit (Kemp and McLaverty, 1995). Meanwhile, a study of HMO tenants in Glasgow found that eight out of ten had paid a deposit (Kemp and Rhodes, 1994a).

Seven out of ten private tenants are also required to pay their rent in advance, according to the *Survey of English Housing*. In Glasgow, just over half of HMO tenants had paid rent in advance, the great majority of whom had also paid a deposit (Kemp and Rhodes, 1994a). Payment of rent in advance can be especially difficult for housing benefit recipients since local authorities normally pay benefit in arrears. The problem is compounded when there are problems with the administration of the scheme, something that is discussed in more depth in Chapter 10.

The social security system now provides very little help with deposits or rent in advance. Relatively little use is made of the Social Fund for this purpose. A minority of low-income tenants do receive some financial assistance to help them pay these access costs. Where help is received, it is families and friends that generally provide it (Kemp and McLaverty, 1995; Kemp and Rhodes, 1994a; McLaverty and Kemp, 1998). Thus, tenant's 'social capital' – in this case, whether or not they are able to draw on the resources of families and friends – can affect their ability to gain access to the private rental market.

For low-income tenants, payment of deposits and rent in advance can prove a barrier to securing accommodation in the private rental housing market. A number of studies have shown that some tenants find it difficult to raise the money to pay these costs. For example, Kemp and McLaverty (1995) found that just over half of the tenants in their survey had found it difficult to pay these upfront access costs. Tenants on housing benefit were about twice as likely to find it difficult as tenants who were not receiving benefit. The study also reported that three out of ten had turned down places because they could not afford the deposit or rent in advance, even though they could have afforded the regular rental payments. More recently, using similar questions, the *Survey of English Housing* found that one in six tenants had turned down suitable places despite being able to afford the rent (Green *et al.*, 1998). Thus, lack of savings to cover deposits and rent in advance can be an important barrier to access within the private rental housing market.

Those unable to afford to pay a deposit or rent in advance may find it difficult to get access to the formal housing market at all. They may consequently have to resort to hostels or bed and breakfast accommodation, as these forms of temporary housing tend not to charge deposits or rent in advance (see Kemp and Rhodes, 1994a). Homeless people in particular can find it very difficult to obtain privately rented housing because of the upfront payments that landlords and agents commonly demand (Anderson *et al.*, 1993). This difficulty has prompted some voluntary organisations and local authorities to set up 'access schemes' that aim to help homeless people with these advance payments (Rugg, 1996).

Access schemes have grown in importance, especially since the early 1990s. The growth of such schemes was given considerable impetus by the introduction in England and Wales in 1995 of a general consent for local authorities to provide financial assistance – directly themselves or via another organisation – with rent in advance and deposits. Although much slower to develop in Scotland, a similar general consent was introduced by the Scottish Executive in 1998. By 2002, two out of three local authorities in Scotland were funding access schemes, mostly via voluntary organisations (Houston *et al.*, 2002b). It appears that, whereas access schemes run by voluntary organisations tend to target their efforts on single homeless people, local authority schemes focus more on families with children (Rugg, 1996), a group for whom they might otherwise have a statutory duty to provide accommodation.

As well as help with rent in advance or deposits, access schemes often provide assistance with the completion of housing benefit claims. Some schemes run registers of accommodation owned by private landlords that are willing to accept homeless people as tenants. Access schemes may not necessarily hand over a *cash* deposit, but may instead provide a deposit *guarantee*: a promise to pay should the tenant cause damage or default on the tenancy in some way. Research into access schemes has found that they can play a valuable and cost-effective way of helping homeless or potentially homeless people to gain access to the private rental housing market (Randall, 1994; Rugg, 1996).

As well as paying the deposit, getting it back at the end of the tenancy can also be a problem for some tenants. Landlords and agents ask for deposits as a form of security in case the tenant causes damage to the property or its fixtures and fittings, or fails to pay rent, or leaves the property in a dirty or untidy state at the end of the tenancy. If any of these contingencies arise, some or all of the deposit money may be withheld when the tenant leaves. Problems arise where tenants disagree with the landlord or agent about the existence or extent of any damage or about the state of cleanliness of the property at the end of the tenancy. As the landlord or agent usually holds the money, rather than an independent organisation, the tenant is in a weak bargaining position if a dispute arises about whether the deposit should be returned in full or in part. It is difficult for managing agents to take a neutral position when disputes arise between landlord and tenant because they are paid by one of the parties involved (i.e. landlords).

There have been claims that landlords and managing agents abuse their position as deposit holders and fail to return the money owed to the tenant. The National Association of Citizens Advice Bureaux (Phelps, 1998), for example, reported that disputes over the non-return of rent deposits are among the most common concerns about the private rental sector reported by their member bureaus. The *Survey of English Housing* found that about seven out of ten deposits are returned in full, with the remainder split roughly equally between cases where the deposit is returned in part and those where it is not returned at all (Table 9.3). The most frequently cited reasons for withholding deposits related to cleaning of the property and damage. As NACAB (Phelps, 1998) has pointed out, these are areas that are highly subjective and hence a likely source of dispute. One Scottish study found that some landlords even withhold deposit money for normal wear and tear on their property (Houston *et al.*, 2002b). Perhaps it is not surprising, therefore, that about half of the tenants or households interviewed by the *Survey of English Housing* whose deposit had not been returned in full felt that the landlord was unjustified in withholding the money. Meanwhile, about a quarter felt the landlord was justified in withholding *some* of the deposit; and the remainder that the landlord was justified in withholding as much as he or she did. For low-income tenants, failure to get the deposit returned can have serious implications for their ability to pay the deposit on new accommodation.

Table 9.3: Whether the landlord or agent had returned the deposit

Deposit	%
Returned in full	70
Returned in part	15
Not returned	13
Total	100

Source: ODPM, *Survey of English Housing 2001/02* (www.odpm.gov.uk).
Note: This question was asked of tenancy groups or households who had moved from PRS accommodation in the previous three years and had paid a deposit at that address.

In England, the New Labour government established a short-lived pilot rent deposit scheme administered by the Local Government Ombudsman. Use of this scheme by landlords and agents was voluntary rather than mandatory. Naturally, landlords and agents – who hold the deposit money and, therefore, the upper hand where disputes arise – see little need for such a scheme and especially not for a mandatory one (ODPM, 2002a). A mandatory rent deposit scheme could be just as easily described as protecting tenants or as imposing 'red tape' on landlords, depending upon whose interests are being considered. In Wales, the Welsh Assembly Government has funded the Cardiff Bond Board since July 2001. This was set up in 1992 and operates on a voluntary rather than a mandatory basis. It is a custodial scheme in which the deposit is lodged with the bond board for the duration of the tenancy and then returned to the tenant unless the landlord makes a claim against the deposit, thereby triggering an independent adjudication process.

Landlord letting strategies

A further obstacle that confronts some tenants seeking to obtain accommodation in the private rental market is the letting strategies employed by private landlords. For although private landlords do not generally have written letting policies of the sort devised by social landlords, many of them tend to prefer some types of households as tenants and not others. In some cases, these letting preferences simply reflect the kind of accommodation that they have (though this may itself reflect a view about the types of tenant they wish to cater for). For example,

HMOs are generally not suitable as accommodation for families with children and, consequently, landlords letting this type of property tend to focus on single people as tenants. More generally, landlords' letting preferences may reflect their experiences of letting to certain kinds of tenant or even their prejudices about who would or would not make a 'good tenant'.

In fact, surveys of private landlords and letting agents reveal that a significant minority say they do not have preferences for or against particular types of tenant when letting their accommodation (Kemp and Rhodes, 1994a, b; Bevan *et al.*, 1995; Crook *et al.*, 1995; Crook and Kemp, 1996b). Nevertheless, most landlords and agents do admit to having preferences one way or the other in terms of the household type or employment status of their tenants. When asked which is the household type they would *most* prefer to have as tenants, more landlords and agents say it is childless couples than any other type of household. The *least* preferred type of household tends to be single people, despite the fact that (as we saw in Chapter 8) they are the largest demand group in the private rental housing market. So far as employment status is concerned, where landlords express a preference it is most commonly in favour of people in paid work. By contrast, unemployed people and students are the two main categories of tenant that most landlords and agents would least like to have. However, some landlords do target the singles' market and others focus on students (Rugg *et al.*, 2000). As discussed in Chapter 8, students account for a significant share of the rental housing market and some landlords specialise in letting to this group of tenants.

Tenants in receipt of housing benefit face more problems in finding accommodation in the private rental market than non-recipients. This partly reflects their weaker bargaining position and lower incomes, but it also reflects the very fact that they are claiming housing benefit (even though in some cases it covers all of their rent). Surveys of landlords and agents have asked them about their preferences when it comes to letting accommodation to people on housing benefit. These consistently show that, while a large minority have no preference either way, a majority prefer not to let to them. Only a small minority say they actually prefer people on housing benefit as tenants. To some extent, this bias against tenants on housing benefit reflects the fact that many landlords have experienced problems in letting to them. These problems appear to be fairly common. For instance, Kemp and Rhodes (1994b) found that the landlords or managing agents at two out of five privately rented addresses in Scotland had experienced difficulties when letting to tenants on housing benefit.

The reasons why a majority of landlords and agents say they prefer not to let their accommodation to tenants on housing benefit fall into three main categories (Crook and Kemp, 1996b):

- administration-related factors,
- claimant-related reasons, and
- other factors.

Administration-related reasons include: long initial delays in the processing of housing benefit claims; the recovery of overpaid housing benefit from the landlord, which may occur where it has been paid directly to them instead of to the tenant; the benefit payment cycle, especially the fact that it is paid in arrears; and (rather more vaguely) the 'red tape' that they perceive to be associated with the scheme. *Claimant*-related reasons include the fact that tenants on housing benefit are less financially secure than those paying the rent wholly out of their own pocket; and the fact that some landlords and agents feel that benefit claimants are in some sense 'undesirable'. Finally, among the *other* reasons, the most commonly mentioned is the restrictions in 'eligible rents', that is, the shortfall between the rent the landlord wishes to charge and the amount that the local authority will consider as eligible for housing benefit. These restrictions are considered in more detail in Chapter 10.

A small minority of landlords and agents report that they have not let accommodation to tenants on housing benefit or that they refuse to do so. In some cases this reflects the fact that they are operating at the upper end of the rental market and rarely if ever come across tenants on housing benefit. In other cases it reflects previous bad experience of letting to this client group or simply prejudice against them. However, there is evidence from Scotland that, while some landlords say they do not let to tenants on housing benefit, they are in fact doing so (Kemp and Rhodes, 1994b). This may be because they do not know that the tenant is on housing benefit. Whatever their preferences, however, some landlords have little alternative to housing benefit claimants as tenants, especially those who operate at the bottom end of the market and in areas of low demand or high unemployment. In these circumstances, a tenant on housing benefit may be considered better than none at all.

Conclusions

The privately rented sector fulfils an important 'easy access' role within the housing market and one that is not particularly well performed by either owner occupation or social housing. This role is especially important for households that are mobile, need immediate access to accommodation, are not yet a priority for social housing, or are unable to afford house purchase. However, particularly at times of, and in localities characterised by, excess demand, privately rented housing may in practice prove to be less than easy for low-income tenants to obtain. The need to pay rent in advance and a deposit can be a problem for low-income tenants whatever the state of the local housing market. Being a housing benefit claimant can also be an obstacle for low-income tenants looking for accommodation, even though it helps them to pay the rent.

CHAPTER 10:
Affordability and housing benefit

Introduction

This chapter looks at three issues that are especially critical for the privately rented sector in Britain. The first section looks at rent levels. The second examines the affordability of privately rented accommodation as well as rent arrears. The third section examines housing benefit, including its role and importance for private renting, the administration of the scheme, and the restrictions in the level of rents eligible for benefit.

Rents

On average, rents in the private sector are much higher than those in the social sector. In England they are about double those in social housing. According to the *Survey of English Housing* for 2000/01, the average weekly private rent in England was £97 per week while the average for social housing (local authorities and housing associations together) was only £52. In Scotland, the rent differential between private and social housing is rather lower than in England, but is still substantial. In 2001, the median private rent (£67pw) was about 50 per cent higher than the median for local authorities (£40) and housing associations (£44) (Scottish Executive, 2002).

The fact that rents are significantly lower in social housing than in the private sector is hardly surprising and reflects a number of important differences between private and social housing landlords. Generally speaking, local authorities and housing associations aim to provide below market rent accommodation for people in housing need and do not aim to make a profit. They also tend to pool their costs and rental incomes across their stock, which enables them to cross-subsidise between their newer, more expensive stock and their older, cheaper dwellings (Malpass, 1990). Most importantly, local authorities and housing associations have benefited from substantial 'bricks and mortar' subsidies that have enabled them to reduce the rents they charge to sub-market levels. By contrast, private landlords in Britain (unlike those in western Europe) have only rarely received bricks and mortar subsidies or tax incentives (Harloe, 1985). It is hardly surprising, therefore, that rents are significantly higher in the privately rented sector than in social housing.

While rents are higher in the private sector, they vary significantly by the type of tenancy on which the property is let. The most obvious distinction is between regulated tenancies and deregulated (assured and assured shorthold) tenancies, as the former are subject to the Rent Act while the latter are not. In fact, the average rent on assured and assured shorthold tenancies taken together is more than double that on regulated tenancies. However, not all regulated tenancies have a rent that is registered with (i.e. set by) the Rent Service and, perhaps surprisingly, registered rents are on average higher than unregistered ones (Table 10.1). This difference is discussed further below. The average rent on resident landlord lettings (which are not subject to the Rent Act) is much lower than that on assured lettings and this will in part reflect the fact that the former are much more likely than the latter to involve shared accommodation.

Table 10.1: Mean rents by type of private tenancy[1]

	£ p/w
Assured	99
Assured shorthold	114
All assured	111
Regulated – rent registered	66
Regulated – rent not registered	43
All regulated	57
Not accessible to the general public – rent paid	77
Resident landlord	59
All tenancies	103

Source: ODPM (2002b) *Housing Statistics Summary*, no. 13, table 11, p13.
Note: 1. Among tenancies where rent is charged.

One aim of the rent deregulation measures included in the 1988 Housing Act was to raise private rent levels in order to make letting more financially attractive and thereby induce new investment in the sector (Whitehead and Kleinman, 1989; Crook, 2002). Since deregulation, average private rents have risen much faster than either retail price inflation or average earnings (Table 10.2). However, the rate of rent increase has differed across the different types of tenancy. Among regulated tenancies, rents have increased much faster on properties where the rent is registered with the Rent Service than where the rent is not registered. Indeed, although the average registered rent is now higher than the average unregistered rent on regulated tenancies, before and immediately after deregulation in 1989 it was the other way around. In 1990, for example, the average weekly rent in England was £24 on registered properties and £33 on unregistered ones. But by 2002/03 the figures were £68 and £59 respectively (ODPM, website). As a result, the average increase over this period was 79 per cent among unregistered tenancies but as much as 183 per cent among registered ones. As noted in Chapter 5, the New Labour government introduced restrictions on the rate at which registered rents could be increased relative to retail price inflation.

Table 10.2: Index of average house prices and private rents, 1990 to 2000[1]

Year	House prices	Deregulated rents	All private rents
1990	100	100	100
1995[2]	133	142	175
2000[2]	170	171	230

Sources: ODPM, *Housing Statistics* and *Survey of English Housing*: on-line tables (www.odpm.gov.uk).

Notes: 1. Data is non-mix adjusted.
2. Rent data for 1995 is for the financial year 1995/1996; for 2000, the financial year 2000/2001.

Average rents for the sector as a whole, or for particular types of tenancy, do not indicate the amount of rent that someone would have to pay if they took out a tenancy today. The average for all assured tenancies, for example, relates to all households with such a tenancy, irrespective of the date at which it commenced. However, surveys show that average rents in the privately rented housing market vary according to the date at which the household moved into the accommodation, with the older the tenancy the lower the rent. This time/rent gradient reflects the fact that many landlords effectively grant what economists call a 'length of tenure discount'. That is to say, it is common for landlords not to regularly increase the rent for their existing tenants each year in line with changes in market levels. (The reasons why landlords may grant length of tenure discounts are explored in Chapter 11.) This means that, while new tenants will usually be expected to pay the market rent, existing tenants will not.

The existence of length of tenure discounts has led some analysts to make a distinction between 'current rents' and 'market access rents' (Mudd, 1998). The *current rent* is the average rent being charged in the privately rented sector or particular parts of it (for example, assured tenancies). The *market access rent* is the amount that prospective tenants have to pay in order to gain access to private rental accommodation at any point in time. Market access rents are likely to be more volatile than current rents (Mudd, 1998). For example, at the time of writing, press reports indicate that the rents on new lettings in parts of London have been falling as a result of over-supply from the buy to let market. In general, however, market access rents will tend to be higher than current rents. Therefore, data on average rents will understate the rents that tenants had to pay in order to obtain privately rented accommodation in the year in question.

Affordability

The ability to pay upfront access costs and fit in with landlord letting preferences (as discussed in Chapter 9) are not the only constraints facing people who wish to move into or remain in privately rented accommodation. It is also necessary to be able to afford the regular rental payments once the tenancy has been taken.

The higher rents in the private sector compared with social housing, and the increase in average rents since they were deregulated in January 1989, have led to concerns about the affordability of privately rented accommodation.

On average, private tenants spend a larger proportion of their incomes on housing than social sector tenants or owner occupiers buying their home with a mortgage. For example, in Scotland in 2001, the median proportion of *net* income (including any housing benefit) spent on rent was 28 per cent among tenants renting from private landlords. This compared with 22 per cent among people renting from local authorities or Scottish Homes, and 23 per cent among those renting from housing associations and co-operatives. Mortgaged house buyers were spending only 15 per cent. These are of course average figures, around which there was considerable variation. In fact, a fifth of private tenants were paying over half of their net income on rent (Scottish Executive, 2002). These high rent-to-income ratios raise a series of questions about rents, such as what tenants think about their rent level, how easy it is for them to pay it, and whether they are able to keep up with the rental payments.

According to the *Survey of English Housing*, about half of private tenants paying rent think that the amount they pay is 'about right'. Meanwhile, a third consider it to be high and the remaining sixth think it is low. Perhaps not surprisingly, tenants renting on assured and assured shorthold tenancies are more likely than other tenants to consider their rent to be high. Compared with regulated tenants with an unregistered rent, those with a registered rent are twice as likely to say their rent is high. Indeed, a third of regulated tenants with an unregistered rent say their rent is low. These patterns broadly reflect the differences in rent levels between the different types of tenancy discussed above, the existence of length of tenure discounts among long-standing tenants, and the fact that some landlords are not primarily motivated by financial returns.

Although rents are higher in the private sector, the proportion of tenants experiencing difficulty in paying the rent is no greater than in the social housing sector. One study found that, between 1991 and 1997, the average percentage of tenants (excluding full-time students) in Britain reporting problems paying their rent was 12.0 per cent among private tenants compared with 14.7 per cent among social housing tenants (Böheim and Taylor, 2000).

One key indicator of difficulty in affording the rent is arrears. It might be thought that, since private rents have risen considerably since deregulation, rent arrears will have increased as well. That certainly was the expectation of many critics of rent deregulation, though the then Conservative government argued that housing benefit, rather than low-income tenants, would 'take the strain'. In fact, despite rising rents, arrears have fallen rather than increased. Whereas in 1993/94, nine per cent of private tenants admitted to having been in arrears on their rent during the previous 12 months, by 2000/01 this had fallen to six per cent. Despite lower rent-to-income ratios, the rate of rent arrears in social housing is more than double that in the private rental sector (Table 10.3). Almost all of the rent arrears in the private sector are among tenants on assured, assured shorthold and resident landlord lettings, that is, the open market part of the private rental sector. The incidence of arrears is very low among tenants living in accommodation not accessible to the general public and those with regulated tenancies.

Table 10.3 : Households who said they were in arrears with their rent by tenure

	Private tenants %	Social tenants %
Currently in arrears	4	10
Not in arrears but has been in the last year	2	6
Not in arrears in last year	94	84
Total	100	100

Source: Bates *et al.* (2002) *Housing in England. A Report of the 2000/01 Survey of English Housing*, London: The Stationery Office, Table A4.17.

The incidence of rent arrears varies by the type of household. We can illustrate this point using data from the *2000/01 Survey of English Housing* on the percentage of tenants who had been in arrears at some point during the year. As noted above, the average among all private tenants was six per cent. Arrears during were relatively *high* among:

- lone parents (12%)
- young people under 25 (8%)
- part-time workers (14%)
- unemployed people (10%).

Arrears were relatively *low* among:

- childless couples (3%)
- people living in multi-adult households (3%)
- retired people (2%)
- full-time employees (3%).

Not surprisingly, arrears varied inversely by income, being highest among tenants with a low-income and lowest among those with a high income. For example, 12 per cent of tenants with a gross income of under £100 per week admitted having been in rent arrears during the previous 12 months. This compares with only two per cent among tenants with more than £400 gross weekly income. The incidence of rent arrears was generally higher among private tenants whose net rent (i.e., after housing benefit has been deducted) was low than among those whose net rent was high. Even among tenants whose net rent was nil (i.e., housing benefit covered all of the rent) arrears were relatively high, with seven per cent having been in arrears during the year and six per cent currently being in arrears.

The shortfall that arises from restrictions in eligible rents for housing benefit (see below) is one possible reason why many tenants whose net rent is less than £10 are in arrears. But how can tenants who have no rent to pay out of their own pocket be in arrears? It could be that a minority of tenants who are receiving full housing benefit are not using that money to pay the rent to their landlord; but, if so, that could only ever be a short-term strategy, because ultimately the landlord will evict them. Much more important is likely to be the administration of housing benefit and especially delays in the processing of claims. Low-income tenants can run up considerable rent arrears while waiting for their housing benefit claim to be processed. Some may find it difficult to pay off the arrears when the benefit finally comes through, especially if they have other debts.

Table 10.4 shows the reasons for falling behind with the rent given by tenants who had been in arrears at some point during the previous 12 months. The most commonly cited reason, mentioned by a third of all tenants who had been in arrears, was problems with housing benefit. A quarter of tenants mentioned other debts as a reason for falling behind with the rent, while a fifth cited unemployment. About one in twenty said that an increase in their rent was a reason for their arrears. Thus, it is clear that housing benefit is paradoxically an important factor helping to explain rent arrears. While the scheme enables low-income tenants to afford the rent, the way it is administered and the restrictions in eligible rents, can make it difficult for some claimants to keep up with their rental payments.

Table 10.4: Reasons for rent arrears in the previous twelve months among private tenants

	%
Problems with housing benefit	32
Debts	24
Unemployment	19
Other job related reasons	9
Domestic reasons	10
Illness problems	11
Increase in rent	6
Other reasons	23

Source: Bates *et al.* (2002) *Housing in England. A Report of the 2000/01 Survey of English Housing*, London: The Stationery Office, Table A4.24.

Ultimately, tenants who fail to pay their rent will be evicted. Although the incidence of tenants reporting difficulty in paying their rent is broadly the same in the private and social housing sectors, private tenants are much more likely to be evicted. One study found that, in Britain between 1992 and 1997, some 5.3 per cent of private tenants compared with only 0.6 per cent of social housing tenants were evicted on average per year (Böheim and Taylor, 2000). This study excluded full-time students (who are less likely to be in arrears), which probably means that the eviction figures for private tenants are somewhat over-estimated, but even so the difference is still quite large. The number of evictions in social housing has increased in recent years and this is likely to have narrowed, but probably not eliminated, the difference between the two sectors. It seems likely that many of the tenants evicted from social housing end up in the privately rented sector.

Housing benefit

A central objective of the housing benefit scheme is to help low-income tenants afford their rent. The scheme was mentioned in Chapter 9 as an important factor affecting access to accommodation, while earlier in the present chapter it was discussed in relation to the affordability of rents charged in the private rental housing market. This section examines housing benefit in a little more detail, beginning first with the administration of the scheme.

The administration of housing benefit

Housing benefit is an income-related social security benefit administered by local authorities in Britain on behalf of the Department for Work and Pensions (DWP). It is a mandatory national scheme, the rules of which are laid down in an enabling Act of Parliament and detailed regulations that have the force of law. The DWP publishes a guidance manual that provides advice to local authorities about how to interpret the regulations and administer the scheme more generally. The manual is supplemented by housing benefit circulars, which focus on particular topics and are issued as and when the need arises. The need arises very often, however, as currently the DWP publishes one or more circulars a week on average.

The housing benefit scheme suffers from major and widespread problems (Hills, 2001; Kemp, 1998). These difficulties encompass not only the structural design of this social security benefit, but also the way in which it is administered. As the Audit Commission has reported, 'Delays in processing new claims have led to increasing hardship, stress and even eviction for people who are already on low incomes' (Audit Commission, 2002). The New Labour government has accepted that the scheme is highly problematic and in need of reform (DETR/DSS, 2000; DWP, 2002).

The rules governing housing benefit are highly complex, which causes confusion for claimants and makes the scheme difficult for local authorities to administer. The scheme is very finely tuned to individual circumstances. Moreover, benefit entitlement is recalculated when even quite minor changes in circumstances occur; which causes particular problems for claimants whose income changes regularly or who frequently move in and out of work. There are many errors in the amount of benefit paid to recipients and the level of fraud is believed to be high (DETR/DSS, 2000). The level of administrative performance varies considerably across the 409 local authorities administering the scheme. Although some local authorities do a reasonably good job in implementing this complex scheme, many others struggle to achieve anything like an acceptable service. Indeed, 'chaos' and 'crisis' are words that are frequently used to sum up the current state of the scheme.

In the second half of the 1990s, the standard of service delivery appeared to deteriorate. Statistics produced by the Department for Work and Pensions showed that the percentage of new housing benefit claims taking more than 14 days to determine doubled: in 1995/96, local authorities in Britain failed to process one in six claims within the 14-day target time, but by 2000/01 the figure was over one in three. This deterioration in performance occurred despite a sharp fall over this period in the number of new claims being processed each year (Kemp *et al.*, 2002). In 2000/02, the average time taken to decide a claim was nine weeks across local authorities in Britain as a whole, while in inner London it was 13 weeks. It is estimated that in one in twenty local authorities the average exceeded 100 days (DWP, 2002). These delays in processing housing benefit claims can make it difficult for claimants to pay the rent in the meantime and undermine their relationship with the landlord.

In order to address these deep-seated, problems, the New Labour government introduced a raft of initiatives, amendments and advice, which should eventually improve matters (DWP, 2002). Indeed, the latest administrative performance statistics do in fact show some signs of improvement, though performance overall is generally still poor. Ultimately, small measures are likely to produce only modest changes and more radical reform will probably be required to substantially improve performance. A major structural reform is being introduced for private tenants and eventually for social housing tenants and this is discussed later in the chapter.

Given the administrative problems, it is hardly surprising that (as discussed in Chapter 9) many landlords prefer not to let their accommodation to housing benefit recipients. These problems also help to explain why, quite apart from their low-income, claimants are disadvantaged in the housing market when compared with tenants paying the rent wholly out of their own pocket. A further difficulty that affects private tenants claiming housing benefit is the restrictions in the amount of rent that may be taken into account when calculating their housing benefit entitlement. This issue is discussed further below, after the role and importance of housing benefit has been examined.

The role of housing benefit

The aim of housing benefit is to enable low-income tenants in private and social housing to afford their rent. The importance of this scheme in the private rental sector is reflected in the fact that 400,000 households in England, or about one in five tenants paying rent, receive help from the scheme.

The large number of privately rented tenants on housing benefit reflects the low-incomes and economic status of many households within this part of the housing market. Table 10.5 shows the economic activity status of private tenants on housing benefit. Two-thirds of these recipients are economically inactive and a further one in seven are unemployed. The remaining fifth are in work, of whom just over half are working part-time. The rate of housing benefit receipt among different types of tenant varies, ranging from only four per cent of private tenants in full-time work to

83 per cent among the 'other economically active' group which includes people who were long-term sick or disabled and lone parents (Table 10.6). Altogether, eight out of ten lone parents within the privately rented sector are on housing benefit and they account for a third (34 per cent) of all recipients.

Table 10.5: Economic status of private tenants receiving housing benefit

	% of total
Working full-time	10
Working part-time	12
Unemployed	14
Retired	15
Permanently sick or disabled	18
Other economically inactive	32
Total	100

Source: Bates *et al.* (2002) *Housing in England. A Report of the 2000/01 Survey of English Housing*, London: The Stationery Office, Table A4.3.
Note: Economic status of head of tenancy group.

The importance of housing benefit also varies between the different types of tenancy within the private rental sector, reflecting differences in income and rent level. A third of regulated tenants, a quarter of all assured tenants, one in six tenants of resident landlords, and one in twenty tenants of lettings not accessible to the general public were receiving housing benefit in England in 2000/01. It is obvious from these figures that housing benefit is an important determinant of effective demand within the privately rented sector, especially at the bottom end of the market (Whitehead and Kleinman, 1988). Changes in benefit levels can therefore influence the effective demand for accommodation from private tenants on housing benefit and this is likely to be particularly important in localities where claimants account for a substantial share of the market (Kemp, 1994).

Table 10.6: Proportion of private tenants receiving housing benefit by economic status

	% receiving HB
Working full-time	4
Working part-time	31
Unemployed	61
Retired	42
Full-time education	14
Other economically active	83
All	23

Source: Bates *et al.* (2002) *Housing in England. A Report of the 2000/01 Survey of English Housing*, London: The Stationery Office, Table A5.47.
Note: Economic status of head of tenancy group.

Rent restrictions

Housing benefit entitlement is currently determined by the claimant's net income, the composition of their household, and their rent. Claimant's whose income is at or below the level of the income support and jobseeker's allowance benefit rates (the 'applicable amount') receive a housing benefit payment that is equal to all of their 'eligible' rent. In cases where net income is above the relevant applicable amount, housing benefit entitlement is reduced by 65 per cent of the excess.

For example, a household whose net income is £10 in excess of their applicable amount receive a payment of housing benefit that is equal to their rent minus 65 per cent of £10. Their contribution to the rent net of housing benefit is therefore £6.50, irrespective of the level of their rent (provided their rent is not 'restricted' – see below). The rest of the rent – whether high or low – is soaked up in housing benefit. Thus if the rent is £70, their housing benefit entitlement is £70 minus £6.50, which is £63.50; if the rent is £80, their housing benefit is £80 minus £6.50, which is £73.50; and so on. As a result, housing benefit recipients are fully insulated from changes in their rent (Hills, 1991).

What this means is that, if recipients' rent goes up (e.g. because they have moved to a more expensive property), so too does their housing benefit and by the same amount, so that they are no worse off. Likewise, if their rent goes down – e.g. following a move to a smaller property or a cheaper locality – so too does their housing benefit, so that they are no better off. In other words, the marginal cost of housing is nil for housing benefit recipients. They neither gain nor lose from a change in their rent. As a result, concerns have been expressed that housing benefit gives recipients little direct incentive to:

- shop around for cheap accommodation,
- bargain a lower rent with the landlord,
- move to smaller accommodation if their present home is larger than they need.

This lack of price sensitivity has led to concerns that, in the privately rented sector, housing benefit recipients might move upmarket to more expensive accommodation (e.g., Hills, 1991; Gibb, 1995). But despite the lack of a shopping incentive, research has also found very little evidence of 'upmarketing' by private tenants receiving housing benefit or that recipients are paying 'over the odds' for their accommodation (Kemp and McLaverty, 1995, 1998). Only a minority of housing benefit recipients in the privately rented sector are aware that the marginal cost of housing is nil for them. Most recipients are under the impression that they have to pay all, or at least part, of any rent increase or do not know what the rules are on this (Kemp and Rhodes, 1994a; Kemp and McLaverty, 1995).

In order to prevent 'upmarketing', the scheme has rules to prevent housing benefit from being paid on accommodation that is:

- unreasonably large,
- has a rent that is over the market value,
- in the upper part of the market,
- has a rent in excess of the 'local reference rent' or the 'single room rent'.

Where the tenant remains in the same accommodation, rules also prevent housing benefit being paid on rent *increases* that are deemed to be unreasonably large or unreasonably soon.

Thus although the *structure* of the housing benefit scheme gives recipients no financial incentive to economise on their housing costs, *administrative rules* exist to prevent benefit from being paid on unreasonable rents. Consequently, when private tenants apply for housing benefit, part of their rent may be ignored if it is deemed to be too high. On deregulated tenancies, the local authority refers the claimant's rent to the Rent Service, which decides what amount of rent should be used to calculate housing benefit in that particular case.

Prior to 1996, the rent could be restricted if it was above the market level for that dwelling, if the accommodation was too large, or if the dwelling was exceptionally expensive. In 1996, *additional* rent restrictions were introduced: the local reference rent (LRR) and the single room rent (SRR). The LRR is an average market rent for dwellings of a particular size in the locality, and acts as a ceiling on the amount of rent that is taken into account for housing benefit purposes. The SRR is similar to the LRR but relates to shared accommodation and applies only to single people under 25 years (Kemp and Rugg, 2001). These rent restrictions apply to different households depending on their age, the date their tenancy began, and when they first claimed housing benefit on the accommodation in question. It is only once tenants' applications have been processed that they find out whether, and if so by how much, their rent has been restricted for housing benefit purposes.

Kemp *et al.* (2002) analysed cases referred to the Rent Service by local authority housing benefit officials in England and Wales in 1999. They found that, under the rules then in place, 70 per cent of cases referred to the Rent Officer were subject to at least one form of restriction to the rent that is taken into account in calculating housing benefit entitlement. The average restriction was £19 per week. It was especially large in London and on cases subject to the single room rent. Although critics of the rent restrictions such as Shelter focused on the local reference rent and the single room rent, the pre-1996 restrictions remain important (see Table 10.7). It was found that 39 per cent of the rents eligible for housing benefit were reduced under the pre-1996 restrictions, and a further 37 per cent under both sets of restrictions. Only 24 per cent were reduced solely under the 1996 restrictions (i.e., the LRR and SRR).

Table 10.7: Restrictions in rents referred to the Rent Service[1]

	Number of referrals	% of referrals	% of restrictions
No restriction	180,606	30	
Restriction under:			
– pre-1996 rules only	161,165	27	39
– 1996 rules only	98,412	17	24
– both pre-1996 and 1996 rules	154,233	26	37
Total	594,416	100	100

Source: Kemp *et al.* (2002).
Note: 1. England and Wales, 1999.

Because of these restrictions, most new claimants with deregulated tenancies face a shortfall between their contractual rent and the amount used to calculate their housing benefit. As a result, tenants may experience financial hardship or end up with rent arrears and face possible eviction. This makes housing benefit recipients a more risky client group for private landlords letting accommodation.

Since the 1996 rent restrictions were introduced, the number of private tenants receiving housing benefit has fallen. The numbers of young single people in deregulated private tenancies dropped particularly sharply, from 114,000 in November 1996 to just 31,000 in May 2000. This has led some commentators to suggest that the decline in the number of recipients is a direct consequence of, and largely attributable to, these restrictions (Wilcox, 2002). However, over the same period there was also a fall in unemployment, a rise in employment, the introduction of tax credits, increases in social security benefit rates, and renewed efforts to reduce housing benefit fraud. Each of these factors is likely to have reduced the number of tenants claiming housing benefit.

The purpose of these rent restrictions is to prevent private tenants living in unreasonably expensive or overlarge accommodation, or paying 'over the odds' for the property. But because they are not very transparent, they as act as hidden 'trip wires' for housing benefit claimants. An alternative would be to design the housing benefit scheme in such a way that tenants have an incentive to shop around for reasonably priced accommodation without the need for rent restrictions (Kemp, 2000b).

As noted in Chapter 5, in 2002 the New Labour government announced plans to introduce a local housing allowance to replace housing benefit for private tenants in order to provide a shopping incentive, make the scheme more transparent and simplify administration. The scheme is being tested out in nine 'pathfinder' local authority areas before being rolled out nationally. Instead of being calculated on the claimant's actual rent (or on a restricted amount if the rent is unreasonably high) the local housing allowance is based on an average rent in the locality. In the pathfinders, this average is the local reference rent and the single room rent. This system is obviously much more rough and ready than housing benefit. Instead of their benefit being calculated on their actual or reasonable rent, claimants will be paid a standard amount, which may be more or less than the amount they pay their landlord.

The local housing allowance eliminates the need for rent restrictions. This is because claimants will pay all of any increase (and gain all of any decrease) in rent. To that extent, the local housing allowance gives tenants a financial incentive to shop around for accommodation. It will be far more transparent than the existing scheme and that will make it easier for recipients and landlords to understand. It should also be easier to administer and the time taken to process claims may be reduced as a result, which could help to remove some of the barriers to work for benefit claimants. However, the local housing allowance will leave unresolved many of the administrative problems from which the current scheme suffers.

It is not yet clear how tenants and landlords will respond to the local housing allowance or how it will affect rents. Roughly half of all existing claimants will gain from the reform and none will lose at the point of change (DWP, 2002). A significant minority of recipients will be paid a local housing allowance that is in excess of their rent (Kemp and Wilcox, 2003). The local housing allowance will create a complex set of incentives for landlords and tenants and this may well prompt behavioural changes by some of them, but the precise outcomes of which will not be clear until the evaluation of the pathfinder experience is completed.

At the time of writing, most of the opposition to the reform is focused, not on the local housing allowance, but on the fact that the money will normally be paid to the claimant rather than to their landlord. The exceptions will be 'vulnerable' tenants who are unable to manage their budgets and tenants who are eight or more weeks in arrears on their rent. Under the current housing benefit scheme, tenants can opt for the money to be paid directly to their landlord and about 60 per cent of them do so (in some cases, landlords make it a condition of the tenancy that the tenant will opt for payment to the landlord). Landlords' organisations argue that tenants cannot be trusted to pay the rent, while the poverty lobby argues that tenants are too poor to do so and will use the money for other purposes if it is paid to them rather than to their landlord. As a result, it is claimed, arrears and evictions will inevitably increase. Only time will tell if they are right, but it does seem unlikely that the vast majority of the 400,000 English private tenants currently receiving housing benefit will choose not to pay their rent and risk the prospect of losing their home. It seems more likely that, once the dust has settled from the reform, landlords and housing benefit recipients will adjust to the situation and that any increase in arrears will affect only a minority of them.

Conclusions

Rising real rents following rent deregulation may have helped to increase the supply of lettings, but have also reduced the affordability of accommodation for tenants paying the rent out of their own pocket. But affordability is also a problem for tenants claiming housing benefit. Although housing benefit can cover up to 100 per cent of the rent, the restrictions in the amount of rent eligible for benefit mean that the majority of recipients have a shortfall to make up out of their other income even when they are on income support or jobseeker's allowance. These restrictions, combined with the difficulties with administration help to undermine the bargaining power of housing benefit recipients within the private rental market, quite apart from any limitations arising from their low income. The local housing allowance should help to empower housing benefit recipients within the rental market as they will know in advance how much rent they can afford and many of them will be better off (at least initially). But unless there are significant improvements in the speed and accuracy of processing claims, housing benefit recipients will always be in a weaker position than tenants with a similar level of income who are paying the rent out of their own pocket.

CHAPTER 11:
Landlord-tenant relations

Introduction

Landlord-tenant relations have always been one of the most problematic features of private renting. The relationship has sometimes descended into conflict and spilled over from the market into the political realm. Governments have consequently found themselves intervening in the private rental market, usually to reinforce or increase the rights of tenants against their landlords. This asymmetry in government intervention partly reflects an opposite asymmetry in landlord-tenant relations: that landlords tend to have more power than tenants in the market place. It also reflects the fact that the number of tenants far outweighs the number of landlords when it comes to votes in the electoral ballot box. This chapter explores some of the most significant aspects of landlord-tenant relations in the contemporary private rental housing market.

The landlord-tenant relationship

The defining feature of the landlord-tenant relationship is that the landlord assigns to the tenant the right to occupy and use the accommodation for the duration of the tenancy, while retaining its ownership.[1] In return, the tenant undertakes to pay rent to the landlord, though in a minority of cases the accommodation is provided rent-free. The right to occupy the accommodation and the terms on which it is granted are critical features of landlord-tenant relations. This is especially so given that the transaction between landlord and tenant is not a one-off or occasional act of exchange, but part of a continuing relationship enacted over the life of the tenancy.

As well as the rent and the respective responsibilities for repairs and maintenance of landlord and tenant, the relationship involves other rights and responsibilities, such as tenants' right to quiet enjoyment and freedom from interference by their landlord. In multi-occupied property, the situation is more complex still, in that any one tenant's occupation of the accommodation is affected, not only by the landlord, but also by the other tenants who live at the address. Finally, and most critically, what for the landlord may be an investment is for the tenant their home, a fact that imbues the property with an emotional value that sharpens the landlord-tenant relationship. In the case of resident landlord lettings, the relationship becomes still more personal, and hence more emotive, as the property is also the landlord's home and one that she or he is sharing with the tenant (Allen and

---

1.   In some cases the tenant is granted a license to occupy the dwelling rather than a lease (Partington, 1980a).

McDowell, 1989). For both resident landlord and tenant, the relationship may have financial, personal and emotional overtones.

Under feudalism, the landlord-tenant relationship seems to have been governed by custom. Subsequently, common law and, since the 19th century, statute have provided the formal rules within which this relationship is played out. The law has intervened mainly, but not exclusively, to protect the tenant and regulate the landlord-tenant relationship in key areas of public interest (Morgan, 2002). The matters affected by this legislation include the key areas of landlord-tenant conflict (Duclaud-Williams, 1978):

- Rent setting.
- Security of tenure.
- Responsibility for repairs and maintenance.

The impact of legislation has not always been that which policy makers intended. As well as unanticipated consequences, the law has often had relatively little affect on landlord and tenant beliefs and behaviour. The gap between law and practice is the result of a variety of factors, including lack of knowledge of the legislation on the part of both landlords and tenants. Tenants make relatively little use of legal advice (Partington, 1980a, b). Landlords tend to rely on solicitors for their legal knowledge and advice (Crook and Kemp, 1996b; ODPM, 2003c). Law centres, citizens advice bureaux and housing advice centres have developed in order to provide help and advice to low-income tenants and others who would not normally be able to buy the services of a solicitor.

There is considerable evidence from surveys and qualitative studies to indicate that a significant minority of landlords and many tenants are largely ignorant of the law or have an incorrect understanding of it. For example, Crook and Kemp (1996b) found that a quarter of privately rented addresses in England were owned by landlords who did not know what tenancy agreement they had used (5 per cent) or described a type of tenancy that is not recognised in law (20 per cent). Ignorance of the law among landlords and tenants is not just confined to Britain but is common in Western Europe and North America (Harloe, 1985) and probably elsewhere as well. In the absence of correct knowledge, landlords and tenants appear to construct their own 'common sense' understanding of their legal rights and responsibilities, which may in fact be at odds with the law. One seemingly common example of this is about security of tenure, which some tenants believe to be weaker than it actually is in law (Lister, 2002).

One reason why many tenants and some landlords are not well informed about the law is that it is complex. The Law Commission (2003) has recently suggested reforms to the law regulating the relationship between landlords and occupiers of residential accommodation. It proposed to shift the basis of regulation away from the principles of property law, towards one based on consumer law principles of fairness and transparency. Social housing landlords would be expected to let their accommodation using what the Commission called Type I letting agreements, which would give relatively strong security of tenure to the tenant. Private landlords would be expected to let their accommodation under Type II agreements, which would give tenants much less security of tenure. Landlords would be required to provide tenants with a written statement setting out their respective rights and obligations. Some of the terms of these agreements would be compulsory, such as landlords' statutory repairing obligations, and could only be changed if it was in favour of the occupier. While the idea of a clearly written letting agreement is a good one, it may also be idealistic in practice (Hughes and Lowe, 2002) given the messy reality of people's lives and the fact that the balance of power in the private rental market has tended to favour landlords over tenants.

Quite apart from the law and their knowledge of it, landlord-tenant relations and especially their respective power are affected by the state of the local housing market and in particular the level of demand relative to supply. We saw this in Chapter 2 in relation to the privately rented market in late nineteenth century Britain. When there was excess demand in the local housing market, the landlord was in a strong position, being more able to pick and choose among tenants. When there was excess supply, tenants held more power and were able to be more choosey about what accommodation they were willing to accept, were often able to secure some improvement in the condition or amenities offered, and bargain more easily over the rent to be paid. Somewhere in between these extremes the bargaining position of landlords and tenants was more evenly balanced (cf. Daunton, 1983; Kemp, 1982b, 1987a).

However, in most places and for most of the time since the First World War, the privately rented housing market has been characterised by significant excess demand (DoE, 1977), leaving the landlord in a position to dictate terms to the tenant. However, in some localities since rent deregulation, there have been periods of excess supply in recent years (such as parts of the flat market in London where there had been an excess of buy to let investment), in response to which rents have fallen (Centre for Housing Policy, 2002). Much of the legislation affecting the landlord-tenant relationship has been introduced to tackle problems that stem from, or are exacerbated by, the imbalance in the market power of landlords relative to tenants (Morgan, 2002).

Managing agents

Generally speaking, housing to let is not a passive investment (Kemp, 1982a, b). Tenants must be found, repairs and decorations carried out, rents collected, any arrears of rent chased up and, on occasion, evictions undertaken. One way in which these 'hassles' can be minimised is by employing an agent either to find tenants or to manage the property on a day-to-day basis. Agents manage about half of all lettings in England (ODPM, 2003c) and Scotland (Kemp and Rhodes, 1994b).

Sideline landlords are more likely to contract out the management of their lettings than business or institutional landlords (Crook and Kemp, 1996b). Many full-time or business landlords believe that agents would not manage the property as well as they would do themselves. Meanwhile, many sideline landlords feel that managing agents are too expensive and some believe that they can do the job just as well. Landlords often use an agent where the property is located some distance away from their own home, though it is not uncommon for them to use relatives or friends in preference to a professional agent (Bevan et al., 1995; Rhodes and Bevan, 2003; Thomas and Snape, 1995).

Generally speaking, landlords are more likely to use agents for finding tenants and deciding on the rent to be charged than for any other aspect of property management. They are also more likely to leave rent collection to the agent, while retaining responsibility for key investment decisions like major repairs and whether or not to re-let the property. Deciding about minor repairs and giving notice to quit is more evenly balanced between landlords and agents, though more landlords take responsibility for these than leave it to their agent (Kemp and Crook, 1996b).

The use of managing agents has significant implications for the landlord-tenant relationship. Although employed by landlords, they act as an intermediary between the two parties. Agents tend to be more knowledgeable about the law than landlords (Crook and Kemp, 1996b) and can bring a level of professionalism that many landlords do not have. In addition, they can help to remove some of the sharpness of landlord-tenant conflict and hence dilute some of the emotion that the landlord (as the owner of the property) and the tenant (as the occupier of it) can bring to the relationship. That said, not all agents are professional in their operations (DETR/DSS, 2000).

Many private landlords manage their property in their spare time. Few landlords appear to have any training in property management or belong to one of the professional bodies such as the Royal Institution of Chartered Surveyors and the Chartered Institute of Housing. Only a minority belong to organisations representing landlords, such as the British Property Federation, the National Association of Residential Landlords, or the Small Landlords Association (Crook and Kemp, 1996b; Crook et al., 2000). The most commonly used sources of information for landlords are solicitors, managing agents, reading the legislation and newspapers. Landlords at one in six privately rented addresses in England claim to have no sources of general information (Crook and Kemp, 1996b).

In the absence of training or professional advice, self-managing landlords must rely on a combination of guesswork, experience on the job, press articles and informal contacts to inform their management practices. To that extent, many of these self-managing landlords can be fairly described as 'amateur housing managers' (Crook et al., 1995), though that does not necessarily mean they are bad ones. The point is rather that anyone who owns a residential property may let it out and manage it themselves, irrespective of whether they have any of the requisite knowledge, skills or expertise. One simply needs to own (or be able to sub-let) a property in order to become a landlord. No licence, qualifications or training is required. The one exception to this is HMOs, in respect of which landlords in Scotland (and in due course elsewhere in Britain) are required to obtain from the local authority a licence to let the accommodation. While it may be of little public interest whether or not individual landlords go out of business because they are not up to the task, the consequences of their lack of skills or knowledge in property management may be borne, in part at least, by the tenant who is unfortunate enough to rent the property from them.

Management policies and practices

Much more is known about the housing management policies and procedures of social housing landlords than about those employed by private landlords and their agents. Nevertheless, sufficient quantitative (Kemp and Rhodes, 1994; Crook and Kemp, 1996b) and qualitative evidence (Bevan *et al.*, 1995; Rhodes and Bevan, 2003; Thomas and Snape, 1995) exists to outline the broad process of property management in the private rental housing market.

Setting the rent

In the case of regulated tenancies with a registered rent, the rent is determined by the Rent Service rather than by negotiation between landlord and tenant. Among deregulated tenancies, the rent is much more likely to be firmly fixed in advance by the landlord or agent than it is to have been negotiated with the tenant. Where it is negotiated, however, it is much more likely to negotiated downwards than upwards, other things being equal (Crook and Kemp, 1996b). One can speculate that negotiation is more likely to occur when the housing market is in a state of flux than when it is relatively stable, for in the former circumstances it will be less clear than in the latter, what rent the market will bear.

Bevan *et al.* (1995) found that there were differences between different types of landlord in the way that they decided upon rent levels. Informal sideline landlords were much less likely than other types of landlord to rely upon evidence about market rent levels in deciding what rent to charge. While most did consult local newspapers, some set the rent to cover their costs (such as their mortgage repayments and perhaps other outgoings), while a few asked the prospective tenant what they had paid at their previous accommodation or thought they should pay. Formal sideline landlords relied on the agent's advice if they used one; those that did not generally checked sources such as local newspapers to see what other landlords were charging and some had a 'reserve price', that is, a minimum rent they wished to charge in order to cover their mortgage repayments or other costs. Business landlords, as the name implies, had a business-like attitude to setting the rent. They looked at what other landlords were charging for similar properties in the locality.

Several studies have found that some landlords charged whatever the Rent Officer decided, for housing benefit purposes, was a 'reasonable market rent' for the property (Bevan *et al.*, 1995; Kemp and Rhodes, 1994a). This strategy tended to be pursued by non-investment oriented sideline landlords who were unsure what rent to charge and the tenant happened to be a housing benefit claimant, and by investment oriented landlords who mainly let to benefit recipients and knew there was no point in charging above the Rent Officer's determination (Bevan *et al.*, 1995). Meanwhile, some landlords deliberately seek to pitch their rent at below the market level in order to help them *attract* or *retain* 'good tenants'. In effect, these landlords are 'turnover minimisers' rather than 'profit maximisers' (Bevan *et al.*, 1995). This turnover-minimising strategy is generally employed for two sets of reasons: first, in order to save the hassle, anxiety and risks associated with taking on new tenant; and second, to prevent any loss of rent due to void periods and to save on advertising and other expenses that arise when a tenant leaves and has to be replaced (Kemp, 1998).

Finding tenants

Landlords employ a wide range of methods to find tenants for their vacant properties. Many landlords use letting agents to obtain tenants and both landlords and letting agents advertise in newspapers. However, many landlords find their tenants through less formal methods, such as direct approaches from prospective tenants, contact with their existing tenants, or friends and relatives. Other methods include placing advertisements in newsagents' windows and on university or hospital notice boards. Where landlords manage the property themselves, informal methods account for a larger share of lettings than formal methods (Crook and Kemp, 1996b).

Finding prospective tenants is one thing, but choosing which one to let the property to is quite another. Landlords typically employ a range of strategies to help them decide which tenant to give the tenancy to (where they have a choice in the matter). Some attempt is often made to match the type of tenant to the size or other characteristics of the property and, as discussed in Chapter 9, landlords and agents often have preferences over the type of tenant. As well as credit checks and character references, landlords take into account personal appearance, politeness and the attitude of prospective tenants. They often rely on 'gut instinct' about whether or not the person could be trusted or would turn out to be a 'good tenant'. So far as landlords are concerned (Bevan *et al.*, 1995; Thomas and Snape, 1995), a 'good tenant' is someone who:

- Pays the rent (and other bills) regularly, promptly and in full.
- Looks after the property and keeps it clean and tidy.
- Does not annoy the neighbours or (in shared housing) the other tenants.

In practice, however, landlords do not find out whether new tenants are good, bad or indifferent until they take up occupation. This is one reason why some landlords prefer word of mouth methods to finding tenants: it reduces the risk of letting to what may turn out to be a 'problem tenant'. One advantage for private landlords of using six month assured shortholds is that they can be used as a kind of 'probationary tenancy' (Bevan *et al.*, 1995).

Repairs and maintenance

In general, landlords see themselves as being largely responsible for property repairs and maintenance (see Table 11.1). The great majority say that they are also responsible for internal non-structural repairs, internal structural repairs, external decoration, and external repairs. However, landlords tend to say that the tenant is responsible for internal decorations (Crook *et al.*, 2000). Responsibility for internal decorations may well depend upon whether the tenancy is furnished or unfurnished, with tenants renting furnished accommodation being less likely to be responsible than the latter.

Table 11.1: Responsibility for decorations and repairs at privately rented addresses in England

	Landlord %	Tenant %	Shared %	N/A %	All[1] %
Internal decorations	37	57	6	1	100
Internal non-structural repairs	87	9	4	1	100
Internal structural repairs	93	3	2	3	100
External decoration	94	3	2	1	100
External repairs	96	1	2	1	100

Source: Crook *et al.* (2000), p107.
Note: 1. Totals may not run to exactly 100 due to rounding.

In general, landlords can decide to be either proactive or reactive when it comes to undertaking repairs and maintenance (Crook *et al.*, 1998b, 2000). Proactive strategies may involve regular property inspections, cyclical maintenance (for example, re-painting external windows every five years) and other planned repair and improvement actions. Reactive strategies may rely on tenant requests or complaints, lack of any repair and improvement policy, and haphazard repair and maintenance work. Crook *et al.* (2000) found that most landlords had a reactive or even haphazard approach to repairs and maintenance.

Crook *et al.* (2000) found that landlords pursuing a proactive approach were more likely to undertake repair and improvement work and spend more than those pursuing a more reactive approach. As one might expect, business and institutional landlords were more likely to be proactive towards repairs and maintenance than were sideline landlords. Those with large letting portfolios were more likely than those with small portfolios to be proactive. More surprisingly, there appeared to be no relationship between landlords' repair and improvement strategies and the condition of their properties. This is because of some key differences in investment orientation between business and institutional landlords. Business landlords tended to have properties which were in relatively poor condition but which had high rents and high returns. By contrast, institutional landlords tended to let properties in good condition but which had low rents and low returns (Crook *et al.*, 2000; Crook, 2002a).

Experience of rent arrears

We saw in Chapter 7 that one of the worst things about being a landlord, according to landlords themselves, is dealing with rent arrears. Having to ask the tenant about arrears of rent may be awkward or embarrassing and perhaps even irritating, quite apart from the extra time and effort it may entail. Crook and Kemp (1996b) found that landlords and agents had not been able to collect all of the rent due at 13 per cent of addresses at which rent was being charged (11 per cent of all privately rented addresses). Rent arrears were three times as common among furnished as among unfurnished lettings (21 per cent compared with 7 per cent respectively). The amount uncollected was equal to 19 per cent of the amount of rent due on the property when averaged across lettings in arrears, or 2.4 per cent when averaged across all lettings where rent was collectable. The latter figure is broadly comparable to the level of arrears on social housing.

Although only a minority of landlords experience rent arrears at any time, the number who have had such difficulties during their letting career is much higher. Crook and Kemp (1996b) found that four out of ten addresses where landlords were interviewed had respondents who had had problems with rent arrears. Meanwhile, eight out of ten addresses where managing agents were interviewed had respondents who had experienced such problems. Not surprisingly, the larger the landlord's letting portfolio, the more likely they were to have experienced problems with tenants being in rent arrears. Business landlords were more likely than sideline landlords, and sideline investors more likely than sideline non-investment oriented landlords, to have experienced such problems.

Different landlords respond to rent arrears in different ways, but some responses seem to be fairly common. Perhaps the most common way of tackling rent arrears initially is to negotiate with the tenant and try to come to some kind of informal arrangement about repayment. For tenants waiting for their housing benefit claim to be processed, many landlords appear to accept that arrears are a hazard associated with letting to claimants. They must hope that the debt will be repaid once benefit starts to be received (Bevan *et al.*, 1995). The first payment of housing benefit is normally made directly to the landlord.

One reason why many landlords prefer housing benefit to be paid directly to them rather than to the tenant is that it ensures that they get the money; and, once the claim is eventually processed, reduces the risk of the tenant subsequently falling behind with the rent. That said, if the benefit does not cover all of the rent, then residual payments still have to be paid by the tenant, which landlords sometimes claim are very difficult to collect from the tenant in practice. An additional advantage of direct payments for landlords is that they reduce their rent collection costs. In effect, the housing benefit system is providing a free rent collection service for landlords.

An important drawback of direct payments can occur when housing benefit is overpaid. This may happen where, for example, the tenant has failed to notify the local authority of a relevant change of circumstances. Once the overpayment comes to light, the local authority can recoup the excess from the landlord (Bevan *et al.*, 1995). In this way, overpayments of housing benefit become converted into uncollected rents. If the change of circumstances was a change of address and the tenant has therefore moved, it may be especially difficult for the landlord to get back the rent they are owed. Naturally, landlords are not happy when overpayments of benefit paid direct to them are reclaimed, as all they have received is the equivalent amount of money that is due to them in rent from the tenant (Bevan *et al.*, 1995; Thomas and Snape, 1995). Nevertheless, what they have received from the local authority is not the rent, but housing benefit. Had the housing benefit been paid to the claimant, the overpayment would have been recovered from the tenant and not the landlord.

The local housing allowance currently being piloted in nine 'pathfinder' local authority areas (see Chapter 10) involves payment to the claimant except where the tenant is eight weeks or more in rent arrears or is 'vulnerable' and unable to manage their financial affairs. Some landlords have threatened to cease letting to tenants on housing benefit in these areas, but whether they will do so in practice remains to be seen and may depend, among other things, on whether there is sufficient demand for their property from tenants paying the rent out of their own pocket.

Evictions

There can be few more powerful signs that the relationship between a landlord and tenant has gone wrong than the eviction (or attempted eviction) of the latter. If a tenant refuses to move when asked to leave, the landlord may have to resort to legal action to repossess the property. Taking possession action can take a considerable amount of time and often involves considerable costs for the landlord, if not for the tenant. If the landlord takes the action rather than a managing agent, it can also be a very stressful experience. It is certainly a situation that most landlords are likely to wish to avoid wherever possible. From the tenant's perspective, it can of course be far more stressful as it involves them losing their home, sometimes before they have secured another one and often before they wish to move.

Crook and Kemp (1996b) found that the landlords of almost half of privately rented addresses had asked a tenant to leave since 1988, while agents at nine out of ten addresses had done the same. Sideline landlords were less likely to have asked a tenant to leave than business or institutional landlords. As one might expect, the larger their lettings portfolio the more likely it was that the landlord had asked a tenant to leave (Table 11.2). By far the most common reason given for having asked a tenant to leave was rent arrears. Anti-social behaviour such as noise, damage to the property, violence and abuse was also important. Scarcely any landlords and hardly any agents mentioned 'non-payment of housing benefit' as a reason for asking a tenant to leave. Two out of five addresses that had either a landlord or an agent who had had experience of asking tenants to leave, said they had gone so far as to take court action to get the tenant out. Altogether, three out of ten addresses had either a landlord or an agent that had at some point taken court action against a tenant since 1988 (Crook and Kemp, 1996b).

Table 11.2: Proportion of privately rented addresses in England where landlords and agents have asked tenants to leave

	%
Landlords	47
Agents	90
Type of landlord:	
Business	62
Sideline	42
Institutional	59
Size of letting portfolio:	
1	13
2 to 7	38
8 to 40	64
41+	76

Source: Crook and Kemp (1996b) p156.

Private landlords and agents commonly complain about the time it takes to evict tenants from a property and the legal bills they incur in doing so (Snape and Thomas, 1995). In order to tackle this perceived problem, in 1993 the Conservative government introduced an accelerated possession procedure for cases where the landlord had incontrovertible evidence of their entitlement to repossess the property. The procedure applied mainly to assured shorthold tenancies, though in certain very limited circumstances it could also be used for assured tenancies as well. Subsequent research indicated that about a quarter of possession actions taken by private landlords in England and Wales involved use of the accelerated possession procedure. It was found that, in the great majority of cases, use of the procedure produced a quicker outcome for the landlord than under the ordinary possession procedure. Eight out of ten accelerated possession actions resulted in the landlord being granted possession (Levison et al., 1998).

Thus, the accelerated possession procedure had improved matters for landlords with the right to repossess the property, but at the expense of the tenants, most of whom were given just 14 days to leave.

Harassment and illegal eviction

Security of tenure is one of the most critical issues affecting the landlord-tenant relationship. At one extreme, tenants may wish to have an unfettered right to occupy their home as long as they would like. At the other extreme, landlords may wish to have an unfettered right to repossess their property, without delay, whenever it happens to suit them or if the tenant fails to adhere to the obligations of their lease. In practice, common law and statute have placed the balance somewhere between these two extremes. Over time, the balance between landlords and tenants has been shifted in one direction or the other, but generally within limits. In recent years, one exception to this generalisation is lettings by resident landlords, where occupiers have almost no security of tenure, either in law or in the minds of landlords and their occupiers (Cowan and Marsh, 2001). Within the privately rented sector as a whole, security of tenure in practice has probably been governed more by the balance of power in the market place between landlords and tenants than by the law and their knowledge of it (Harloe, 1985).

Harassment and unlawful eviction are two significant breaches of tenants' security of tenure. Both are areas of the landlord-tenant relationship where the state has intervened. The imposition of rent control was necessarily accompanied by strong security of tenure, for without the latter the former would have been of much less benefit to the tenant (Duclaud-Williams, 1978). Difficulties often arose in the aftermath of rent deregulation, especially where it took the form of decontrol on vacant possession, for this gave the landlord an incentive to get rid of the tenant in order to charge a market rent. The Rachman scandal discussed in Chapter 4 arose in part because the rent decontrol provisions of the 1957 Rent Act were implemented in the context of severe housing pressure in Greater London. An Act of 1958, introduced by the Conservative government, made it illegal to evict without a court order, but that measure was a temporary one that applied only until 1961. It is no coincidence that the incoming Labour government immediately introduced a Prevention of Eviction Act after taking office in 1964. This temporary measure made it an offence to evict a tenant without first obtaining a court order. The provisions of the 1964 Act were incorporated into Part III of the Rent Act 1965. The latter also created the criminal offences of harassment and unlawful eviction (Morgan, 2002).

'Harassment' is a term that is difficult to pin down and an activity the existence of which is even more difficult to prove. It can take many forms, may involve a single act or a series of actions (or failures to act), but is something that disturbs or creates pressure on the part of the recipient (DETR, 2000b). What is more, different people may have different perceptions about whether an act (or failure to act) constitutes harassment or reasonable behaviour (Morgan, 2002). As a government publication on harassment and unlawful eviction (DETR, 2000b, p4) noted:

> *Many tenants consider that a single act would not typically be harassment, but there are some actions – such as disconnecting the electricity – that are so blatant as to constitute harassment. Tenants often feel that only deliberate acts should constitute harassment: you can't harass someone unintentionally. Others think that if you felt harassed by a landlord's actions then it was harassment, whether or not the landlord knows or intends it.*

Unlawful eviction is more clear cut and easier to prove. It occurs where an occupier is evicted without the proper legal procedure for terminating the right to occupation being followed by the landlord or their representative (Morgan, 2002, p111). Thus, an unlawful eviction is not necessarily an act of ill intent but may arise simply because a landlord has not followed the strict letter of the law to the full in seeking to bring a tenancy to an end. The fact that a substantial minority of landlords are poorly informed about the law relating to landlords and tenants increases the possibility of unlawful evictions taking place, even if unwittingly. However, some landlords do admit to evicting tenants while knowingly not following the proper legal procedure (Cowan and Marsh, 2001). According to a study by Marsh *et al.*(2000) the most common reason for unlawful action by landlords was non-payment of rent, which was itself principally due to delays in the processing of housing benefit claims or failure of housing benefit to cover all of the rent (see Chapter 10).

Perhaps not surprisingly, problems of harassment and illegal eviction are more common 'at the lower income end of the privately rented sector: housing benefit, bedsit land, HMOs' (DETR, 2000b, p5), though are by no means confined to that part of the market. Consequently, the people who are most affected are the poorer and more vulnerable tenants in the sector – groups of people who have relatively little financial muscle or power in the marketplace. Moreover, in high demand housing markets, tenants are likely to have less choice over what behaviour they will or will not put up with on the part of their landlord. As Cowan and Marsh (2001, p838) have noted, 'The excess demand for rented properties in many areas means that strong competitive pressure does not exist within the market to discipline inappropriate behaviour.' Harassment can be particularly distressing for elderly tenants (Izuhara and Heywood, 2003).

The number of prosecutions for harassment is low. As noted above, harassment is difficult to prove. Moreover, tenants may be reluctant to testify against their landlord for fear of the consequences (Nelkin, 1983). The majority of offences of harassment are not reported and tenants may simply leave. Indeed, private tenants renting on a six month assured shorthold tenancy do not have very long until they are contractually free to leave (Jew, 1994). Equally, the replacement of protected tenancies by assured shortholds means that landlords have less incentive than they did before 1989 to harass their tenants in order to persuade them to leave. Morgan (2002, p122) has argued that the 1988 Housing Act resulted in '...the replacement of insecurity via extra-legal means with legally sanctioned insecurity.' However, insecurity can cut both ways, as six month tenancies also mean that tenants are not tied down very long to the same property and can move relatively often should they wish to do so. As we saw in Chapter 8, most private tenants move because they choose to rather than because they are forced to leave by the landlord. This is hardly surprising as, provided the landlord wishes to continue letting the property, it is generally in their interest to keep good tenants rather than take the risk (and incur the costs associated with) taking on new tenants. Nevertheless, six month assured shortholds can be very insecure for tenants who have little market power and wish to stay in their present accommodation. Landlords of regulated tenancies have more financial incentive to get rid of their tenant than those with assured and assured shorthold tenancies (Izuhara and Heywood, 2003).

Many local authorities employ tenancy relations officers (TROs) to intervene in disputes between landlord and tenant and tackle cases on unlawful eviction and harassment. The introduction of TROs had been a recommendation of the Francis Committee (1971) on the Rent Acts. In general, it seems that TROs seek to mediate between landlords and tenants, with the aim of achieving compliance with the law rather than prosecution (Morgan, 2002).

Cowan and Marsh (2002) found that local authorities had recently shifted in their approach to private landlords more generally, moving from a confrontational approach to a more co-operative one. Where previously they had seen private landlords as almost an historical anachronism, increasingly they were seeing them as a valuable resource able to play a useful role in local housing provision. The result was to make prosecutions even less likely. Instead, local councils were seeking to develop a preventative approach to harassment. In high demand areas, private landlords were being seen as 'partners in meeting housing need' including helping them to fulfil their statutory obligations under the homelessness legislation. Even in low demand areas, where councils saw themselves as being in competition with private landlords, many had developed private rented sector strategies and begun to engage in dialogue with them (Cowan and Marsh, 2002). A number of local authorities have set up local landlord forums and some have developed accreditation schemes as part of an attempt to encourage a 'healthy private rented sector' (DETR/DSS, 2000).

Conclusions

Landlord-tenant interaction is not a one-off transaction but a continuing relationship over the period of the lease. Conflict can occur over the price (rent), control and use of the landlord's property and the tenant's home. Both 'property' and 'home' are terms that are imbued with emotional and symbolic meaning, quite apart from the practical significance they may have as investment and shelter respectively. It is not surprising, therefore, that landlord and tenant conflict can be sharp and even personal, especially when not mediated by a managing agent. In fact, research suggests that most landlord and tenant relationships are amicable and relatively problem-free. Yet when problems do arise they can cause misery to tenants, as well as to landlords (for just as there are difficult landlords, so there are also difficult tenants).

The state has stepped in to regulate the landlord-tenant relationship, but with mixed success. This is partly because it is an inherently difficult relationship to regulate and to police, but also because a significant minority of landlords, and probably most tenants, are relatively ignorant of the law. Moreover, in practice the relationship is influenced by the market power of landlords and tenants, which is affected by the balance of supply and demand in the local housing market or sub-market. During the late nineteenth century (see Chapter 2), the balance of power shifted in response to the cycles of boom and slump within the largely unregulated rental housing market. But for most of the twentieth century, excess demand has meant that the balance of power arguably lay with landlords rather than tenants, mitigated somewhat by the fact that the latter had relatively strong security of tenure under the Rent Acts. More recently, following rent deregulation, tenants' security of tenure has been substantially weakened. Meanwhile, the increase in supply of privately rented accommodation and the shift towards younger and more mobile tenants has helped to reduce the imbalance to some extent. However, at the bottom end of the market, especially in high demand areas, the upper hand remains firmly with landlords.

CHAPTER 12:
Retrospect and prospect

Over the past century, the privately rented sector has undergone a profound transformation. One hundred years ago, it was the housing tenure in which most people lived for most or all of their lives. Renting from a private landlord was the normal way to obtain living accommodation (Kemp, 1987a). That private renting would remain the tenure for the majority of the population was so taken for granted that it was scarcely discussed or questioned. Some commentators hoped to encourage growth in working-class owner occupation and some radical socialists campaigned for the introduction of subsidised municipal housing (Merrett, 1979). But at that time few people would have predicted the scale and speed of the sector's subsequent decline.

The collapse of house-building in Edwardian Britain, the accommodation shortage created by the First World War, the extension of the franchise in 1918 and the post-war boom and slump, transformed the political economy of housing provision. After the war, new investment in the privately rented more or less dried up and did not recover until the early 1930s. By then, owner occupation and subsidised council housing had developed as strong competitors to the private landlord.

After the Second World War, the stock of privately rented dwellings began to shrink quite rapidly in numbers – mainly via sales into owner occupation and slum clearance – and was not replenished by new construction. New building was almost entirely confined to council housing and owner occupation, two tenures that gradually over took the privately rented sector in size. The Conservative's attempt to revive private renting through the Rent Act 1957 seemed merely to highlight the seeming inevitability of the sector's decline and the politically perilous nature of rent decontrol.

By the 1970s, the question had become how far the decline would go, or even if the private landlord would disappear altogether. 'The landlords' slow goodbye' (Eversley, 1975) and 'the private landlord is dead, but he won't lie down' (Finnis, 1977) were the titles of just two articles in this vein at the time. Private landlords had never been popular, particularly in Scotland (Englander, 1983), but the image of private renting deteriorated in tandem with the sector's physical decline. For many, the prevailing impression seemed to be one of poor quality or slum housing, let at high rents by unscrupulous or at least untrustworthy individuals intent on milking the property or evicting the tenants in order to sell into the owner occupied market. While this was a caricature, there was enough evidence in house condition surveys and in the client files of housing advice centres to suggest that it had sufficient substance to give it some credence. The reality was undoubtedly more complex and the solutions not easy to find. At best, the policy goal appears to have become how to manage the seemingly inevitable decline and avoid political controversy of the sort associated with the 1957 Rent Act.

Attempts were made to new breath life into the privately rented sector when the Conservatives were re-elected to government in 1979 under Mrs Thatcher. Despite the radicalism of her government, the measures contained in the 1980 Housing Act were too modest to make a substantial difference (Crook, 1986), though the shorthold tenancy that it introduced became more significant following a new legal interpretation of the lease/license distinction in 1985 (see Chapter 5). The deregulation of new lettings in 1989 was very important because it allowed landlords to come out of the shadow of the Rent Acts. They could now legitimately let residential property at market rents. Moreover, if they did so using shorthold tenancies, they could be sure of being able to gain vacant possession should they need to. Although deregulation meant higher rents for new tenants, the new tenancy arrangements were arguably more secure than the uncertainties over whether they had a lease or a licence that had previously prevailed. New Labour's commitment to retain the deregulatory framework introduced by the Conservatives was also an important turning point and helped to minimise the high political risk that had surrounded the privately rented sector since the 1950s.

Rent deregulation and the emerging political consensus over the importance of private renting in meeting certain types of housing need (Best *et al.*, 1992) provided a viable legal and political framework for the sector, but were not by themselves necessarily sufficient to attract substantial amounts of investment. In addition, growth in the supply of, and demand for, privately rented properties was partly fuelled by the slump in the owner occupied housing market that took place in the late 1980s and early 1990s. Subsequently, low interest rates, increased competition among mortgage lenders, a fall in share values at the turn of the century and uncertainty over pension provision, all added to the relative attractions of rental housing to people with money to invest.

Meanwhile, the growth in higher education, the shift from grants to repayable loans in student maintenance, the growing number of single person households – partly fuelled by divorce and relationship breakdown and by an increase in the average age of partnering – all helped to sustain tenant demand. The rapid inflation in house prices from the mid-1990s, which helped to raise the cost of entry into owner occupation, also helped to sustain demand for privately rented accommodation among younger people who might otherwise have become first-time buyers.

The privately rented housing sector in Britain seems to have entered a new phase in its development. Private renting is seen both by the Labour government and the Conservative opposition as a sector to encourage and foster. Consequently, the political risk involved in investing in this part of the housing market has virtually disappeared. Although the modest growth in private renting that occurred in the first half of the 1990s has come to an end, the sector has levelled out at about 10 per cent of the total stock. Perhaps of more significance than size, is the transformation *within* the privately rented sector (Bailey, 1999). The number of regulated lettings has rapidly declined as older tenants died or moved elsewhere. The privately rented market is increasingly dominated by deregulated tenancies and by younger people. Meanwhile, the rate of mobility within the sector, which was already quite high, has increased still further over the past decade.

At the same time, the reputation of private renting has improved. The stigma of being a private landlord or a private tenant seems to have reduced if not disappeared. By regularly carrying articles on investing in rental housing and on the merits and demerits of renting versus buying one's home, the newspapers have helped to normalise the image of private landlords. The emergence of buy to let has brought back into the sector highly geared, investment-orientated private individual landlords. Helped by the surge of buy to let investment, there has been an influx of new and modern dwellings into the privately rented sector. There has also been significant improvement in the condition of the privately rented housing stock more generally in terms of fitness, disrepair and heating and insulation. While some of this change is due to improvement in existing privately rented dwellings, the evidence indicates that it is mainly a consequence of the transfer into private renting of reasonably good condition dwellings from the owner occupied sector (Crook *et al.*, 2000). It may also be the result of sales by private landlords to the owner occupied sector of newly vacant, poor quality dwellings that had previously been let on regulated tenancies.

Nevertheless, there remain substantial numbers of non-decent dwellings in the privately rented sector, including many in the Scottish cities and towns in the north of England. In some low demand localities, private landlords have bought up older terraced housing and let the property to tenants on housing benefit. The government has expressed concern about the behaviour of some anti-social tenants and landlords in such areas (DETR/DSS, 2000) and the planned introduction of selective licensing (see Chapter 5) is intended to help tackle this problem.

More generally, the problem of non-decent housing reflects the level of rents that tenants are able to pay at the lower end of the private rented sector. As discussed in Chapter 6, part of the problem is also that the market does not necessarily provide landlords with sufficient incentive to improve the condition of their properties. Short-stay tenants appear to be more concerned about decorations, white goods and furniture than they are about the structural condition of the dwelling. As a result, rents do not always reflect property conditions and, consequently, landlords who carry out improvement works do not necessarily gain a sufficiently large uplift in rents to compensate them for the investment they have made (Crook *et al.*, 2000).

New Labour's approach to housing policy is to rely on the market to work and intervene only when it is convinced that it is necessary to do so (Armstrong, 1998; Crook, 2002b). In this sense, 'necessary' is as likely to mean politically necessary, as necessary to solve a deficiency in the operation of the market. Some interventions may be symbolically important, whether that is to appease party supporters or to head off criticism from opponents. Whatever the impetus to take action, however, the very fact of intervention does not itself guarantee the efficacy of the measure being introduced. The introduction of HMO licensing is probably important symbolically as well as instrumentally for New Labour, but is unlikely by itself to be sufficient to tackle what are deep-seated problems with no easy solution. Nor is it evident that local authorities have sufficient staff and financial resources to take action that will clearly produce a significant improvement in the condition of HMOs. Better regulation of the bottom end of the market (Rugg and Rhodes, 2001; Shelter, 2002) would be more effective if combined with financial assistance for landlords willing to improve their properties and manage them professionally (Crook *et al.*, 2000).

Fiscal incentives, if carefully designed, could help to encourage new investment in the privately rented sector by financial institutions, property companies and private individuals. This is most likely to work in the centres of major cities and towns in Britain and also in the South-east of England, where housing demand – especially from young and single people – remains strong, house prices are relatively high and social rented housing in short supply. The size of the privately rented sector may not increase very much even with fiscal incentives for private landlords (assuming there is no major privatisation of social housing or collapse of owner occupied house prices). But it could help to drive out some of the poorer landlords and stock by attracting new landlords and better dwellings into the rental market. That would help to further transform and normalise the privately rented housing market in Britain.

References

Adams, R. (2003) 'Investment trust plan to increase property supply', *The Guardian*, 11 December, p23.

Aldcroft, D.H. and Richardson, H.W. (1969) *The British Economy 1870-1939*, Macmillan.

Allen, J. and McDowell, L. (1989) *Landlords and Property: Social Relations in the Private Rented Sector*, Cambridge: Cambridge University Press.

Anderson, G. (1982) 'Some aspects of the labour market in Britain, c.1870-1914', in C Wrigley (ed.) *A History of British Industrial Relations 1875-1914*, Brighton: Harvester Press, pp1-19.

Anderson, I., Kemp, P.A. and Quilgars, D. (1993) *Single Homeless People*, London: HMSO.

Armstrong, H. (1997) 'Speech by Minister for Housing at the Annual Conference of the Association of Residential Letting Agents', *Agreement: The Journal of ARLA*, 4, p5.

Ashworth, H. (1957) *Housing in Great Britain*, London: Thomas Skinner.

Audit Commission (2002) *Learning from Inspection: Housing Benefit Administration*, London: Audit Commission.

Bailey, N. (1999) 'Deregulated private renting: a decade of change in Scotland', *Netherlands Journal of Housing and the Build Environment*, vol. 14, pp363-384.

Ball, M. (1981) 'The development of capitalism in housing provision', *International Journal of Urban and Regional Research*, vol. 5, pp145-177.

Ball, M. (1983) *Housing Policy and Economic Power*, London: Methuen.

Ball, M. (1986) 'Housing research: time for a theoretical refocus?', *Housing Studies*, vol. 1, pp147-165.

Banting, K.G. (1979) *Poverty, Politics and Policy*, London: Macmillan.

Barker, K. (2003) *Review of Housing Supply. Interim Report – Analysis*, London: The Stationery Office.

Barker, K. (2004) *Review of Housing Supply. Final Report and Recommendations*, London: The Stationery Office.

Barnett, M.J. (1969) *The Politics of Legislation*, London: Weidenfeld and Nicolson.

Bates, B., Joy, S., Kitchen, S., Perry, J., Swales, K., Thornby, M., Kafka, E., Oliver, R. and Wellington, S. (2002) *Housing in England 2000/1. A Report of the 2000/2001 Survey of English Housing*, London: The Stationery Office.

Bates, B., Joy, S., Roden, J., Swales, K., Grove, J. and Oliver, R. (2001) *Housing in England 1990/00*, London: HMSO.

Beck, U. (1992) *Risk Society: Towards a New Modernity*, London: Sage.

Benwell, CDP (1978) *Private Housing and the Working Class*, Benwell: Community Development Project.

Best, R., Kemp, P.A., Coleman, D. Merrett, S. and Crook, A.D.H. (1992) *The Future of Private Renting,* York: Joseph Rowntree Foundation.

Bevan, M., Kemp, P.A. and Rhodes, D. (1995) *Private Landlords and Housing Benefit*, York: Centre for Housing Policy, University of York.

Bevan, M. and Rhodes, D. (1997) *Can the Private Rented Sector House the Homeless?*, York: Centre for Housing Policy, University of York.

Bevan, M. and Sanderling, L. (1996) *Private Renting in Rural Areas*, York: Centre for Housing Policy, University of York.

Böheim, R. and Taylor, M.P. (2000*) My Home was my Castle: Evictions and Repossessions in Britain*, University of Essex, Colchester: Institute for Social and Economic Research.

Boviard, E., Harloe, M. and Whitehead, C.M.E. (1985) 'Private rented housing: its current role', *Journal of Social Policy*, 14, 1, pp1-23.

Bowers, S. (2002) 'Unite uses bond to pay for affordable housing', *The Guardian*, 15 March, p29.

Bowley, A.L. (1947) *Wages, Earnings and Hours of Work, 1914-1947, United Kingdom*, London and Cambridge Economic Service.

Bowley. M (1945) *Housing and the State 1919-1944*, London: Allen and Unwin.

Bramley, G., Satsangi, M. and Pryce, G. (1999) *The Supply Responsiveness of the Private Rented Sector: An International Comparison*, London: Department of the Environment, Transport and the Regions.

Bull, J. (1995) *The Housing Consequences of Relationship Breakdown*, Discussion Paper 10, York: Centre for Housing Policy, University of York.

Burrows, R. (1998a) *Contemporary Patterns of Residential Mobility in Relation to Social Housing in England*, York: Centre for Housing Policy, University of York.

Burrows, R. (1998b) 'Residential mobility and the owner-occupied market in England', *Housing Finance*, 37, February, pp15-23.

Burrows, R. (1999) 'Residential mobility and residualisation in social housing in England', *Journal of Social Policy*, 28(1), pp27-52.

Byrne, D. and Damer, S. (1980) 'The State, the Balance of Class Forces, and Early Working-Class Housing Legislation' in *Housing, Construction and the State*, Political Economy of Housing Workshop, pp63-70.

Cairncross, A.K. (1953) *Home and Foreign Investment: Studies in Capital Accumulation*, Cambridge: Cambridge University of Cambridge.

Cannan, E., (1914) 'The Land Report: Urban', *Economic Journal*, vol. 24, pp551-56.

Carey, S. (1995) *Private Renting in England 1993/94*, London: HMSO.

Centre for Housing Policy (2002) *The University of York Index of Private Rents and Yields. Fourth Quarter 2001*, York: Centre for Housing Policy, University of York.

Clark, W.A.V. and Dieleman, F.M. (1996) *Households and Housing*, New Brunswick, NJ: Centre for Urban Policy Research, Rutgers University.

Cleary, E.J. (1965) *The Building Society Movement*, London: Elek Books.

Communities Scotland (2003) *Scottish House Condition Survey 2001*, Edinburgh: Communities Scotland.

Conway, J. and Kemp, P.A. (1985) *Bed and Breakfast: Slum Housing of the Eighties*, Policy Paper 7, London: SHAC.

Coopers and Lybrand (1993) *Fiscal Incentives to Regenerate the Private Rented Sector*, London: Coopers and Lybrand.

Coopers and Lybrand (1996) *The Outlook for Housing Investment Trusts*, London: Coopers and Lybrand.

Council of Mortgage Lenders (2003) 'Buy-to-Let lending grows strongly', *Press Release*, 24 September.

Cowan, D. and Marsh A. (2001) 'There's regulatory crime, and then there's landlord crime: from '"Rachmanites" to "partners"', *Modern Law Review,* vol. 64, pp831-854.

Cox, A., (1853) *Landlord and Tenants Guide* (Privately published by the author).

Crook, A.D.H. (1986) 'Privatisation of housing and the impact of the Conservative Government's initiatives on low-cost home ownership and private renting between 1979 and 1984 in England and Wales: 4. Private renting', *Environment and Planning A,* 18, pp1029-1037.

Crook, A.D.H. (1989) 'Multi-occupied housing standards: the application of discretionary powers by local authorities', *Policy and Politics*, 17, 1, pp41-58.

Crook, A.D.H (1992) 'The revival of Private Rented Housing: a comparison and commentary on recent proposals', in: R. Best, P.A. Kemp, D. Coleman, S. Merrett and A.D.H Crook, *The future of Private Renting: Consensus and Action*, York: Joseph Rowntree Foundation.

Crook, A.D.H. (2002a) 'Housing conditions in the private rented sector within a market framework' in S. Lowe and D. Hughes (eds.), *The Private Rented Sector in a New Century: Revival or False Dawn?*, Bristol: The Policy Press.

Crook, A.D.H. (2002b) 'Private Renting in the 21st century: lessons from the last decade of the 20th century' in S. Lowe and D. Hughes (eds.), *The Private Rented Sector in a New Century: Revival or False Dawn?*, Bristol, The Policy Press.

Crook, A.D.H and Bryant, C.L (1982) *Local Authorities and Private Landlords*, Sheffield: Sheffield Centre for Environmental Research.

Crook, A.D.H., Henneberry, J.M. and Hughes, J.E.T. (1998b) *Repairs and Improvements to Privately Rented Dwellings in the 1990s*, London: Department of the Environment Transport and the Regions.

Crook, A.D.H., Henneberry, J.M., Hughes, J.E.T. and Kemp P.A. (2000) *Repair and Maintenance by Private Landlords*, London: Department of the Environment, Transport and the Regions.

Crook, A.D.H. and Hughes, J.E.T. (2001) 'Market signals and disrepair in privately rented housing', *Journal of Property Research*, vol. 18, pp21-50.

Crook, A.D.H., Hughes, J. and Kemp, P.A. (1995) *The Supply of Privately Rented Homes: Today and Tomorrow*, York: Joseph Rowntree Foundation.

Crook, A.D.H., Hughes, J. and Kemp, P.A. (1998a) 'Housing investment trusts and the returns from residential lettings', *Journal of Property Research*, vol. 15, pp229-248.

Crook, A.D.H. and Kemp, P.A. (1996a) 'The revival of private rented housing in Britain', *Housing Studies*, vol. 11, pp51-68.

Crook, A.D.H. and Kemp, P.A. (1996b) *Private Landlords in England*, London: HMSO.

Crook, A.D.H. and Kemp, P.A. (1999) *Financial Institutions and Private Rented Housing*, York: Joseph Rowntree Foundation and York Publishing Services.

Crook, A.D.H. and Kemp, P.A. (2002) 'Housing investment trusts: A new structure of rental housing provision?', *Housing Studies*, vol. 17, pp741-753.

Crook, A.D.H., Kemp, P.A., Anderson, I. and Bowman, S. (1991) *Tax Incentives and the Revival of Private Renting*, York: Cloister Press.

Crook, A.D.H. and Kemp, P.A. with Barnes, Y. and Ward, J. (2002) *Investment Returns in the Private Rented Sector*, London: British Property Foundation.

Crook, A.D.H. and Martin, G.J. (1988) 'Property speculators, local authority policy and the decline of private rented housing in the 1980s' in P.A. Kemp (ed.), *The Private Provision of Rented Housing*, Aldershot: Avebury.

Cullingworth, J.B. (1963) *Housing in Transition*, London: Heineman.

Cullingworth, J.B. (1979) *Essays on Housing Policy*, London: George Allen and Unwin.

Currie, H. (2002) 'The Scottish system of licensing houses in multiple occupation' in S. Lowe and D. Hughes (eds.) *The Private Rented Sector in a New Century: Revival or False Dawn'*, Bristol: The Policy Press.

Currie, H. and Miller, B. (1987) *A Home of my Own: A Survey and review of Multiple Occupancy in Scotland*, Edinburgh: Scottish Council for Single Homeless.

Currie, H., Third, H., Satsangi, M. and Brown, A. (1998) *Good Practice in the use of Licensing Schemes for Homes in Multiple Occupation in Scotland*, Edinburgh: Scottish Office.

Damer, S. (1976) *Property Relations and Class Relations in Victorian Glasgow*, Discussion Paper in Social Research No.15, Glasgow: University of Glasgow.

Damer, S. (1980) 'State, Class and Housing: Glasgow 1885-1919' in J.Melling (ed.) *Housing, Social Policy and the State*, London: Croom Helm, pp73-112.

Daunton, M.J. (1977) *Coal Metropolis: Cardiff 1870-1914*, Leicester: Leicester University.

Daunton, M.J. (1983) *House and Home in the Victorian City*, London: Arnold.

Daunton, M.J. (1984) 'Introduction' in M.J. Daunton (ed.) *Councillors and Tenants*, Leicester: Leicester University Press.

Davis, M. and Hughes, D. (2002) 'Changing rooms: the legal and policy implications of a burgeoning student housing market in Leicester' in S. Lowe and D. Hughes (eds.) *The Private Rented Sector in a New Century: Revival or False Dawn'*, Bristol: The Policy Press.

Deacon, A. and Bradshaw, J. (1983) *Reserved for the Poor: The Means Test in British Social Policy*, Oxford: Basil Blackwell and Martin Robertson.

Dennis, R. J. (1984) *English Industrial Cities of the Nineteenth Century*, Cambridge: Cambridge University Press.

Department of the Environment (DoE) (1977) *Housing Policy Review*, Parts I to III, London: HMSO.

DoE (1982) *English House Condition Survey 1981, Part 1*, London: HMSO.

DoE (1984) *Assured Tenancies*, Housing Booklet No.17, London: HMSO.

DoE (1987a) *Housing: The Government's Proposals,* London: HMSO.

DoE (1987b) *New Directions for Council Housing*, London: HMSO.

DoE (1991) *Housing and Construction Statistics 1980-1990*, London: HMSO.

DoE (1993) *English House Condition Survey 1991*, London: HMSO.

DoE (1995) *Our Future Homes: Opportunity, Choice, Responsibility,* London: HMSO.

Department of the Environment, Transport and the Regions (DETR) (1998) *English House Condition Survey 1996*, London: The Stationery Office.

DETR (1999) *Houses in Multiple Occupation in the Private Rented Sector*, London: Department of the Environment, Transport and the Regions.

DETR (2000a) *The Way Forward for Housing*, London: Department of the Environment, Transport and the Regions.

DETR (2000b) *Harassment and Unlawful Eviction of Private Sector Tenants and Park Home Residents*, London: Department of the Environment, Transport and the Regions.

DETR (2001) *Selective Licensing of Private Landlords*, London: Department of the Environment, Transport and the Regions.

DETR (2002) *A Decent Home*, London: Department of the Environment, Transport and the Regions.

Department of the Environment, Transport and the Regions (DETR) and Department of Social Security (DSS) (2000) *Quality and Choice: A Decent Home for All*, London: Department of the Environment, Transport and the Regions.

Department for Work and Pensions (DWP) (2002) *Building Choice and Responsibility: A Radical Agenda for Housing Benefit*, London: Department for Work and Pensions.

DWP (2003) *Housing Benefit Sanctions and Anti-Social Behaviour: A Consultation Paper*, London: Department for Work and Pensions.

Dickins, P. (1978) 'Social Change, Housing and the State: Some Aspects of Class Fragmentation and Incorporation 1915-1946', in M. Harloe (ed.) *Urban Change and Conflict*, London: Centre for Environmental Studies, pp336-96.

Dieleman, F.M., Clark, W.A.V. and Deurloo, M.C. (1995) 'Falling out of the home owner market', *Housing Studies*, vol. 10, pp3-15.

Dodd, T. (1990) *Private Renting in 1988*, London: HMSO.

Doling, J. and Davies, M. (1982) 'The two privately rented housing sectors', *Housing Review*, vol. 31, November-December, pp192-194.

Doling, J. and Davies, M. (1984) *The Public Control of Privately Rented Housing*, Aldershot: Gower.

Donnison, D.V. (1967) *The Government of Housing*, Harmondsworth: Penguin.

Donnison, D.V., Cockburn, C. and Corlett, T. (1961) *Housing Since the Rent Act*, Welwyn Garden City: Codicote Press.

Dorling, D. and Cornford, J. (1995) 'Who has negative equity? How house prices falls in Britain have hit different groups of home buyers', *Housing Studies*, vol. 10, pp151-178.

Down, D., Holmans, A.E. and Small, H. (1994) 'Trends in the size of the private rented sector in England', *Housing Finance*, 22, pp7-11.

Duclaud-Williams, R. (1978) *The Politics of Housing in Britain and France*, London: Heinemann.

Dunleavy, P. (1989) 'Paradoxes of an ungrounded statism' in F.G. Castles (ed.) *The Comparative History of Public Policy*, Cambridge: Polity Press.

Dwyer, P. (1998) 'Conditional citizens: welfare rights and responsibilities in the late 1990's', *Critical Social Policy*, vol. 18, pp519-543.

Dyos, H.J and Reeder, D.A. (1973) 'Slums and Suburbs' in H.J Dyos and M. Wolff (eds.), *The Victorian City: Images and Realities*, vol. 1, London: Routledge and Kegan Paul, pp359-86.

Englander, D. (1983) *Landlord and Tenant in Urban Britain 1838-1918*, Oxford: Clarendon Press.

English, J., Madigan, R. and Norman, P. (1976) *Slum Clearance: The Social and Administrative Context in England and Wales*, London: Croom Helm.

Ernest, R. (1905) *How to Become A Successful Estate Agent*, London: Ernst and Co.

Eversley, D. (1975) 'Landlords' slow goodbye', *New Society*, vol. 31, pp119-21.

Finnis, N. (1977) 'The private landlord is dead but he won't lie down', *Roof*, vol. 2, pp109-12.

Ford, J. and Burrows, R. (1999) 'To buy or not to buy? A home of one's own', in R. Jowell *et al.* (eds.) *British Social Attitudes: The 16th Report*, Aldershot: Ashgate.

Forrest, R. and Kemeny, J. (1980) 'Middle-class housing careers: the relationship between furnished renting and home ownership', *Sociological Review*, vol. 30, pp208-221.

Forrest, R. and Murie, A. (1994) 'Home ownership recession', *Housing Studies*, vol. 9, pp55-74.

Francis Committee (1971) *Report of the Committee on the Rent Acts*, London: HMSO.

Gauldie, E. (1974) *Cruel Habitations: A History of Working-Class Housing 1780-1918*, London: Allen and Unwin.

Gibb, K. (1994) 'Before and after deregulation: market renting in Glasgow and Edinburgh', *Urban Studies*, vol. 31, pp1481-1495.

Gibb, K. (1995) 'A housing allowance for the UK? Preconditions for an income-related housing subsidy', *Housing Studies*, vol. 10, pp517-532.

Gibb, K., Istephan, N. and Kemp, P.A. (1997) *An Evaluation of GRO Grants for Market Rent Housing*, Edinburgh: Scottish Homes.

Giddens, A. (1994) *Beyond Left and Right*, Cambridge: Polity Press.

Goodchild, B. and Syms, P. (2003) 'Developing and managing market renting schemes by housing associations', *Findings*, York: Joseph Rowntree Foundation.

Green, H., Deacon, K. and Down, D. (1998) *Housing in England 1996-1997*, London: The Stationery Office.

Green, H. and Hansbro, J. (1995) *Housing in England 1993-1994*, London: The Stationery Office.

Griffin, H. (1893-4) 'Weekly property as an investment', *Transactions of the Surveyor's Institution*, vol. XXVI, pp331-76.

Gunn, N.B. (1902) 'Life assurance investments', *Journal of the Insurance Institute of Great Britain and Ireland*, vol. 5, pp217-34.

Hamnett, C. and Randolph, B. (1988) *Cities, Housing and Profits*, London: Hutchinson.

Hancock, P. (2002) 'The private rented sector in rural areas' in S.Lowe and D.Hughes (eds.) *The Private Rented Sector in a New Century: Revival or False Dawn?*, Bristol: The Policy Press.

Harloe, M. (1985) *Private Rented Housing in the United States and Europe*, London: Croom Helm.

Harloe, M. (1995) *The People's Home? Social Rented Housing in Europe and America*, Oxford: Blackwell.

Harloe, M., Issacharoff, R. and Minns, R. (1974) *The Organization of Housing*, London: Heineman.

Heath, S. and Kenyon, L. (2001) 'Single young professionals and shared household living', *Journal of Youth Studies*, vol. 4, pp83-100.

Hedges, A. and Clemens, S. (1994) *Housing Attitudes Survey*, London: HMSO.

Heron, J. and Stevens, S. (1999) 'From deregulation to Buy-to-Let: developments in the private rented sector', *Housing Finance*, no. 44, pp27-34.

Hills, J. (1991) *Unravelling Housing Finance*, Oxford: Oxford University Press.

Hills, J. (1998) 'Housing: a decent home within the reach of every family?', in H.Glennerster and J. Hills (eds.) *The State of Welfare: The Economics of Social Spending*, 2nd edition, Oxford: Oxford University Press.

Hills, J. (2001) 'Inclusion or exclusion? The role of housing subsidies', *Urban Studies*, vol. 38, pp1887-1902.

Hirschmann, A.O. (1970) *Exit, Voice and Loyalty*, Cambridge MA, Harvard University Press.

HM Treasury and Inland Revenue (2004) *Promoting More Flexible Investment in Property: A Consultation*, London: The Stationery Office.

Holmans, A.E. (1987) *Housing Policy in Britain*, London: Croom Helm.

Holmans, A.E. (1995) 'Where have all the first-time buyers gone?', *Housing Finance*, February.

Holmans, A.E (1996) 'Meeting housing need in the private rented sector', in S.Wilcox (ed.) *Housing Finance Review 1996/97*, York: Joseph Rowntree Foundation.

House of Commons Environment Committee (1982) *The Private Rented Housing Sector, Volume 1. Report*, London: HMSO.

Houston, D., Pryce, G. and Kemp, P.A. (2002a) *Review of the Private Rented Sector in Wales*, Cardiff: Welsh Assembly Government.

Houston, D., Barr, K. and Dean, J. (2002b) *Research on the Private Rented Sector in Scotland*, Edinburgh: Scottish Executive.

Hughes, J. (1995) 'The impact of the Business Expansion Scheme on the supply of privately rented housing', *Journal of Property Finance*, vol. 6, no.2, pp21-33.

Hughes, D. and Lowe, S. (2002) 'New law, new policy' in S. Lowe and D. Hughes (eds.) (2002) *The Private Rented Sector in a New Century: Revival or False Dawn?*, Bristol: The Policy Press.

Inquiry into British Housing (1985) *Inquiry into British Housing: Supplement*, London: National Federation of Housing Associations.

Ivatts, J. (1988) 'Rented housing and market rents: a social policy critique', *Social Policy and Administration*, vol. 1, no.3.

Izuhara, M. and Heywood, F. (2003) 'A life-time of inequality: a structural analysis of housing careers and issues facing older private tenants', *Ageing and Society*, vol. 23, pp207-244.

Jackson, A.A. (1973) *Semi-detached London: Suburban Development, Life and Transport 1900-1939*, Allen and Unwin.

Jew, P. (1994) *Law and Order in Private Rented Housing*, London: Campaign for Bedsit Rights.

Jones, G. (1995) *Leaving Home*, Buckingham: Open Press.

Kemp, P. A. (1980) *Housing Production and the Decline of the Privately Rented Sector: Some Preliminary Remarks*, Urban and Regional Studies Working Paper 20, Brighton: University of Sussex.

Kemp, P.A. (1981) *The Changing Ownership Structure of the Privately Rented Sector: A Case Study of Partick East 1964-1978*, Discussion Paper in Planning, Glasgow: University of Glasgow.

Kemp, P.A. (1982a) 'Housing landlordism in late nineteenth century Britain', *Environment and Planning A*, vol. 14, pp1437-47.

Kemp, P.A (1982b) *House Property as Capital: Private Rental Housing in the Late Victorian City*, Urban and Regional Studies Working Paper 28, Brighton: University of Sussex.

Kemp, P.A. (1984) *The Transformation of the Urban Housing Market in Britain c.1885-1939*, DPhil Thesis, Brighton: University of Sussex.

Kemp, P.A. (1987a) 'Some aspects of housing consumption in nineteenth century England and Wales', *Housing Studies*, vol. 2, pp3-16.

Kemp, P.A. (1987b) 'The ghost of Rachman', *New Society*, 6 November, pp13-15.

Kemp, P.A. (1988a) *The Future of Private Renting*, Occasional Monograph in Environmental Health and Housing, Salford: The University of Salford.

Kemp, P.A. (1988b) 'The impact of the assured tenancy scheme, 1980-1986', in P.A. Kemp (ed.) *The Private Provision of Rented Housing,* Aldershot: Avebury.

Kemp, P.A. (1988c) 'New proposals for private renting: creating a commercially viable climate for investment in rented housing?' in P.A. Kemp (ed.) *The Private Provision of Rented Housing*, Aldershot: Avebury.

Kemp, P.A. (1989) 'The demunicipalisation of rented housing' in M. Brenton and C. Ungerson (eds.) *Social Policy Review 1988-89*, pp46-66, Harlow: Longman.

Kemp, P.A. (1990) 'Deregulation, markets and the 1988 Housing Act', *Social Policy and Administration*, vol. 24, pp145-155.

Kemp, P.A. (1991) 'From solution to problem? Council housing and the development of national housing policy', in S. G. Lowe and D. J. Hughes (eds.) *A New Century of Social Housing*, Leicester: Leicester University Press, pp44-61.

Kemp, P.A. (1992) 'Housing' in D. Marsh and R.A.W. Rhodes (eds.) *Implementing Thatcherite Policies*, Buckingham: Open University Press.

Kemp, P.A. (1993) 'Rebuilding the private rented sector?' pp59-73 in P. Malpass and R. Means (eds) *Implementing Housing Policy*, Buckingham: Open University Press.

Kemp, P.A. (1994) 'Housing allowances and the fiscal crisis of the welfare state', *Housing Studies*, vol. 9, pp531-542.

Kemp, P.A. (1997) 'Ideology, public policy and private rental housing since the war' in P. Williams (ed.) *Directions in Housing Policy*, London: Paul Chapman Publishing, pp68-83.

Kemp, P.A. (1998) 'Private Renting in England', *Netherlands Journal of Housing and the Built Environment*, vol. 13, pp233-253.

Kemp, P.A. (1999) 'Making the market work? New Labour and the housing question', in H. Dean and R. Woods (eds) *Social Policy Review 11*, London: Social Policy Association, pp166-186.

Kemp, P.A. (2000a) 'Images of council housing', in R. Jowell *et al.* (eds.) *British Social Attitudes: the 17th Report – Focusing on Diversity*, London: Sage, pp137-154.

Kemp, P.A. (2000b) *Shopping Incentives and Housing Benefit Reform*, Coventry: Chartered Institute of Housing and Joseph Rowntree Foundation.

Kemp, P.A. and Keoghan, M. (2001) 'Movement into and out of the private rented sector in England', *Housing Studies*, vol. 16, no. 1, pp21-37.

Kemp, P.A. and McLaverty, P. (1993) *Rent Officers and Housing Benefit*, Centre for Housing Policy Discussion Paper No.3, York: University of York.

Kemp, P.A. and McLaverty, P. (1995) *Private Tenants and Restrictions in Rent for Housing Benefit*, Centre for Housing Policy Research Report, York: University of York.

Kemp, P.A. and McLaverty, P. (1998) 'Private tenants and "perverse incentives" in the housing benefit scheme', *Government and Policy: Environment and Planning C: Government and Policy*, vol. 6, no. 4, pp395-409.

Kemp, P.A. and Rhodes, D. (1994a) *The Lower End of the Private Rented Sector: Glasgow Case Study*, Edinburgh: Scottish Homes.

Kemp, P.A. and Rhodes, D. (1994b) *Private Landlords in Scotland*, Edinburgh: Scottish Homes.

Kemp, P.A. and Rhodes, D. (1997) 'The motivations and attitudes to letting of private landlords in Scotland', *Journal of Property Research*, vol. 14, pp117-132.

Kemp, P.A. and Rugg, J. (1998) *The Single Room Rent: Its Impact on Young People*, York: Centre for Housing Policy, University of York.

Kemp, P.A. and Rugg, J. (2001) 'Young people, housing benefit and the risk society', *Social Policy and Administration*, vol. 35, no.6, pp688-700.

Kemp, P.A. and Wilcox, S. (2003) 'Housing benefit reform: who gains?', *Benefit*, May, pp10-12.

Kemp, P.A., Wilcox, S. and Rhodes, D. (2002) *Housing Benefit Reform: Next Steps*, York: Joseph Rowntree Foundation.

Kemp, P.A. and Williams, P. (1991) 'Housing management: an historical perspective', in S. Lowe and D. Hughes (eds.), *A New Century of Social Housing*, Leicester: Leicester University Press, pp121-141.

Kenyon, E. and Heath, S. (2001) 'Choosing *This Life*: narratives of choice amongst house sharers', *Housing Studies*, vol. 16, pp619-637.

Kleinman, M. and Whitehead, C.M.E (1985) 'The geography of private renting', *Housing Review*, vol. 34, no. 1, pp13-16.

Lamont, N. (1988) 'The business of renting', *Housing Review*, November-December.

Law Commission (2003) *Renting Homes*, London: Law Commission.

Levison, D., Barelli, J. and Lawton, G. (1998) *The Accelerated Possession Procedure: The Experience of Landlords and Tenants*, London: Department of the Environment, Transport and the Regions.

Lister, D. (2002) 'The nature of tenancy relationships: landlords and young people' in S. Lowe and D. Hughes (eds.) *The Private Rented Sector in a New Century: Revival or False Dawn*, Bristol: The Policy Press.

Lloyd, T.H. (1978) 'Royal Leamington Spa', in M. Simpson and T.H. Lloyd (eds.), *Middle Class Housing in Britain*, Newton Abbot: David and Charles, pp114-52.

Maclennan, D. (1982) *Housing Economics*, Harlow: Longman.

Maclennan, D. (1988) 'Private rental housing: Britain viewed from abroad' in P.A. Kemp (ed.) *The Private Provision of Rented Housing: Current Trends and Future Prospects*, Aldershot: Avebury.

Malpass, P. (1990) *Reshaping Housing Policy*, London: Routledge.

Malpass, P. (1998) 'Housing Policy' in N. Ellison and C. Pierson (eds.) *Developments in British Social Policy*, Basingstoke: Macmillan.

Malpass, P. (2000) *Housing Association and Housing Policy*, Basingstoke: Macmillan.

Malpass, P. and Murie, A. (1999) *Housing Policy and Practice*, 5th Edition, Basingstoke: Macmillan.

Marsh, A., Niner, P., Cowan, D., Forrest, R. and Kennet, P. (2000) *Harassment and Unlawful Eviction of Private Rented Sector Tenants and Home Park Residents*, London: DETR.

Marsh, A. and Riseborough, M. (1998) 'Explanding private renting: flexibility at a price?' in A. Marsh and D. Mullins (eds.) Housing and Public Policy: *Citizenship, Choice and Control*, Buckingham: Open University Press.

Mason, C., Harrison, J. and Harrison, R. (1988) *Closing the Equity Gap?* London: Small Business Research Trust.

McCarthy, P. and Simpson, B. (1991) *Issues in Post-divorce Housing*, Aldershot: Avebury.

McDowell, L. (1978) 'Competition in the private rented sector: students and low-income families in Brighton, Sussex', *Transactions of the Institute of British Geographers*, vol. 3, pp55-65.

McLaverty, P. and Kemp, P.A. (1998) 'Housing benefit and tenant coping strategies in the private rental housing market', *Environment and Planning A*, vol. 29, pp355-366.

Melling, J. (1980) 'Clydeside housing and the evolution of state rent control', pp139-67, in J. Melling (ed.) *Housing, Social Policy and the State*, London: Croom Helm.

Merrett, S. (1979) *State Housing in Britain*, London: Routledge and Kegan Paul.

Merrett, S. (1985) *The Right to Rent*, London: Greater London Council.

Merrett, S. (1992) 'Housing legislation and the future of the private rental sector' pp48-57 in R. Best *et al. The Future of Private Renting*, York: Joseph Rowntree Foundation.

Merrett, S. with Gray, F. (1982) *Owner-Occupation in Britain*, London: Routledge and Kegan Paul.

Milner-Holland Committee (1965) *Report of the Committee on Housing in Greater-London*, Cmnd 2605, London: HMSO.

Ministry of Housing and Local Government (1953) *Housing: The Next Steps*, London: HMSO.

Money, L.C. (1912) *Insurance Versus Poverty*, London: Methuen.

Morgan, J. (2002) 'Unlawful eviction and harassment' in S. Lowe and D. Hughes (eds.) *The Private Rented Sector in a New Century: Revival or False Dawn?*, Bristol: The Policy Press.

Morgan, N. and Daunton, M.J. (1983) 'Landlords in Glasgow: a study of 1900', *Business History*, vol. XXV, pp264-286.

Mudd, W. (1998) 'A Standard Rent? Context and Considerations', *Social Security Journal*, 1998/1, pp147-170.

Murie, A. (1997) Beyond state housing, in P.Williams (ed.) *Directions in Housing Policy*, London: Paul Chapman Publishing.

Murie, A., Niner, P. and Watson, C. (1976) *Housing Policy and the Housing System*, London: George Allen and Unwin.

Murphy, M. (1990) 'Housing consequences of marital breakdown and remarriage', in P. Symon (ed.) *Housing and Divorce*, Studies in Housing No.4, Glasgow: Centre for Housing Research, University of Glasgow.

Nelkin, D. (1983) *The Limits of the Legal Process: A Study of Landlords, Law and Crime*, London: Academic Press.

Nevin, E.T. (1955) *The Mechanism of Cheap Money: A Study of British Monetary Policy 1931-1939*, Cardiff: University of Wales Press.

Nevitt, A.A. (1966) *Housing, Taxation and Subsidies: A Study of Housing in the United Kingdom*, Nelson.

Nevitt, A.A. (1970) 'The nature of rent-controlling legislation in the UK', *Environmental and Planning A*, vol. 2, pp127-36.

Oakes, C. and McKee, E. (1997) 'The market for a new private rented sector', *Findings*, June, York: Joseph Rowntree Foundation.

Offer, A. (1981) *Property and Politics, 1870-1914*, Cambridge: Cambridge University Press.

Office of the Deputy Prime Minister (ODPM) (2002a) *Tenancy Money: Probity and Protection*, London: Office of the Deputy Prime Minister.

ODPM (2002b) *Housing Statistics Summary*, no. 13, London: Office of the Deputy Prime Minister.

ODPM (2003a) *English House Condition Survey 2001: Building the Picture*, London: Office of the Deputy Prime Minister.

ODPM (2003b) *English House Condition Survey 2001: Supporting Tables*, www.odpm.gov.uk.

ODPM (2003c) *English House Condition Survey 2001: Private Landlords Survey*, London: Office of the Deputy Prime Minister.

ODPM (2003d) 'Survey of English Housing Provisional Results: 2002– 03, *Housing Statistics Summary*, no.18, London: Office of the Deputy Prime Minister.

Onslow Committee (1923) *Final Report of the Departmental Committee in the Increase of Rent and Mortgage (Restrictions) Act 1920*, London: HMSO.

Paley, B. (1978) *Attitudes to Letting in 1976*, London: HMSO.

Pannell, B. and Heron, J. (2001) 'Goodbye to Buy-to-Let?', *Housing Finance*, no. 52, pp18-25.

Partington, M. (1980a) *Landlord and Tenant*, 2nd Edition, London: Weidenfeld and Nicolson.

Partington, M. (1980b) 'Landlord and tenant: the British experience', in E.Kamenka (ed.) *Law and Social Control*, London: Edward Arnold.

Patten, J. (1987) 'Interview with John Patten, Minister for Housing', *Roof*, January-February.

Phelps, L. (1998) *Unsafe Deposit: CAB Clients' Experiences of Rental Deposits*, London: National Association of Citizens Advice Bureaux.

Pieda (1996) *Third Survey of Consumer Preference in Housing*, Edinburgh: Scottish Homes.

Pollard, S. (1969) *The Development of the British Economy 1914-1967*, 2nd Edition, London: Edward Arnold.

Pooley, C. (1979) 'Residential Mobility in the Victorian City', *Transactions of the Institute of British Geographers*, vol. 4, pp258-77.

Power, A. (1997) *Estates on the Edge: the Social Consequences of Mass Housing in Northern Europe*, Basingstoke: Macmillan.

Priemus, H. and Maclennan, D. (eds.) (1998) 'Private rented housing: special issue', *Netherlands Journal of Housing and the Built Environment*, 13, pp195-407.

Property Research Unit, University of Cambridge (1998) *Institutional Investors' Attitudes Towards Residential Investment and Prospective Controls on Regulated Rents*, London: British Property Foundation.

Randall, G. (1994) *Private Renting for Single Homeless People: An Evaluation of a Pilot Rent Deposit Fund*, London: HMSO.

RCHWC (1884-85) *Report of the Royal Commission on the Housing of the Working Classes*, London: HMSO.

Rhodes, D. (1999) 'A testing time? Students in the private rented sector' in: J. Rugg (ed.) *Young People, Housing and Social Policy*, London: Routledge.

Rhodes, D. and Bevan, M. (2003) *Private Landlords and Buy to Let*, York: Centre for Housing Policy, University of York.

Rhodes, D. and Kemp, P.A. (2002) 'Rents and returns in the residential lettings market' in S.Lowe and D.Hughes (eds) *The Private Rented Sector in a New Century: Revival or False Dawn?*, Bristol: The Policy Press.

Richardson, H.W., and Aldcroft, D.H. (1968) *Building in the British Economy Between the Wars*, London: Macmillan.

Ridley Committee (1945) *Inter-Departmental Committee on Rent Control Report*, London: HMSO.

Robinson, R. (1979) *Housing Economics and Public Policy*, Basingstoke: Macmillan.

Rooney, B. (1997) 'The viability of furnished tenancies in social housing', *Findings*, October, York: Joseph Rowntree Foundation.

Rose, D. (1981) *Home Ownership and Industrial Change: The Struggle for a Separate Sphere*, Urban and Regional Studies, Working Paper 25, Brighton: University of Sussex.

Rowntree, B.S. (1901) *Poverty: A Study in Town Life*, London: Macmillan.

Rugg, J. (1996) *Opening Doors: Helping people on low income secure private rented accommodation*, York: Centre for Housing Policy, University of York.

Rugg, J. (1999) 'The use and 'abuse' of private renting and help with housing costs' in J.Rugg (ed.) *Young People, Housing and Social Policy*, London: Routledge.

Rugg, J. and Burrows, R. (1999) 'Setting the scene: young people, housing and social policy' in J.Rugg (ed.) *Young People, Housing and Social Policy*, London: Routledge.

Rugg, J. and Rhodes, D. (2001) *Chains or challenges? The Prospects for Better Regulation of the Private Rented Sector*, Coventry: British Property Federation, Chartered Institute of Housing.

Rugg, J. and Rhodes, D. (2003) 'Between a rock and a hard place: The failure to agree on regulation for the private rented sector in England' in *Housing Studies*, vol. 18, no. 6, pp937-946.

Rugg, J., Rhodes, D. and Jones, A. (2000) *The Nature and Impact of Student Demand on Housing Markets*, York: Joseph Rowntree Foundation.

Rugg, J., Rhodes, D. and Jones, A. (2002) 'Studying a niche market: UK students and the private rented sector', *Housing Studies*, vol. 17, pp289-303.

Sargant, C.H. (1886) *Ground Rents and Building Leases*, London: Swan Sonnenschien.

Satsangi, M. (2002) 'Rental housing supply in rural Scotland: the role of private landowners' in S. Lowe and D. Hughes (eds.) *The Private Rented Sector in a New Century: Revival or False Dawn?* Bristol: The Policy Press.

Saul, S.B. (1962) 'House-building in England, 1890-1914', *Economic History Review*, 2nd Series, vol. XV, pp119-37.

Saunders, P. (1990) *A Nation of Home Owners*, London: Allen and Unwin.

Scottish Executive (2002) *Scottish Household Survey Bulletin*, no.8, Edinburgh: Scottish Executive.

Scottish Office (1999) *Investing in Modernisation – An Agenda for Scotland's Housing*, Edinburgh: The Stationery Office.

Select Committee on Town Holdings (1888) *Minutes of Evidence*, London: HMSO.

SHAC (1981) *Good Housekeeping: An Examination of Housing Repair and Improvement Policy*, London: SHAC.

Shelter (2002) *Private Renting: A New Settlement*, London: Shelter.

Sokoll, T. (1997) 'Old age in poverty: the record of Essex pauper letters, 1780-1834' in T. Hitchcock, P. King and P. Sharpe (eds) *Chronicling Poverty: the Voices and Strategies of the English Poor, 1640-1840*, Basingstoke: Macmillan.

Spensley, J.C. (1918) 'Urban housing problems', *Journal of the Royal Statistical Society*, vol.1 xxxi, pp163-95.

Stafford, B. and Doling, J. (1981) *Rent Control and Rent Regulation in England and Wales 1915-1980*, Centre for Urban and Regional Studies Occasional Paper No.2, New Series, Birmingham: University of Birmingham.

Stedman Jones, G. (1971) *Outcast London: A Study in the Relationship Between Classes in Victorian Society*, Oxford: Clarendon Press.

Sullivan, O. (1986) 'The housing movements of the separated and divorced', *Housing Studies*, vol. 1, pp35-48.

Swenarton, M. (1981) *Homes for Heroes: The Politics and Architecture of Early State Housing in Britain*, London: Heineman.

Thomas, A.D. (1986) *Housing and Urban Renewal*, London: George Allen and Unwin.

Thomas, A.D. with Hedges, B. (1987) *The 1985 Physical and Social Survey of HMO's in England and Wales*, London: HMSO.

Thomas, A. and Snape, D. (1995) *In From the Cold: Working with the Private Landlord*, London: HMSO.

Thomas, W.A. (1978) *The Finance of British History*, London: Methuen.

Todd, J. (1986) *Recent Private Lettings 1982-84*, London: HMSO.

Todd, J.E., Bone, M. and Noble, I. (1982) *The Privately Rented Sector in 1978*, London: HMSO.

Todd, J.E and Foxon, J. (1987) *Recent Lettings in the Private Rented Sector 1982-94*, London: HMSO.

Treble, J.H. (1971) 'Liverpool working-class housing 1801-51', in S.D. Chapman (ed.) *The History of Working-Class Housing: A Symposium*, Newton Abbott: David and Charles.

Treble, J.H. (1979) *Urban Poverty in Britain 1830-1914*, London: Batsford.

Treen, C. (1982) 'The Process of Suburban Development in North Leeds, 1870-1914', in F.M.L Thompson (ed.) *The Rise of Suburbia*, Leicester: Leicester University Press, pp157-209.

Urlin, R.D. (1902) *A Handbook of Investment in Houses and Lands*, 4th Edition, Effingham: Wilson.

van Weesep, J. (1987) 'The creation of a new housing sector: condominiums in the United States', *Housing Studies*, vol. 2, pp122-133.

Waldegrave, W. (1987) *Some Reflections on Housing Policy*, London: Conservative News Service.

Walker, A., O'Brien, M., Traynor, J., Fox, K., Goddard, E. and Foster, K. (2003) *Living in Britain: Results from the 2001 General Household Survey*, London: The Stationery Office.

Weber, B. (1960) 'A New Index of House Rents for Great Britain, 1874-1913', *Scottish Journal of Political Economy*, vol. VII, pp232-37.

Whitehead, C.M.E. (1978) 'Private landlords in London: who stays, who goes?' *CES Review*, no. 4, pp48-52.

Whitehead, C.M.E. (1979) 'Why owner-occupation?', *CES Review*, no. 7, pp37-50.

Whitehead, C.M.E. (1999) 'Economic flexibility and the private rented sector', *Scottish Journal of Political Economy*, 45(4), pp361-375.

Whitehead, C.M.E. and Kleinman, M. (1985) 'The private rented sector: A characteristics approach', *Urban Studies*, vol. 22, pp507-220.

Whitehead, C.M.E. and Kleinman, M. (1986) *Private Rented Housing in the 1980's and 1990's*, Cambridge: Granta Publications.

Whitehead, C.M.E. and Kleinman, M. (1987) 'Private renting in London: Is it so different?', *Journal of Social Policy*, vol. 16, pp139-348.

Whitehead, C.M.E. and Kleinman, M. (1988) 'Capital value rents: an evaluation' pp124-146, in P.A. Kemp (ed.) *The Private Provision of Rented Housing*, Aldershot: Avebury.

Whitehead, C.M.E. and Kleinman, M. (1989) 'The private rented sector and the Housing Act 1988', pp65-84 in M. Brenton and C. Ungerson (eds.) *Social Policy Review 1988-9*, Harlow: Longman.

Wicks, M. (1973) *Rented Housing and Social Ownership*, Fabian Tract 421, London: Fabian Society.

Wilcox, S (ed.) (1997) *Housing Review 1997-98*, York: Joseph Rowntree Foundation.

Wilcox, S (2002) 'Housing benefit and social security', in S. Lowe and D. Hughes (eds.) *The Private Rented Sector in a New Century: Revival or False Dawn?*, Bristol: The Policy Press.

Wilding, P. (1972) 'Towards Exchequer Subsidies for Housing 1906-14', *Social and Economic Administration*, vol. 6, pp3-18.

Williams, P. (1978) 'Gentrification in Islington', *Transaction of the Institute of British Geographers*, New Series, vol. 3.

Worthington, T.L. (1893) *Dwellings of the People*, London: Swan Sonnenschien.

Wulff, M. and Maher, C. (1998) 'Long-term renters in the Australian housing market', *Housing Studies*, vol. 13, pp83-98.

Young, G. (1989) 'Review of "The Future of Private Renting"', *Search*, 1, February, pp27-28.

Young, G. (1991) 'Speech by Sir George Young', presented to a seminar on *The BES and Rented Housing: What Next,* July, London.

Index

Notes:

1. Acts of Parliament are only included in the index in cases where there is more than one reference in the text.
2. Proper names are not included except where related to important issues in the text.
3. The index covers the main text but not the references.
4. Where there are many references to one item, **bold** numbers indicate places in the text where the subject is covered in more depth.

Chartered Institute of Housing Policy and Practice Series

For details of all CIH publications, and information on postage and packing charges and discounts for CIH members and students, contact CIH publications (tel 024 7685 1752, email pubs@cih.org).

Introducing social housing

Stephen Harriott and Lesley Matthews

The provision and management of social housing demands a wide range of knowledge and expertise. This important book provides a stimulating introduction for both students and staff needing to understand *what social housing is* and *how it can be most effectively provided.*

'Partnering' approaches to social housing provision are very high profile, therefore it is not only housing staff who need to be aware of recent and anticipated changes in housing finance, development, management and the law. Planners, social workers, developers and many other professionals need to understand what social housing is all about.

Introducing Social Housing offers a readable description and thorough analysis of:

- how social housing has evolved;
- the range of tenures;
- the nature of running a 'social business' and achieving Best Value;
- the social context of changing priorities for lettings and meeting the needs of different tenants;
- core housing management functions and skills such as rent setting and collection, maintenance and dealing with anti-social behaviour;
- achieving customer involvement and satisfaction;
- dealing with housing supply and demand questions, and
- how the provision of social housing forms an important element in regeneration, what the government calls 'liveability' and future economic growth.

This book is ideal for those studying for the Chartered Institute of Housing recognised qualifications, and also for other social policy courses where an understanding of social housing policy and practice is required. But it will also be invaluable for professionals in housing and other fields who need to have a good understanding of the background to current policy.

Order no: 122
ISBN: 1 903208 54 8
Price: £22.00

Housing and public policy in post-devolution Scotland

Edited by Duncan Sim

In less than five years since its new Parliament was declared open, Scotland has seen the beginnings of radical moves away from the social policies previously decided in Westminster. For the Scottish Parliament and Executive, housing was an early priority. A housing green paper was soon followed by legislation, and controversial changes in the right to buy and the future for council housing. Change of ownership in the social housing sector – a feature of Scottish housing policy for some years – took on a new dimension with moves towards wholesale transfers of council housing to new community ownership, notably in Glasgow. Communities Scotland was created, there is now a single tenancy for social housing and, more recently, homelessness legislation has been reformed.

This book comprehensively and critically reviews the developments in housing and related policy that have taken place under devolved government. It brings together many of the leading experts on Scottish housing to consider in detail such topics as:

- Housing rights and responsibilities
- Developments in housing management
- Housing investment
- Affordability of housing
- Rural housing
- Regeneration of declining neighbourhoods
- The changing roles of housing agencies

Some of the chapters have a strong 'people' focus, dealing with issues such as homelessness and the needs of vulnerable people for care and support.

The book does not ignore the context of the changes in Scotland – an important chapter compares the developments with those in the UK as a whole and the continuing constraints imposed by Whitehall. This book is for any reader wanting the only wide-ranging and up-to-date assessment of housing policy and related changes since Scotland gained its new government.

Order no: 118
ISBN: 1 903208 63 7
Price: £20.00

Forthcoming titles

Housing, 'race' and community cohesion

Malcolm Harrison and others

Although there have been many research reports and good practice guides on race and ethnicity in relation to housing, there have been few books which look comprehensively at all the issues. This book will both look back at how race has been dealt with in the past – especially given the history of discrimination in housing and how the promotion of race equality came to the fore – as well as looking at recent issues like community cohesion and the impact of new immigration, such as asylum seekers and refugees.

The authors have a wealth of experience in this field and this book will be the definitive text both for students and for professionals who need to know about the background to present day concerns and the programmes that aim to address them. The book will offer a considered critique of the effectiveness of current policy at both national and local levels, and make suggestions about how it should change.

Order no: 114
ISBN: 1 903208 21 1
Price: £22.00
Available: Winter 2004

Housing finance

Third Edition
David Garnett and John Perry

The definitive guide to Housing Finance in the UK has been a best seller since its first publication more than a decade ago. Now a completely rewritten edition will be the first book to take account of the major changes which took effect in April 2004 – prudential borrowing for local authorities in England, Wales and Scotland, changes in housing benefit, new investment arrangements for housing associations, the Barker Review of the UK private housing market, and much more. With over 400 pages of detailed text, this book is the definitive student textbook on all aspects of housing finance, and is also invaluable to practitioners wanting the full background to current changes.

Order no. 121
ISBN 1 903208 53 X
Price: £25.00
Available: Autumn 2004